DOING BUSINESS IN THE US

DOING BUSINESS IN THE US
Legal Opportunities and Pitfalls

Lawrence B. Landman

JOHN WILEY & SONS

Chichester • New York • Brisbane • Toronto • Singapore

Published in 1996 by John Wiley & Sons Ltd,
Baffins Lane, Chichester,
West Sussex PO19 1UD, England

National   01243 779777
International   (+44) 1243 779777
e-mail (for orders and customer service enquiries): cs-books@wiley.co.uk
Visit our Home Page on http://www.wiley.co.uk
or http://www.wiley.com

Other Wiley Editorial Offices

John Wiley & Sons, Inc., 605 Third Avenue
New York, NY 10158-0012, USA

Jacaranda Wiley Ltd, 33 Park Road, Milton,
Queensland 4064, Australia

John Wiley & Sons (Canada) Ltd, 22 Worcester Road,
Rexdale, Ontario M9W IL1, Canada

John Wiley & Sons (Asia) Pte Ltd, 2 Clementi Loop #02-01,
Jin Xing Distripark, Singapore 129809

Library of Congress Cataloging-in-Publication Data
Landman, Lawrence B.
   Doing business in the US: legal opportunities and pitfalls / Lawrence B. Landman.
      p.   cm.
   Includes index.
   ISBN 0 471 96160 4 (soft)
   1. Business law—United States.   2. Businessmen—United States—Handbooks, manuals, etc.
I. Title.
   KF390.B84L36   1996
   346.73'07—dc20   96–35879
   [347.3067]   CIP

British Library Cataloguing in Publication Data
A catalogue record for this book is available from the British Library

ISBN 0 471 96160 4

Typeset in 11/13 pt Times by Poole Typesetting (Wessex) Ltd, Bournemouth, Dorset
Printed and bound in Great Britain by Biddles Ltd, Guildford and King's Lynn
This book is printed on acid-free paper responsibly manufactured from sustainable forestation, for
which at least two trees are planted for each one used for paper production.

To Helle, for all her support,
and to Elizabeth and Benjamin

CONTENTS

2   Bringing Goods into the United States
     Handling customs effectively   49

PART II   Establishing a Presence in the US Market   73

3   Corporations, Partnerships, and Joint Ventures
Establishing a business in the United States   75

PART III   Selling Ideas

4   Commercial Intellectual Property
Protecting valuable ideas

PART IV   The Business Environment   201

6   Product Liability
Managing risk   203

7 Contracting
Creating binding obligations

Purpose of this book
Making informed decisions

"Everything should be made as simple as possible, but not simpler."
                                                        – Albert Einstein

This book will help the non-American manager operate his business knowledgeably and efficiently in the United States. Each chapter contains the basic information attorneys tell clients regarding that area of the law or type of business deal. If the manager knows these basics, then his meetings with his attorneys will be shorter and less frequent, and he will be better able to deal with other firms.

If the manager keeps the warnings of the book in mind when thinking through all the implications of a possible business deal, then he will have a better sense of whether he should enter into the agreement. He will make a more informed decision. The practicalities of the lawsuit process, for example, may make a manager seriously consider the true security a contract term offers. This may help the manager avoid a long and costly legal battle.

The book will also tell those considering doing business in the United States not only what risks they run, but also what risks they do not run. Many non-American managers fear doing business in the United States when they should not. The book will help non-American managers see which of their fears are justified and which are not.

The book will help managers negotiate the important points of a possible business deal before they turn to their attorneys. The world is so complex, and each deal has so many unique aspects, that the managers must turn to their attorneys before signing any contract. But if the managers have negotiated the main parts of the contract themselves, the lawyer's job will be easier and quicker. And if these initial discussions show that the managers will not reach a deal, then at least they will know this before retaining attorneys.

To help managers focus on the important points, the chapters which review a type of contract list only these important points. The book does not mention standard, uncontroversial, terms. For example, the parties usually agree that if the licensee declares bankruptcy, then it forfeits its right to the exclu-sive use of the licensor's technology. This is typically an uncontroversial provision, one which the attorneys will include when they finalize the contract. Managers should focus on the important points of the possible deal, and so this book identifies only those important points.

Other chapters provide practical, step-by-step, overviews of an area of law relevant to doing business in the United States. By keeping the book close at hand the manager will be able to quickly get a general understanding of that area of law. This will allow the manager to quickly prepare for a meeting, wherever and whenever the meeting may be.

This book provides an overview of the law of all 50 states. The law in all the various states is broadly the same. Indeed, law students learn these general principles of law. However, the laws of the states do vary. This is another reason why the book cannot substitute for an attorney.

The book offers a brief and understandable introduction to American commercial law. It contains the least possible jargon. Keeping the discussion brief and understandable inevitably leads to small, technical, distortions. This should cause no problem because the book presents only an overview of American law but it is another reason why this book is no substitute for qualified legal advice tailored to a specific problem or transaction.

The book often uses "he" to refer to a person who could be either male or female. The book consistently uses "he" simply to avoid confusion.

Finally, **much thanks goes to** Michael Greenberg. His research assistance made writing this book much easier and more pleasant than it otherwise would have been.

PART I   Exporting Goods to the United States

1. AGENT AND DISTRIBUTOR AGREEMENTS
Selling in America

1. AGENT AND DISTRIBUTOR AGREEMENTS
Selling in America

(i) Introduction

(a) Agents and distributors are different

Distributors own the goods they sell and agents work for others. This distinction is crucial. Distributors own the goods they sell. They earn profits. These profits are the difference between the price they pay the manufacturer for the goods and the price they charge customers for the same goods.

The agent, by contrast, never owns goods. The agent finds customers for the manufacturer. It works on behalf of the manufacturer. The manufacturer pays the agent a commission, and then sells the goods directly to the customer the agent found. The agent could be a firm or an individual.

Although the agent works on behalf of the manufacturer, it is not the manufacturer's employee. The agency is an independent business. The agent is an "independent contractor," not an employee of the manufacturer. See Practical appendix, Section (iv).

(b) Agent and distributor agreements

Manufacturers tend to enter into more formal and detailed agreements with distributors than they do with agents. Distributors usually have well-developed businesses, and are therefore more likely to negotiate formal contracts with other firms. Agents, on the other hand, are usually individuals and they therefore tend to enter into informal agreements. Not every relationship will of course conform to these general tendencies. Some agents are firms, for example. In any case seemingly informal agreements are nevertheless binding contracts courts will enforce. See Contracting, Chapter 7.

This chapter discusses first the more elaborate distributor agreement. Because agents usually face the same issues that distributors face, this discussion applies to agents as well. There are, however, some issues which agents, but not distributors, typically face. The final section of this chapter discusses those issues.

ii   Distributor agreements

(a)   Introduction

Unlike some other countries, the United States does not apply any law specifically to distributor agreements. Rather, general commercial law, such as the Uniform Commercial Code (UCC) and antitrust law, regulate distributor agreements. While some states do apply special rules relating to specific industries, such as the alcoholic beverage industry, these specific rules are not common. Thus, the law generally allows the parties to enter into any agreement they wish. In the United States, the free market reigns.

To the extent that the law restrains the parties' freedom, antitrust law imposes the greatest restraints. This chapter therefore discusses the antitrust laws quite extensively. Antitrust law ensures that markets function properly, and therefore that the forces of free competition set prices. The antitrust law forbids managers from *unreasonably* restraining trade. It forbids a manufacturer, for example, from *unreasonably* restraining its distributor's right to conduct its business. See Licensing, Chapter 5 (i)(c).

When negotiating a distributorship or any other agreement, the parties must remember that they cannot possibly list in their contract every expectation each party has of the other. Nor can the parties agree in their contract how they will solve every potential future problem.

For this reason the law includes in all contracts some implied terms. The most important of these implied terms is the term of good faith. The law reads into all contracts a term in which each party agrees to act "fairly" with the other. Thus while the parties cannot anticipate many future situations, they have agreed that they will each do what is commercially appropriate, what is "fair," in these unpredictable situations. See Contracting, Chapter 7 (v).

(b)   Parties

Issue

The contract should identify all the different parties to the contract. Parties can be either:

● corporations, or

● individuals.

Commentary

Identify All Parties

Before the parties can define the responsibilities of each party to the contract they must define the parties to the contract. In particular, the parties must decide which parent and subsidiary corporations are parties to the contract. The law treats parent and subsidiary corporations as separate entities. Thus the contract must identify each parent or subsidiary corporation which is a party to the contract.

Non-American manufacturers in particular should distinguish between their American marketing subsidiary and their parent corporation. Any American marketing subsidiary which they may establish will typically have far fewer assets than the non-American parent manufacturer. Thus, the non-American manufacturer will usually want its American marketing subsidiary, and not its parent corporation, to assume legal responsibility for dealing with American distributors.

(c)   Products

Issue

Which products will the distributor sell?

Commentary

Less than manufacturer's full product line

The contract should very clearly identify which products the distributor
will sell. Some manufacturers want different distributors to sell different
products. These manufacturers believe that using different distributors
increases the flexibility of their distribution system. They also believe it
increases their bargaining leverage over any one distributor.

Products not yet developed

The contract should also discuss the distributor's possible rights to sell
products which the manufacturer may develop later. Distributor agreements often fail to discuss this issue, and this failure causes many disputes.
The agreement should therefore clearly state what rights, if any, the
manufacturer is giving the distributor to sell products the manufacturer
may develop later. If the manufacturer is giving the distributor no such
rights, then the agreement should state that clearly. The manufacturer
should be sure that the contract does not imply that it is giving the
distributor rights which it does not intend to give.

Expand distributor's product line

The contract should also discuss any rights the distributor may later have
to distribute other products which the manufacturer currently produces.
The manufacturer could offer the distributor the right to sell these
products under certain conditions. For example, the manufacturer may
give the distributor the right to sell some or all of these additional
products if the distributor meets its minimum sales requirement or other
quota. Manufacturers often use such promises as incentives to motivate
the distributor. See Best efforts and minimum sales and marketing
requirements, Section (f) below.

Sale of manufacturer's entire product line

Some manufacturers want their distributors to sell their entire product line.
In particular, non-American manufacturers just entering the American
market often want a well-established American distributor to sell all their
products. A manufacturer requiring a distributor to carry its full product
line is engaging in "full-line forcing." This "full-line forcing" may violate
the antitrust laws.

Antitrust

If a manufacturer requires a distributor to sell its entire product line, then it may, as a practical matter, be stopping the distributor from selling products of a competing manufacturer. If this is the case, then the "full-line forcing" requirement would have the same effect as one requiring the distributor to sell only the manufacturer's products. The two requirements would therefore raise the same antitrust issues. See Exclusive territory and right to exclusively carry manufacturer's products, Section (d) below.

Manufacturers commonly avoid the antitrust problems of "full line forcing" by requiring the distributor to carry only a "representative" line.

Shortages

The parties should also discuss the possibility that the manufacturer may not be able to fill all its distributors' orders. Manufacturers at times cannot fill all orders for their popular products. Distribution agreements usually require the manufacturer to equally distribute to all distributors products in short supply.

(d) Exclusive territory and right to exclusively carry manufacturer's products

Issues—reorder

- Does the contract give the distributor the exclusive right to sell within a certain market? If so, does the manufacturer nevertheless retain the right also to sell its products?

- Are the customers to whom the distributor may sell limited by:
  - type (industrial or retail), or
  - geography?

- Does the contract restrict the distributor's warehouses and other selling facilities? If so, are the restrictions by:
  - quantity (number of facilities), or
  - location?

- Do these provisions have any time limits?

- Must the distributor sell only the manufacturer's products?

Commentary

Divide into territories

Non-American manufacturers commonly make the mistake of granting their distributor the entire United States as a territory. The United States is very large, and most distributors cannot sell effectively throughout the entire country. Manufacturers can limit territories in any number of ways and usually do so by region, state or even city.

Manufacturers can also define territory not by geography but by type of purchaser. One distributor may sell to industrial customers, for example, while another may sell to retail stores.

Exclusive territory

The manufacturer could grant its distributors exclusive territories. If it did so, then it would have to restrict its distributors' freedom to sell, so each could not sell in the others' territories. The contract could limit the distributors' freedom to sell in the following ways:

- absolutely forbid sales outside a geographical territory,

- impose financial penalties for selling outside the territory,

- merely "expect" the distributor to concentrate its sales efforts in one territory,

- restrict the distributor to selling from only one or more locations, or

- restrict the distributor to selling to only one type of customer, such as industrial firms.

Restraining trade among distributors and the antitrust laws

All these restrictions restrain competition among the manufacturer's distributors. The first three do so explicitly: they give the distributor a monopoly in one territory. The latter two do so just as effectively. A distributor will not be able to compete against another distributor, for example, if it cannot open an outlet in the first distributor's territory.

Although these restrictions restrain trade, parties often succeed in convincing a court that they do not violate the antitrust laws. The parties first point out that the law only prohibits contracts which *unreasonably* restrain trade. These restrictions are reasonable, parties usually argue, because they stop one distributor from taking advantage of another's investment in advertising, showrooms, and general marketing. Without these restrictions, the parties argue, one distributor could make the investments necessary to develop a market, and the other could then enter the market, offer a lower price, and steal customers. This reasoning is particularly applicable to products just entering the American market, for which distributors may have to make considerable marketing investments.

According to this argument, restrictions of this type actually increase, not decrease, competition. They stop distributors from taking unfair advantage of each other's efforts. They therefore encourage distributors to develop the relevant market. They help to bring new products to the market and therefore increase, rather than decrease, competition.

Generally accepted

Generally speaking, courts accept this argument. They therefore allow restrictions on competition among distributors but they do so only to the extent that they believe such restrictions are reasonable. Courts tend to find that restrictions which hinder, rather than forbid, competition among distributors are reasonable. And courts tend to find that absolute customer and territorial restrictions are unreasonable restraint of trade, and therefore violate the antitrust laws. In short, courts prefer flexible restrictions.

Flexible restrictions and APR's

Manufacturers can usually grant distributors exclusive territories while still avoiding the absolute restrictions courts dislike. Manufacturers can do this in a number of ways. They can, for example, "expect" their distributors to each sell in only one area. Manufacturers commonly do this by assigning "Areas of Primary Responsibility" (APR's).

Manufacturers establish APR's in numerous ways. Some will only consider a distributor's sales within an APR when determining if the distributor met its minimum sales requirement. Others require distributors selling outside their territory to compensate the distributor in whose territory the customer is located. This so-called "profit passover" provides well-targeted compensation. It requires the distributor who sold the product to compensate the distributor who developed the relevant market.

Manufacturers sometimes have difficulty administering these APR provisions. For example, manufacturers often have difficulty deciding how much compensation one distributor should pay another. Also, after one distributor has compensated another the manufacturer cannot be sure which distributor should provide after-sales service.

New products and bankrupt distributors

Courts allow different manufacturers, facing different market conditions, to establish different restrictions on their distributors. For example, courts allow both manufacturers beginning to enter a market and firms on the verge of bankruptcy to impose greater restrictions on their distributors than they would allow other manufacturers. Courts reason that these manufacturers must impose these restrictions to survive in the market. Allowing these firms to survive and compete, courts reason, increases rather than decreases overall competition.

Manufacturer's right to sell

Market coverage or compete with distributor

Even if the manufacturer grants the distributor an exclusive territory, the manufacturer may nevertheless retain the right to sell its own products in the distributor's territory. The manufacturer may want to retain this right for either of two reasons. Some distributors tend to sell only to larger, more profitable, customers. A manufacturer may therefore choose to sell to the smaller customers whom the distributor ignores, and in this way ensure complete market coverage of its product. On the other hand, the manufacturer may itself want to sell to those larger and more profitable customers. To accomplish either of these goals the manufacturer will retain the right also to sell in its distributor's territory.

Distributor could abuse its market power

Problems in this area arise when the distributor claims that the manufacturer is setting an improperly low price. The distributor may claim that the manufacturer is setting so low a price that it is stealing the distributor's customers. The distributor may even claim that the manufacturer is trying to drive it out of business.

Manufacturers are vulnerable to the charge that they are trying to drive their distributor out of business. Manufacturers have to be careful because they set both the distributor's costs and its selling price. The manufacturer sets the distributor's costs because it sets the price the distributor must pay for the goods the distributor resells. The manufacturer also, in effect, sets the distributor's selling price because the distributor's price cannot be higher than the price the manufacturer sets in the distributor's territory. The manufacturer is therefore in a very powerful position to squeeze the distributor's profit margins and drive it out of business. If the manufacturer were to try to drive the distributor out of business to lessen competition among its distributors, then it would be unreasonably restraining trade in violation of the antitrust laws.

Because the manufacturer is vulnerable to such a charge it should, on the one hand, be careful not to create the appearance that it is trying to drive the distributor out of business. On the other hand, it should not overcompensate because the distributor may make such a claim. If the manufacturer were to sell to the distributor for too low a price, it would be unnecessarily sacrificing its own profits. Moreover, the distributor could then underprice the manufacturer and drive the manufacturer from the distributor's territory.

Parties compromise by working together

Perhaps unsurprisingly, distributors usually do not want to compete with manufacturers. Distributors fear not only that the manufacturer will underprice them in their territory, but also that the manufacturer will take undue advantage of their market development efforts. Manufacturers usually want to co-operate with their distributors. The parties often agree to work together, sharing marketing and customer responsibilities. For example, one party may sell to larger customers and the other to smaller customers

Exclusivity expires, but distributor may continue to sell goods

The marketing rationale for granting exclusivity, to encourage agents to invest in and develop a market, is generally more applicable to the marketing of complex products. No one needs to tell consumers the virtues of simple products. Simple products do not require sophisticated after sales service. As product life cycle theory stipulates, however, what were once complex products eventually become simple products. Thus, over time, the rationale for granting *exclusive* distribution rights tends to disappear. The parties could therefore limit *exclusive* distribution rights to a reasonable period of time. After this period expires the distributor may still sell the manufacturer's goods. It will only have lost its *exclusive* right to sell.

Exclusive territory and related terms

Differing interests

The distributor usually asks for an exclusive territory, but the manufacturer is usually reluctant to give exclusive control over a market, particularly a potentially lucrative one, to a distributor that may not exploit the market to its fullest potential. A manufacturer may also prefer to grant nonexclusive territories because it feels that competition among distributors will spur the distributors' sales efforts.

Co-ordinate with related terms

To reach an agreement, the parties usually negotiate this and other related terms at the same time. Typically, at the same time as they negotiate exclusive territories the parties also negotiate:

- the distributor's minimum sales requirements,

- the length of the contract,

- the distributor's obligation to sell the manufacturer's entire product line, and

- the distributor's right to sell competing goods.

The parties must co-ordinate all these related terms. For example, in return for receiving an exclusive territory the distributor will usually agree to meet a minimum sales requirement. This is a common compromise because it gives the distributor the exclusive territory it wants, and it also gives the manufacturer at least some protection against the lazy or ineffective distributor. See Best efforts, minimum sales and marketing requirements, Section (ii)(f).

The length of the contract is also relevant to these discussions. The manufacturer usually prefers a short contract, which allows it quickly to stop doing business with a poor distributor. It also gives the manufacturer the opportunity to change its distributors' responsibilities, should the manufacturer change its distribution strategy. A distributor will of course prefer the security of a long contract. Thus if a distributor were to agree to a shorter contract, it would probably do so only if the manufacturer were to give it a concession, such as an exclusive territory.

Exclusively sell manufacturer's products

In return for the grant of an exclusive territory the distributor will often agree not to sell goods of the manufacturer's competitors.

Probably does not violate antitrust law

A provision stopping the distributor from selling the manufacturer's competitors' products certainly seems to restrain trade. In fact a court would only find that the provision violated the antitrust laws if, by forbidding this one distributor from selling competing products, the manufacturer completely blocked competing goods from entering the market. Thus only in the unlikely event that the distributor has such great market power that no other distributor can compete with it will a court require the distributor to sell the products of the manufacturer's competitors.

Some courts even interpret "best efforts" clauses as requiring the distributor to sell only the manufacturer's products. See Best efforts and minimum sales and marketing requirements, Section (ii)(f) below.

In practice, parties may violate antitrust law

All parties should realize that in actual practice many distribution agreements violate the antitrust laws. Parties do not put all terms of their agreements into their contracts. At times parties leave unwritten, and perhaps even unsaid, terms which violate the law. But each party still knows what the other expects.

Many manufacturers have market power. In many cases, if they terminate the distribution agreement, then the distributor will go out of business. A distributor in such a position will do what the manufacturer expects. Despite what antitrust law and the contract may say, for example, such a distributor will not sell in territories in which the manufacturer does not want it to sell. This is particularly true if the manufacturer granted the distributor a favorable concession, such as an exclusive territory of its own, and in return expected the distributor not to sell in other distributors' territories.

Dispute when contract terminated

If the distributor were to sue the manufacturer for imposing on it an illegal, and unwritten, requirement, then it would probably do so after the manufacturer terminated the distribution agreement. After the manufacturer has terminated the agreement the distributor no longer has to worry about losing its distribution rights, and is usually quite upset. This is a potent combination. See Termination, Section (ii)(o).

(e)   Manufacturer's control of price

Issue

How, if at all, may the manufacturer control the distributor's price?

Commentary

The manufacturer's control over the distributor's price is a very complex subject, and one which the parties should approach with great caution.

In this area the distinction between a distributor and an agent is crucial. A distributor buys and resells goods. An agent merely locates buyers for the manufacturer, who then sells the goods directly to the buyer. In the case of an agent the manufacturer sells directly to the customer. If the manufacturer is selling directly to the customer, then it can clearly set the price the customer will pay.

Manufacturer cannot set distributor's price

In the case of a distributor, the manufacturer does not sell directly to the customer. The manufacturer sells to the distributor who in turn sells to the customer. In this case the law will not allow the manufacturer to set the distributor's price. Agreements which allow the manufacturer to set the distributor's price are called resale price maintenance agreement. Such agreements unreasonably restrain competition among distributors, and the antitrust laws therefore prohibit them.

Same price for all distributors

The manufacturer will always have the power to influence the distributor's reselling price. The manufacturer will always be able to set the price it charges its distributors and the law must always allow the manufacturer to adjust the price it charges its distributors as market conditions change. On the other hand, the law also fears that manufacturers may use their power to set the price their distributors will pay to influence the price their distributors will charge.

To resolve this dilemma, the law requires the manufacturer to charge all its distributors the same price. Thus the law restricts the manufacturer's authority to adjust it price. The manufacturer cannot set different prices for different distributors.

The law still gives the manufacturer considerable power however. It can refuse to grant distribution rights to any potential distributor. It can cancel a distribution agreement. These powers are part of the manufacturer's inherent right to market its products. The manufacturer therefore retains considerable power over distributors and potential distributors.

Consignment sales turn distributor into agent

To avoid the prohibition on controlling their distributors' prices, some manufacturers structure transactions so that their distributors never actually buy the relevant goods. These manufacturers structure transactions so that after their distributors find customers, they, the manufacturers, sell directly to the customers. Since in this case the manufacturer is selling directly to the customer, the manufacturer can set the price the customer will pay.

In these transactions the distributor usually has physical possession of the goods. The parties will therefore have entered into a what is called a consignment sales arrangement. In a consignment sale the manufacturer retains ownership of goods which are in the distributor's physical possession. The buyer will then purchase, directly from the distributor, goods which belong to the manufacturer. See Consignment sales and credit, Section (ii)(i).

The law allows consignment sales. But courts realize that a manufacturer may use a consignment sale structure to hide its attempt to set the distributor's selling price. Courts therefore scrutinize consignment sales to see if the manufacturer is improperly trying to set the distributor's price.

To determine if the parties have entered into a legitimate consignment sale arrangement courts look at the following factors. No one factor is determinative. Courts look at the entire transaction to determine the manufacturer's true intent. These factors are:

- which party sets the selling price,
- which party in reality owns the goods – to determine this courts look at factors such as which party:
  - would incur the loss if the products were not sold,
  - paid taxes for which the owner is legally responsible,
  - paid insurance on the goods,
  - actually delivered the products,
  - performed repairs, and
  - collected delinquent payments
- whether the distributor used the manufacturer's trademark.

Manufacturers should be careful

Manufacturers should proceed with caution in this area, for two reasons. First, the liability for violating the antitrust laws is great–the manufacturer will have to pay three times the distributor's loss, plus attorneys' fees. Secondly, in the case of a dispute with the distributor, even about an unrelated issue, if the distributor can credibly threaten to bring an antitrust case against the manufacturer, then the distributor will have great bargaining leverage. In fact, when a distributor challenges a manufacturer's past attempts to control the distributor's price, it is often doing so because it is angry at the manufacturer for terminating the distribution agreement, not because it is truly upset about the manufacturer's attempts to set its price. See Termination, Section (ii)(o).

Manufacturer's ability to influence distributor's price

Control distributor's costs

Even if the law will not allow the manufacturer to set the distributor's price, the law cannot stop the manufacturer from influencing the distributor's price. The manufacturer will always have the power to greatly influence the distributor's costs. The manufacturer may, for example, be able to require the distributor to invest in certain marketing and promotion activities. See Distributor's capital investment requirements, Section (ii)(g).

Advertising and promotion programs

Further, if the manufacturer develops an advertising program, then it will expect the distributor to sell at the price it advertises. The more the manufacturer makes these and similar programs and campaigns optional rather than mandatory for distributors, the less likely a court is find that they are schemes through which the manufacturer is illegally controlling the distributor's reselling price.

Grant or deny credit

Still another complication in this area regards the manufacturer's power to grant or deny credit. The manufacturer can grant credit not only to the distributor but also to the distributor's customers. The manufacturer's control over credit and financing certainly gives it influence over the distributor's resale price. So long as it makes its decisions to grant or deny credit on a case-by-case basis, and has commercially valid reasons for its decisions, a court will not find that it has illegally used its ability to control credit to control the distributor's resale price.

(f) Best efforts and minimum sales and marketing requirements

Issues

- Must the distributor use its "best efforts" to sell the product?

- Must the distributor sell a specific minimum amount of goods?

- Must the distributor invest a certain sum in:
  - marketing,
  - advertising, or
  - promotion?

- In what other ways can the manufacturer motivate the distributor?

Commentary

Best efforts

All contracts implicitly require the distributor to use its "best efforts." Courts have derived this requirement from the term, implicit in every contract, that each party must act in good faith. Thus, to act in good faith, the distributor must do more than make a bare minimum effort to sell the manufacturer's product. See Contracting, Chapter 7, and Licensing, Chapter 5.

The law, however, cannot adequately define "best efforts." A firm's "best efforts" will vary greatly from situation to situation. A useful definition is that a distributor uses its "best efforts" when it uses its best judgment to sell as many products as it reasonably can.

A court could interpret the "best efforts" clause as requiring a distributor to only sell the manufacturer's products. Whether a court would actually interpret the implied clause in this way depends on the context of the entire transaction. A court would interpret a "best efforts" clause this way if, for example, the industry norm were for one distributor to sell only one manufacturer's products. A court would be even more likely to require the distributor to sell only the manufacturer's goods if the effect of selling the goods of a second manufacturer would be to lower significantly sales of the products which the distributor must use its "best efforts" to sell. See Exclusive territory and right to exclusively carry manufac-turer's products, Section (ii)(d) above.

Minimum sales requirements

Quantifies "best efforts"

Since the law cannot define "best efforts" courts have great difficulty enforcing "best effort" clauses. Many manufacturers therefore include minimum sales requirements in their contracts. In this way they turn the subjective concept of "best efforts" into a measurable, objective standard.

Many possibilities

The parties could set minimum sales requirements in an almost infinite number of ways. Three common ways to establish minimum sales requirements are:

- an explicit target, such as 10,000 units sold, within a period of time;
- a particular market share for a specific territory;
- a target based on past performance. Among the many ways to do this are requiring the same sales as:
  - the previous year, or
  - an average of the past two or three years.

The parties could set other targets as well. They could tie sales growth targets to macroeconomic variables such as GDP growth. Such a provision would appropriately adjust the distributor's sales target to the state of the economy.

The parties could set the distributor's minimum as a percentage of a certain target, such as 90% of the amount sold last year. The parties could increase the minimum over time, as the product establishes itself in the market. The parties could establish a minimum sales requirement which is a combination of several different targets.

Common source of disputes

These requirements often lead to disputes. They do so not only because the distributor will suffer some penalty if it fails to sell the required minimum, but also because parties and lawyers find it so hard to define clearly the minimum sales they require. All minimum sales requirements are, to some degree, ambiguous. For example, the parties who base their minimum sales requirement on market share will not be able to define market share adequately.

Penalties

If the distributor fails to meet its minimum sales requirement it could suffer any one of many penalties. At the extreme, the manufacturer will take from the distributor its right to sell the manufacturer's goods. The manufacturer, however, will probably find that it is not in its interest to impose so severe a sanction. The manufacturer will have to spend a great deal of time looking for a new distributor and the new distributor will lack experience. Furthermore, if the manufacturer were simply to terminate the agreement the distributor would probably sue the manufacturer. See Termination, Section (ii)(o).

Thus the manufacturer would probably impose a less severe sanction on the distributor who failed to meet its minimum sales requirements. The manufacturer could impose the following less severe sanctions:

- loss of the *exclusive* right to sell the manufacturer's products – the distributor would retain the non-exclusive right to sell.

- loss of the right to sell only one product or one product line – the distributor would retain the right to sell other products.

In addition, the manufacturer could terminate the distribution agreement if the distributor failed to meet its minimum sales requirements over an extended period of time, such as two consecutive years.

Often very low

Very often, after the parties have finished negotiating the entire distribution agreement, they find that they have established a minimum sales requirement which is so low that it does not provide adequate motivation to the distributor. Thus, to truly motivate their distributors, manufacturers must usually offer their distributors the opportunity to earn substantial profits. Manufacturers should therefore focus on giving their distributors sound marketing and related assistance. See Marketing assistance provided by manufacturer, Section (ii)(h).

Required marketing expenditures

Manufacturers often require distributors to spend a certain minimum amount to market the manufacturer's products. Other manufacturers develop joint marketing programs in which their distributors must participate. All these requirements define how many resources the distributor must invest to market the manufacturer's products. They define the distributor's "best efforts."

(g) Distributor's capital investment requirements

Issues

1. Must the distributor make the necessary investments to ensure adequate:

- warehouses and physical facilities,

- transportation and delivery systems, or

- inventory?

2. Must the distributor supply:

- after sales service, or

- spare parts?

Commentary

Defines best efforts

Manufacturers often require their distributors to make some of these investments. These required minimum investment provisions really define "best efforts." These, and the other provisions discussed above, require the distributor to make a certain minimum effort to market the manufacturer's products.

Manufacturer's assistance

The manufacturer could help the distributor make the necessary investment. The manufacturer could provide credit, for example, either to help the distributor make the investments the manufacturer requires, or to help the distributor generally. The manufacture could also make an appropriate investment itself, such as building a distribution center. The manufacturer could help the distributor implement its marketing program. For the sake of its long term success, the manufacturer should usually help the distributor in some appropriate fashion.

Co-ordinate all related terms

The parties must co-ordinate their capital investments provision with other provisions of their distribution agreement. A distributor will probably refuse to make a significant capital investment, for example, unless the manufacturer gives the distributor an exclusive territory. The exclusive territory would both increase the distributor's return on its investment and help to ensure that it receives the benefits of its investment.

Distributor investments and termination

If the manufacturer requires the distributor to make a substantial investment, then the law may limit the manufacturer's right to terminate the contract. The distributor should not, however, rely on any such possible legal protection. Before making any substantial investments, the distributor should be sure that the contract limits the manufacturer's right to terminate the contract. The distributor should, at a minimum, ensure that it will have an adequate opportunity to earn back its investment. See Termination, Section (ii)(o).

Distributors making several smaller investments over a period of time, rather than one initial large investment, must be especially careful. When signing the agreement they may not realize how much money they will invest in the future. These distributors must carefully evaluate how much money they will invest during the term of the agreement, and must make sure that the manufacturer cannot terminate the agreement until they have at least had the opportunity to earn back their investment.

Courts protect distributors who make investments

If the manufacturer encouraged the distributor to invest, then a court may later limit the manufacturer's right to terminate the agreement. This is true even if the contract gives the manufacturer the right to terminate the agreement at any time. A court may later feel that the manufacturer abused its power and acted "unfairly."

If a court were to stop a manufacturer from terminating an agreement, it would base its authority to do this on the term, implicit in all contracts, that all parties must act in good faith. The court would find that the manufacturer acted in bad faith. Thus, when deciding whether to ask a distributor to invest, a manufacturer should consider how this may effect a court's view of its possible later decision to terminate the agreement. See Termination, Section (ii)(o)

Manufacturer could reimburse distributor

The parties could agree that the manufacturer will compensate the distributor if the manufacturer terminates the agreement. The manufacturer could agree to pay what is called a "buy-out" fee. The parties typically base this fee on the distributor's investment. Since these terms are "fair" to the distributor, they help manufacturers avoid liability for "unfairly" terminating a distribution agreement.

If the parties have agreed that the manufacturer will not pay a "buy-out" fee, then the contract should state this clearly. This statement will help the manufacturer show that the distributor made an informed business decision to accept the contract without such a clause, and the court should therefore not award the distributor any compensation the contract does not provide it.

(h) Marketing assistance provided by manufacturer

Issue

1. Areas in which the manufacturer could help the distributor include:

● staff training,
    – technical training,
    – sales and marketing training,

● market research,

● market planning,

● customer leads,

● providing sales literature and other promotional material, and sharing the cost of translation and other adjustments for the American market,

● co-operative advertising,

● warranty claims other than repairs, such as exchange of defective goods.

Commentary

Assistance helps both parties

The best distributor is the motivated distributor. It sells the most products, and therefore makes the most money for the manufacturer. The potential for profits, not the threat of sanctions, truly motivates distributors. Thus the manufacturer who helps its distributor is actually helping itself. Manufacturers usually find the marketing assistance they give their distributor to be a good investment. This is particularly true regarding assistance a manufacturer may give to a distributor introducing a new product into the American market.

Distributor keeps information confidential

The manufacturer may give the distributor valuable, confidential information. If the manufacturer does so, then it should of course require the distributor to keep the information confidential. This confidential information could include mailing lists, trade secrets, etc. See Confidentiality, Section (ii)(m).

Joint marketing

The manufacturer and distributor could implement a joint marketing campaign. Such campaigns increase overall promotion efforts and allow the parties to share costs. A non-American manufacturer entering the American market should be particularly interested in working with its American distributor, who can help the non-American manufacturer learn how to market its products in the United States.

Common source of disputes

The contract should clearly describe whatever assistance the manufacturer will provide. This applies both to information the manufacturer may provide and any joint marketing efforts the parties may implement. Clarity always helps to avoid misunderstandings, strained relations, and lawsuits.

(i)   Consignment sales and credit

Issues

- Will the manufacturer supply the distributor with:
    - samples, or
    - inventory?

- If so, who will be responsible for:
    - maintenance (including the cost of periodic inspections)
    - storage, or
    - insurance?

- Will the manufacturer provide credit to the agent?

Commentary

Distributor holds manufacturer's goods

Under a consignment arrangement the distributor holds the manufacturer's goods. Customers will buy the goods from the distributor, but the
goods still belong to the manufacturer until then. If the manufacturer were
to structure its sales efforts in this way, then the distributor would in effect
be the manufacturer's agent.

Consignment sale arrangements allow the manufacturer to retain control
over many aspects of the distributor's business. Most importantly they
allow the manufacturer to control the distributor's selling price. In fact, if
a manufacturer establishes a consignment sale arrangement, it must be
sure to do so in such a way that a court would see it as a legitimate
business arrangement, and not as the manufacturer's illegal attempt to
set the distributor's price. See Manufacturer's control of distributor, Section (ii)(k).

Maintenance costs

If the manufacturer provides goods on consignment, then the parties must
decide how to allocate the costs of maintaining the goods. The contract
may require the distributor, for example, to purchase appropriate insurance.
The parties must also develop procedures so that each party can be sure
that the other has fulfilled its obligations. The contract may require the

distributor, for example, to provide proof that it has purchased the appropriate insurance. See Insurance, Section (ii)(l).

Credit with security

Manufacturers sometimes use consignment sales, in effect, to extend credit to their distributor. The manufacturer could of course extend credit to the distributor directly, by shipping it inventory without receiving payment. If the distributor needed this assistance because it was small and under-capitalized, then the manufacturer would only ship goods to the distributor if someone else guaranteed payment. The logical person to guarantee payment is the person who owns the undercapitalized distributor. But if this person did not have sufficient assets, then his guarantee would not be any more valuable than that of the undercapitalized distributor.

In this case the manufacturer would usually obtain a security interest in the goods. A security interest, similar to a mortgage, would give the manufacturer the right to repossess the goods if the distributor failed to pay. By contrast, if the manufacturer had no security agreement and the distributor failed to pay, then the distributor would merely owe the manufacturer the money.

On the other hand, the manufacturer could sell the goods on consignment. The manufacturer would, in effect, sell the goods on credit, but have complete security. Like a credit sale, the manufacturer would transfer the goods to the distributor, but would not receive payment. The manufacturer would have complete security in the goods because it would still own the goods. If the distributor became bankrupt, then the manufacturer could easily take possession of its goods, which would be its own property.

Sale or return

Some contracts are for "sale or return." The distributor pays for its inventory, but has the right to return unsold inventory. This is very similar to a consignment arrangement. In fact, courts sometimes interpret sale or return arrangements as consignment sale arrangements.

Provides compensation to distributor

Furthermore, the "or return" part of a "sale or return" arrangement will, in effect, force the manufacturer to pay compensation to the distributor should the manufacturer terminate the distribution agreement. If the manufacturer terminated the distribution agreement, then this provision would allow the distributor to return its unsold inventory to the manufacturer. A manufacturer terminating the distribution agreement but then buying back the distributor's unsold inventory would, in effect, be compensating the distributor for terminating the agreement. A "sale or return" provision may therefore help a manufacturer to convince a court that it terminated the distribution agreement "fairly." See Termination, Section (ii)(o).

(j) Trademark use

Issue

● To what extent may the distributor use the manufacturer's trademark?

Commentary

Helps both parties

The manufacturer usually allows the distributor to use its trademark. The trademark usually helps the distributor increase sales.

The distributor could use the trademark, among other places, on:

● buildings and factories,

● cars and trucks,

● stationery and business cards.

Manufacturer's concerns

While the manufacturer should usually allow its distributor to use the manufacturer's trademarks, it must do so carefully. The manufacturer must be careful not to trigger franchise laws, and it must also be careful that a court will not hold it liable for the distributor's acts or violations of product liability law.

Franchise laws

If the distributor uses the manufacturer's trademarks, then federal and state franchise rules may apply to the parties' relationship. Franchising in the US is highly regulated. The Federal Trade Commission implements federal regulations, and many states also impose regulations. These regulations generally protect franchisees. A manufacturer should therefore only allow its distributor to use its trademarks in ways which will not cause franchise laws to apply to the parties' relationship.

Manufacturer liable for distributor's acts

The manufacturer must be careful not to make the distributor its "agent." If the distributor becomes the manufacturer's agent then a court may hold the manufacturer liable for the distributor's acts. As is more fully explained in Manufacturer's control of distributor, Section (ii)(k), when one party is under the control of another, a court may hold the party with the authority liable for the acts of the person under its control. In this context, because the distributor is using the manufacturer's trademark, third parties may reasonably believe that the distributor is under the manufacturer's control. If third parties reasonably believe this, then a court may hold the manufacturer liable for the distributor's acts. See Practical appendix, Section (iv).

The manufacturer should require the distributor to take all appropriate steps so third parties realize that the manufacturer does not control the distributor. The manufacturer could require the distributor, for example, to use with the trademark phrases such "authorized dealer" or "an independent company." The manufacturer should also require the distributor to buy the appropriate insurance. See Insurance, Section (ii)(l).

Strict products liability

Some courts impose strict products liability on trademark owners who allow others to use their trademarks. Courts reason that a trademark is an assurance of quality, and the owner of that trademark, by receiving payment in return for letting another firm use that trademark, must ensure that the firm using the trademark sells products of the appropriate quality. If the firm's products are not of the appropriate quality, then a court may hold the trademark owner responsible. To protect itself from such liability the manufacturer should be sure that it, and its distributor, purchases the appropriate insurance. See Insurance, Section (ii)(l), and Product Liability, Chapter 6.

(k)   Manufacturer's control of distributor

Issues

- What is the distributor's authority to enter into agreements on behalf of the manufacturer?

- The what extent, if at all, must the distributor follow the manufacturer's instructions regarding:
  - price, or
  - other marketing practices?

- When must the distributor report to the manufacturer?

Commentary

Distributor's authority to enter into agreements

The law gives the distributor whatever authority to enter into contracts on the manufacturer's behalf that a third party dealing with the distributor reasonably believes the distributor has. In other words, it is not the contract between the distributor and the manufacturer which limits the distributor's authority. Rather it is the reasonable impression of third parties which limit the distributor's authority. See Practical appendix, Section (iv).

Since third parties' reasonable impressions limit the distributor's authority, the manufacturer should require the distributor to inform third parties that it has only limited authority to act on behalf of the manufacturer. See Trademark use, Section (ii)(j), and Manufacturer's liability for agent's actions, Section (iii)(b).

(l)   Insurance

Issue

- Has the distributor purchased insurance to protect the manufacturer from liability for:
  - the distributor's acts, and
  - product liability?

- Has the manufacturer purchased appropriate insurance for:
  - product liability,
  - related business risks?

Commentary

Each party must buy the appropriate insurance

When the parties divide risks, they are really deciding which party will incur which insurance cost. Each party must then make sure that the other does in fact buy the appropriate insurance.

For example, both parties face the risk that a consumer may bring a product liability lawsuit. The contract should make clear how the parties have agreed to apportion liability for this risk. Each party typically assumes liability for its acts. Thus the manufacturer assumes liability for injuries its products cause, and the distributor assumes liability for injuries related to its efforts to modify or install those products. The manufacturer should be sure that the distributor then purchases the appropriate insurance. In this way the manufacturer can be sure that even if the court were to hold it liable for the distributor's repairs, an insurance company would actually pay the court award.

(m)   Confidentiality

Issue

May the distributor reveal:

- the terms of the contract, or

- underlying business information?

Commentary

Manufacturer should forbid distributor from sharing information

Distributors often share information among themselves. The manufacturer should forbid the distributor from sharing information. It should do so for the following reasons.

- If the distributors are competitors, a court could interpret this exchange of information as collusion among competitors. The antitrust laws forbid such collusion.
- The manufacturer will not want the entire industry to know the terms of its agreement with any particular distributor.
- The information the distributor shares could contain customer lists and other trade secrets which the manufacturer will want to keep confidential.
- If the manufacturer did not require the distributor to keep the trade secrets confidential, then the trade secrets would probably lose their legal protection. See Commercial Intellectual Property, Trade secrets, Chapter 4 (iii).

(n)   Communication between the parties

Issue

- Will the parties develop formal reporting and communication procedures?

Commentary

Distributor reports

The manufacturer will often require the distributor to provide periodic reports. In fact, to develop a good business relationship, not only should the distributor issue frequent reports but the manufacturer should do so as well.

The manufacturer should periodically report business developments to its distributors. The manufacturer should report on items such as the product improvements it expects to make in the near future, its yearly financial reports, and so on. The parties should develop reporting practices which help them communicate and work together.

Regulatory changes

The non-American manufacturer will often ask the American distributor to keep it abreast of appropriate regulatory and legal developments in the United States. The distributor should usually agree to do so.

(o) Termination

Issues

- Does the agreement say when it will end? If so, when will it end?
- Can the agreement be renewed?
- Will one party, such as the manufacturer, be able to terminate the agreement early if the other party, such as the distributor, fails to meet certain criteria, such as a minimum sales requirement? Will the manufacturer be able to terminate the contract early even if the distributor meets all its obligations?

Commentary

The most common source of lawsuits

When the manufacturer terminates the agreement, the distributor is likely to sue. Most distributor agreement lawsuits revolve around the issue of whether the manufacturer properly terminated the agreement. When the manufacturer terminates the distribution agreement, it certainly hurts the distributor's business, and it may put the distributor out of business. The distributor has often invested considerable time and money to develop its market. When the manufacturer takes this market away the distributor usually feels cheated. This emotion and this lost money are a potent combination, and the two together often produce a lawsuit.

Contract must be clear

Because termination can so easily lead to a lawsuit, it is crucial that the contract spell out – absolutely clearly – when and how each party may terminate the agreement. Ambiguous terms cause lawsuits. The contract should therefore clearly specify:

- how long the contract will run,
- the conditions under which a party may choose not to renew the contract,
- the conditions under which a party may cancel the contract, and

● the notice required if a party cancels or fails to renew the contract.

Courts sympathize with terminated distributor

Because termination is so harmful to the distributor's business, courts tend to feel sympathy for the terminated distributor. This is particularly true if the court sees the manufacturer's acts as somehow "unfair." If the court believes that the manufacturer acted "unfairly," then it will find that the manufacturer acted in bad faith. It will find that the manufacturer violated the term, which the law implies in every contract, in which each party agrees to act towards the other in good faith. See Best efforts and minimum sales and marketing requirements, Section (ii)(f).

Courts find bad faith in many different situations. A classic example of a manufacturer acting in bad faith is one who refuses to sell the distributor enough products so it can meet its minimum sales requirement. Courts also tend to find that a manufacturer who terminated a distribution agreement before the distributor has had a reasonable opportunity to earn back its investment has acted in bad faith. Courts treat manufacturers they find acting in bad faith rather harshly. Some have even ordered manufacturers acting in bad faith to pay punitive (punishment) damages. See Distributor's capital investment requirements, Section (ii)(g).

Manufacturer must not even appear to be acting unfairly

Courts will almost always look beyond the manufacturer's explanation for why it terminated the agreement. A court will want to know if a manufacturer is using a seemingly legitimate reason to terminate the agreement as a pretext to terminate for another, improper, reason. For example, a manufacturer may claim that it is terminating the agreement because the distributor failed to meet its minimum sales requirement. The distributor may claim that the manufacturer really terminated the agreement because it wanted to lessen competition in the distributor's territory in violation of the antitrust laws. The court will listen to both arguments and then decide.

Before terminating a distribution agreement, therefore, the manufacturer must consider how a court may later perceive its actions. Even if the manufacturer's acts are legal, if they seem unfair to a court then the court may find that the manufacturer acted in bad faith. For this reason a manufacturer should not, for example, allow a distributor to make a large investment in equipment or facilities when it knows that technological developments will soon make the investment worthless. This is true even if the manufacturer has no legal obligation to tell the distributor of future developments. If the manufacturer should later terminate the agreement, then a court may find that it acted in bad faith.

Manufacturer should protect itself

Keep records

When deciding whether to terminate an agreement, the manufacturer should assume that the distributor will challenge in court its reason for terminating the agreement. And, as with war, preparing for a lawsuit is the best way to avoid it. For example, long before it terminates a contract, a manufacturer should record everything which the distributor does improperly and which may give it a legitimate reason to later terminate the distribution agreement. The manufacturer should therefore continuously monitor the distributor's performance. By doing this the manufacturer will be able to prove that the distributor performed poorly. It will be able to prove in court that it terminated the agreement for valid business reasons.

Give opportunity to improve

Before terminating a contract the manufacturer should consider giving the distributor the opportunity to correct any breach or improve its business performance. The contract may not require the manufacturer to give the distributor this opportunity, but if the manufacturer does so, then it has gone a long way towards protecting itself from the distributor's later claim that it terminated the contract improperly or too quickly.

Distributor should seek contractual protection

While the parties may agree that the manufacturer can terminate the contract at any time, the distributor should resist giving the manufacturer so much power. If the manufacturer forces the distributor to accept such a term, then the distributor should make sure that the contract in some way limits the manufacturer's ability to exercise this power. The contract could require the manufacturer to:

● give the distributor reasonable notice of termination;

● wait a reasonable period of time before terminating – the length of this period is usually related to the amount the distributor will invest;

● give the distributor time to correct any breaches of the contract – in particular, the contract could give the distributor time to pay the manufacturer any money it may owe;

- only for certain specified breaches may the manufacturer terminate immediately.

Contracts with no termination date

Some contracts do not say when they will end. In most states either party may terminate such contracts at any time. In a minority of states, however, a party may only terminate such a contract if it has a good reason. In still other states a party may only terminate such a contract after the contract has been in force for a reasonable period, such as a period long enough to give the distributor a reasonable opportunity to earn back its investment. (See Distributor's capital requirements, Section (ii)(g).)

Expiration instead of termination

Some manufacturers simply wait for their distribution agreements to expire. They do not terminate agreements, and they therefore avoid the related lawsuits. Of course manufacturers can use this strategy only if their distribution agreements expire quickly. Manufacturers therefore prefer short agreements.

(p) Arbitration and mediation

Issues

- Will the parties arbitrate their disputes?
- Will the parties mediate their disputes?

Commentary

Parties should arbitrate and mediate

The parties should try to arbitrate and mediate their disputes. While this is always true, it is particularly true regarding distribution agreements. Parties to distribution agreements have usually developed a working relationship over time, and neither party should want to destroy this relationship. Lawsuits are not only time consuming and expensive, they also distract managers from their primary task of operating their businesses to earn profits. Further, if arbitration or mediation allows the parties to solve their disputes with a minimum of rancor, then the parties can hopefully continue to work together.

Mediation particularly helpful

Parties to distribution agreements may find mediation particularly helpful. A mediator may be able to develop a solution which makes business sense, but which neither a judge nor an arbitrator could impose. It will also help the parties avoid the problem that the antitrust aspects of their dispute may stop them from arbitrating their dispute. See Court system: lawsuits and arbitration, Chapter 9.

(q) Sale of right to distribute

Issue

- As part of the sale of its business, may the distributor sell its right to distribute the manufacturer's products?

Commentary

Manufacturer can usually only reject for good reason

The parties clearly have different interests regarding the distributor's right to sell its business. The distributor wants the flexibility to sell its business to the highest bidder. The manufacturer wants to have at least the authority to approve a new distributor.

Parties often compromise by allowing the manufacturer to approve the new distributor, but they also agree that the manufacturer may not unreasonably withhold its approval. Under this arrangement, if the manufacturer were to refuse to approve the new distributor, then it must explain why. A court would then only stop the sale if it found this explanation reasonable. In fact in some states if the manufacturer does have the right to approve the new distributor, the law itself says that the manufacturer may not unreasonably withhold its approval.

iii.   Agreements with agents

(a)   Introduction

Agents find customers for manufacturers. Unlike distributors, agents never own the manufacturer's goods. Agents are mere intermediaries. Agents earn commissions while distributors earn profits. Agents are independent contractors, not the manufacturer's employees. Firms and individuals can both be agents.

In some respects agents are similar to sales personnel the manufacturer may employ. Like sales personnel, agents sell on behalf of the manufacturer. Like employees, and unlike distributors, agents tend not to enter into formal agreements with manufacturers. However, agents are not employees, and manufacturers have less control over agents than they do over their own sales personnel.

Many people use different terms to describe one who sells for a firm but is not the firm's employee. Broker, sales agent, sales representatives, and manufacturer's representatives are examples of such terms. Some define these terms more specifically. To some, for example, a manufacturer's representative knows more about marketing than does a broker or a sales agent. For simplicity, this discussion simply uses the term agent.

Manufacturers who use agents retain greater control over the marketing process than those who use distributors. Because manufacturers continue to own the goods while they are in the distribution chain, they are often deeply involved in the process of marketing their goods. Most importantly, because manufacturers own the goods, they can set the price customers pay for the goods. Manufacturers therefore tend to work very closely with their agents.

The manufacturer's relationship with its agent will determine how much marketing control the manufacturer exercises. The formal contract and the informal habits which develop over time will together determine each party's role. In fact, each party has to be careful because the expectations the other party develops over time may create terms of the agency agreement which a court will enforce as much as it would terms of a written contract. See Contracting, Chapter 7.

As with distributors, the United States imposes no laws or regulations specifically on manufacturers or agents. Courts generally apply standard commercial law to the manufacturer-agent relationship. The exceptions are a few industries, such as the alcoholic beverage industry, to which special regulations apply. Thus, in general, the law gives the parties wide discretion to structure almost any relationship they wish.

Agents similar to manufacturers

Manufacturers dealing with both agents and distributors must address essentially the same issues. Thus the preceding discussion regarding distributors applies almost equally well to agents.

Agree to all details of working relationship

Manufacturers tend to work closely with agents as the two market the manufacturer's products. To insure that this relationship starts smoothly, before beginning to work together the manufacturer and agent should, as far as possible, agree on the details of their working relationship.

Agents in particular should be sure to discuss all aspects of their working relationship with the manufacturer. Agents tend to be individuals, and individuals tend not to negotiate complete agreements. Agents should realize the importance of their relationship with the manufacturer and should negotiate a complete and proper agreement with the manufacturer.

Areas which tend to cause friction between manufacturers and agents, and which the parties should therefore discuss particularly carefully, are:

- the period of time in which the manufacturer must accept or reject orders from the agent's customers,

- the right of the agent to receive correspondence between the manufacturer and the agent's customers,

- the possible payment of commissions for orders the agent's customers place after the agent is terminated. See Commissions, Section (iii)(c).

(b)   Manufacturer's liability for agent's actions

Tell third parties of limited authority

As with distributors, manufacturers should limit the possibility that a court will hold them liable for their agents' actions. The reasonable impression of third parties determines the extent to which a court will hold the manufacturer liable for an agent's acts. The manufacturer should therefore do all it can to ensure that the public knows the extent of the agent's authority. See Manufacturer's control of distributor, Section (ii)(k).

Manufacturers working with agents should be doubly sure to take this precaution. Because agents and manufacturers work closely together, a court is particularly likely to hold a manufacturer liable for an agent's acts. The manufacturer should therefore be sure that the contract requires the agent to take all appropriate steps to ensure that third parties know the limit of the agent's authority. The contract could require the agent, for example, to use forms which explain the agent's limited authority.

The manufacturer must also make sure that as its relationship with its agent develops over time, the agent does not come to believe that its authority is increasing. One effective way for the manufacturer to do this is to repeat in its correspondence the limited authority of the agent. This is particularly true if third parties will also read this correspondence. It is even more important if the relationship begins to deteriorate. When the relationship turns sour, problems tend to develop. The manufacturer which limits its agents authority will be protecting itself.

Quickly respond to false product claims

An agent will on occasion make an exaggerated claim about the abilities of the manufacturer's product. While the law allows agents to express their glowing opinions of the products they are selling, the law does not allow agents to make untrue factual claims about their products. To protect itself against an agent's untrue factual claim, the manufacturer should tell the customer the truth as soon as it learns of the agent's exaggerated claim. The manufacturer should put this notification in writing. See Contracting, Chapter 7.

(c) Commissions

Issues

- How will commissions be calculated? Possibilities include:
  - percentage of the selling price, or
  - flat rate per unit sold.

- Will the commission rate vary depending on how the goods were ordered? Commissions on orders placed directly to the manufacturer could, for example
  - receive a lower commission (or no commission at all).

- On what price is the commission to be based?
  - On the price at the manufacturer's factory, or a related price?
  - Does the price include insurance and related costs?

- When is the commission earned? Possibilities include:
  - when the order is received,
  - when the goods are delivered, or
  - when the customer makes payment.

- Are commissions still payable if, for example:
  - the buyer cancels the order,
  - the buyer declares bankruptcy,
  - the manufacturer rejects the order?

- When must the manufacturer pay the agent? Possibilities include:
  - within 30 days,
  - four times a year.

- Will the commission rate change? It could, for example:
  - increase as sales increase,
  - increase on more profitable items, or
  - increase for new customers.

Commentary

The law generally allows the parties to enter into any agreement they choose. The manufacturer must be careful, however, not to structure its commission payment system in such a way that a court believes the manufacturer is using the commission structure to circumvent the anti-trust laws and control its distributor's reselling price. See Manufacturer's control of distributor, Section (ii)(k).

Parties frequently dispute the amount of commission the manufacturer must pay. Because this is such a common cause of lawsuits, the contract should lay out the commission structure in great detail. The contract should say, for example, if the manufacturer should pay a commission for orders it rejects.

(d)   Delivery of goods

Non-American manufacturers must be particularly careful to develop a satisfactory way of delivering their goods to their American agents. To solve the problem of long delivery times, the manufacturer may store goods in the United States. It may store the goods in a foreign trade zone or bonded warehouse. See Bringing Goods into the United States, Chapter 2.

(e)   Termination

Agents and distributors face essentially the same issues regarding when they or their manufacturers may terminate the relevant agreements. Agents face a few special problems, however, which the following discussion outlines. The agents who face the greatest problems in this area are those who failed to enter into a formal agreement with their manufacturer. Informal agency agreements leave open many issues. Most importantly, they tend not to discuss how the parties may terminate their relationship.

No termination date

Some agency agreements do not say when they terminate. Because agents are similar to employees courts tend to interpret these agency agreements as they would employment agreements. Since either party can generally terminate an employment agreement at any time, so too they can generally terminate such an agency agreement at any time.

On the other hand, as with the distributor, if the agent has invested considerable sums in developing his business, then a court will usually not allow the manufacturer to terminate the agreement until after a reasonable period of time. This reasonable period of time is usually the time it should take the agent to earn back his investment. See Distributor's capital investment requirements, Section (ii)(g).

Manufacturer must act fairly

Just as manufacturers must be careful to act "fairly" when terminating a distribution agreement, so too must they act "fairly" when terminating an agency agreement. If they do not act fairly, then a court may find that they violated the implied term of good faith. A manufacturer may act in bad faith, for example, if it were to terminate an agency agreement just before the agent was to conclude a major sale. The manufacturer may appear to be trying to avoid paying a sizeable commission to its agent. Finally, while courts look favorably on terminated distributors, they look particularly favorably on terminated agents who are individuals rather than firms.

Customer lists and other trade secrets

The agency agreement usually forbids the terminated agent from using the manufacturer's trade secrets, and in particular its customer lists. However, unless the agent has signed an agreement not to compete, the manufacturer cannot stop the agent from calling on particular clients after the agent has begun to represent a new manufacturer.

Further, in some cases the manufacturer will not own the customer list. If the agent developed the customer list, then it is his, not the manufacturer's. At times each party claims ownership of the relevant customer list and, in fact, also of other trade secrets. This is another common source of disputes and these disputes often lead to lawsuits.

(f)   Agreement not to compete

In an agreement not to compete the agent, usually an individual, agrees that after the parties end their relationship he will not work for the manufacturer's competitors. Courts do not to like these agreements. Courts see these agreements as taking from the agent his right to work in his chosen field.

Many courts will nevertheless enforce these agreements. But they will do so only so long as the contract imposes reasonable restrictions on the agent's future work. While what is reasonable varies with the circumstances, as a general rule courts will not allow these agreements to restrict the agent's right to work for more than two years, and will only allow them to apply to an area slightly larger than the agent's former territory. A few states, however, have completely banned these agreements.

(g)   Antitrust

Courts are not likely to find that a manufacturer and agent have violated the antitrust laws. Manufacturers do not sell to agents. Thus the parties do not engage in any sale to which the antitrust laws could apply. Therefore, while a manufacturer may violate the antitrust laws when terminating a distribution agreement, it is not likely to do so when terminating an agency agreement.

However, over time agents tend to act more and more like distributors. Their business grows, and they take on more and more tasks. As this process develops, the parties may blur the line between agent and distributor. As the agent becomes more like a distributor he is more likely, and more able, to make the antitrust claims distributors usually make.

Furthermore, there are two situations in which a manufacturer terminating an agency agreement may very well face a lawsuit raising antitrust issues.

- The parties used the agency as a sham to hide what was really a distributorship.

- The manufacturer dismissed the agent as part of a conspiracy to restrain trade.

Thus the manufacturer should consider the antitrust implications of just about any action it may take

Practical Appendix
The law of agency
When one is liable for another's acts

(a)   Employer and individuals fully liable

Corporations, partnerships fully liable

The law holds corporations and partnerships fully liable for the actions of their employees and, in the case of partnerships, partners as well. The law calls these corporations and partnerships "principles", and it calls the employees and partners who represent them "agents".

Individuals can create agents

Individuals as well as corporations and partnerships can create agents. Individuals must be particularly careful because principals do not necessarily have to pay their agents. Unpaid agents have just as much authority as paid agents to act on behalf of their principal. An individual may therefore ask another person to do something for him, as a favor. Without realizing it the individual has probably created an agent with broad powers to act on his behalf.

Managers and others must take care

Managers and other must therefore be careful:

● not to accidentally give someone the powers of an agent – a manager could easily, and inadvertently, give a person the authority to act for either their firm or themselves personally

● to whom they do, intentionally, give the powers of an agent. The manager or his firm will be responsible for this agent's acts.

(b)   Scope of employment

Employer liable for act of employee

Corporations and partnerships are liable for the actions of their employees and partners when these persons act within the scope of their employment. An employee certainly acts within the scope of his employment when he does what his employer says. But he also acts within the scope of his employment when he takes steps his employer has not authorized, but which are related to his job. For example, if an employee drives the employer's delivery truck where his employer told him not to go, and along the way causes a traffic accident, a court will still hold the employer liable for the damage its employee caused.

Not liable for acts of independent contractor

By contrast, a court will not hold a corporation or other principal liable for the acts of an independent contractor, even for acts the independent contractor takes while working for the corporation. Thus a court will hold a corporate employer liable for the acts of its employees, but not for the acts of the independent contractors the corporation hires.

Employee v. independent contractor

The law distinguishes between an independent contractor and an employee by the extent to which the corporation can tell him how to do his job. Corporations do not have the authority to tell an independent contractor how to do his job but they can tell an employee how to do his job. For example, a corporation may retain an attorney to handle a lawsuit. Since the corporation cannot tell the attorney exactly what to do, such as when to schedule a court hearing, a court will find that the attorney is an independent contractor.

(c) Agent's authority is what appears reasonable to third party

No documents needed

The agent's authority is whatever appears reasonable to a third party. Agents can have broad powers even if the corporation or other principal signs no written document creating this authority. If a third party acts on the assumption that a person is acting on behalf of a corporation, then a court may hold the corporation liable for the person's acts. The court will hold the corporation liable if the third party's belief that the person was acting on behalf of the corporation was reasonable.

Easy to create broad authority

Managers must therefore be very careful. If their actions lead a third party to reasonably believe that a person has the authority to act on behalf of them or their firm, then a court will hold them or their firm liable for the person's acts. Managers must never, for example, allow unauthorized persons to wear their firm's uniforms. Managers must also be very careful who they allow even to say that they represent them or their firm.

Employers must also be very careful of the titles they give employees. Broad and impressive titles may make employees feel good, and cost their employers nothing, but they may lead a third party to reasonably believe that the employee has considerable authority to act on behalf of the firm.

(d) Distributor can be agent

A corporation can be an agent. A distributor can therefore be a manufacturer's agent. Since a distributor acts through its employees, and particularly through its sales personnel, a court may hold a manufacturer liable for the acts of its distributor's employees and sales personnel. Thus a court may hold a manufacturer responsible for the promises made by its distributor's sales personnel. This is another reason why manufacturers must select their distributors with care.

2 BRINGING GOODS INTO THE UNITED STATES
Handling Customs Effectively

2. BRINGING GOODS INTO THE UNITED STATES
Handling Customs Effectively

(i) Introduction

Managers who break customs laws commit a very serious offense. The United States Customs Service, which controls goods coming into the United States, can obtain search warrants and can seize records, goods, and other valuable items. Courts impose civil penalties on violators. These penalties can be up to eight times the customs duties the violator should have paid. Courts will hold firms liable even if they merely make innocent mistakes. Courts also impose criminal penalties.

All firms, but non-American firms in particular, should be sure that the Customs Service does not even suspect that they have violated customs rules and procedures. If a firm has raised the Service's suspicions then the Service may, among other things, seize the goods the firm intended to sell in the United States. Even if a court should eventually find that the firm did nothing wrong, it may still have suffered through years of courtroom proceedings. It may lose control of its goods for years. All this will waste a lot of time and money, much more time and money than the firm thought it was saving when it took the steps which raised the Customs Service's suspicions.

Thus, all managers, but particularly non-American managers, should ask themselves whether the benefits of violating the customs laws outweigh the risks. For example, the manager who alters documents to change the appearance of a transaction, and thereby lower the payable duty, has committed a crime. All managers should wonder whether saving such a small amount of money is worth the risk of criminal penalties. And if, to lower the apparent value of a transaction, someone should suggest that a manager make a separate wire transfer of funds, which the parties would not record on the invoice accompanying the imported goods, then again the manager should ask himself if the saving is worth the risk.

In short, for even an innocent firm, fighting the Customs Service will harm, and may even kill, the firm's American business. Thus, managers should take the time to be sure they are shipping their goods properly. This is true even for managers of non-American firms which have not assumed legal responsibility for passing their goods through customs. It simply makes good business sense for managers to help those who are importing their products.

Finally, the non-American firm trying to help its American importer may find that, rather than helping the importer, it is actually helping itself. When thinking about customs procedures the firm may, for example, realize that it does not have proper country of origin markings ('Made in Denmark') on its goods. By realizing this problem sooner rather than later the firm can probably solve it more quickly and easily.

(ii) Importer of record

The importer of record is the person or firm which assumes legal responsibility for importing the goods into the United States. The owner of the goods, the seller, usually accepts this responsibility, but the buyer, or even a licensed customs broker, could be the importer of record. The importer of record must pay the customs duty and also assumes liability for any penalties and criminal sanctions courts may impose.

Firms involved in import transactions should therefore make very clear which firm will assume the responsibility of being the importer of record. Managers, particularly non-American managers, should not accept this responsibility without appreciating the consequences. Managers should consider, for example, whether their firm is willing to accept legal responsibility for the accuracy of documents other parties may prepare.

If a non-American firm is the importer of record, the firm must have a registered agent in the state in which it is entering the goods. The non-American firm must authorize this agent to accept the papers, called service of process, which begin lawsuits. See Court System, Chapter 9. The non-American firm could authorize its customs broker as the agent. As is discussed further in Customs brokers, Section (x)(a), customs brokers often provide valuable assistance, particularly to non-American firms.

(iii) Get through customs fast

To help the Customs Service enter goods as soon as possible, the importer should:

- prepare a proper invoice, as described below;

- prepare a detailed packing list, one which contains numbers which correspond to numbers on the boxes or containers to which each document refers;

- make sure the manufacturer has properly marked the country of origin on the goods;

- pack the goods in a way which makes inspection easy;

- avoid mixing different types of goods. If the Customs Service cannot separate different types of goods then it will charge, for all the goods, the highest possible duty.

(iv) Import procedure

(a) Decision based on papers and samples

The Customs service cannot inspect every item every importer brings into the United States. For most goods, therefore, it looks only at the relevant papers to determine the appropriate duty. The Customs Service may also examine a few samples of the imported goods.

(b) Bonds

The Customs Service may wait up to one year after the importer has brought the goods into the United States before determining the appropriate duty. The Customs Service requires importers who intend to sell their goods during this period to post a bond. A bond is a guarantee a bank or similar financial institution issues on behalf of its client. In the bond the bank says that if the importer does not pay the Customs Service, then the bank will make the payment instead.

Through these bonds banks promise to pay the Customs Service all the money that it decides the importer must pay. Thus, by issuing bonds, banks promise to pay not only the appropriate duty but also other charges such as interest. Many customs brokers have bonds which banks have already issued in the custom broker's name, and which the broker may use on behalf of its client. This is another example of the assistance customs brokers offer. See Customs brokers, Section (x)(a).

(c)   Invoice

The commercial invoice is the most important document the importer prepares, and the importer should be sure that it prepares its invoice properly. In most cases the Customs Service uses the invoice to determine the appropriate duty. Furthermore, if an importer submits an improper invoice then the Customs Service will, at a minimum, not allow the goods to enter the United States. It may also impose fines and may even take possession of the goods.

Requirements

The commercial invoice must state the following.

- The port through which the importer will bring the goods into the US.

- If the goods have been sold to an American:
  - the name of the American buyer, and
  - the time and place of the sale.

If, however, a non-American firm will sell the goods on consignment (by offering them for sale in the United States while retaining ownership) then the invoice must contain:

  - the time and place from where the goods began their journey to the United States,
  - the name of the shipper, and
  - the name of the receiver of the merchandise.

- A detailed description of the merchandise. Such a description should include:
  - the name of each type of imported good,
  - the grade or quality level of each good,
  - the trademark or similar name under which the goods were sold in the country from which the goods are being exported,
  - the quantities imported,
  - if an American is buying the goods, the price of the goods – the price should be stated in the currency of the sale, be it dollars, Danish kroner, or another currency,
  - the method of payment.

- If the non-American firm will sell the goods on consignment, the fair market value of the goods, or the usual wholesale price of such goods in the country from which the goods were exported. The invoice should give this price in the currency of the exporting country, and should state the usual method of payment.

- All costs involved in shipping the goods to the United States. These include:
  - cases and containers,
  - insurance,
  - packaging,
  - freight costs, and
  - all commissions relating to the transaction.

- All adjustments to the price which the parties will make later. This includes rebates and drawbacks. (Drawbacks are import duties which are refunded by the Customs Service when the imported goods are later exported from the United States. See Refund of duty when goods are re-exported out of the US, Section (vii).)

- The country of origin of the goods.

- All "assists" not included in the invoice price. Regarding assists, see Section (v)(b). The invoice should contain the following information about each assist:
  - its value, if known (see Valuation, Section (v)(b))
  - who supplied the assist
  - under what terms the assist was supplied, i.e. free of charge, on a rental basis, etc.
  - whether the assist was separately invoiced. If so, then the importer should attach a copy of the invoice.

- If the goods were sold at a discount from a list or other standard price, the value of the discount must be shown. If sellers provide discounts so frequently that the official standard or list price is not in actual fact the true market price, then the importer should also disclose this fact. The Customs Service bases duties on market prices, and the importer should ensure that the Customs Service bases its valuation on this true market price, and not a higher price established for marketing purposes.

- The documents should clearly show what is in each individual package of the shipment. See Invoice, Section (iv)(o).

- The invoice must either be in English, or have an attached English translation.

- Weights and measures may be expressed in either the measurement system of the country from which the exporter is shipping the goods, or in the American system.

Invoice not yet ready

If at all possible, the importer should have the invoice ready to give to the Customs Service when the importer brings the goods into the United States. If the complete invoice is not ready, then the importer must:

- provide a statement, called a pro forma invoice, instead,

- post a bond , and

- complete the invoice within a short period of time.

Disclose all possibly relevant information

To make the importing process as fast as possible, the importer should include in its invoice all possibly relevant information. The importer should never assume that information is not relevant. If the importer is in doubt, then it should include the information.

The importer should include all this information because the Customs Service requires importers to disclose information about many non-dutiable items. The Customs Service does this so it can decide whether the item is in fact non-dutiable. It is for this reason that the Customs Service requires importers, for example, to report commissions in addition to any commissions the buyer may have paid to the seller's agent. See Commissions, Chapter 1, Section (iii)(c). Thus, to speed the process, the importer should err on the side of including in the invoice information which may possibly be relevant.

Other practical considerations

The importer should also:

- use a numbering system which clearly shows which invoice relates to which box or container
- make sure statements regarding the following are complete and accurate.
  - The description of the goods. The importer should be sure that the descriptions are not vague or too abbreviated and that different types or classes of goods are separately described.
  - The price of the goods. The price on the invoice should be the price the American buyer paid and not a previous price paid further up the distribution chain.
  - The value of any price discounts the seller gave the buyer.
  - The value of all assists. (For the definition of an assist see Valuation, Section (v)(b).)
  - All costs of shipping the goods to the United States.
  - All commissions relating to the transaction.
  - The names of the buyers and sellers, **or** consignor and consignee – this can be a problem, in particular, when the person in the United States who receives the goods is acting as either an agent or a reseller, and will transfer the goods to another party.
  - The nature of the full importation transaction, of which this shipment may be only a part.

(v) Valuation

(a) Introduction

The Customs Service usually considers the value of imported goods to be the price the buyer actually paid for the goods. The Customs Service will, however, make sure that the price the buyer paid is the true market price. It will, for example, look to see if the buyer and seller are related persons or firms and, if so, if this relationship influenced the selling price. If the Customs Service believes that the price of the goods is not the fair market value of the goods, then it will use one of several alternative values.

(b) Price actually paid

In the usual case the Customs Service will base the duty on the value of the imported goods. It will consider the value of the goods to be the selling price, plus:

- packing costs incurred by the buyer,
- any commissions the buyer may have paid to the seller's agent,
- the value of any "assist,"
- any related royalty or license fee which the seller requires the buyer to pay,
- any subsequent payments which the seller may receive later for the resale of the goods.

Selling price

The selling price also includes all indirect benefits which the buyer provides to the seller. The buyer may, for example, forgive a debt the seller owes the buyer. If the buyer forgives a debt, the Customs Service will consider this to be the same as the buyer paying that money to the seller.

The selling price does *not*, however, include:

- the cost of shipping the goods to the United States, including insurance and related costs,
- maintenance, technical assistance, and similar charges regarding the product after it has entered the United States,
- federal taxes due on the goods, including customs duties,
- the value of American-made components contained within the product.
- commissions other than commissions paid to the seller's agent.

Packing costs

This includes:

- materials used for packing, such as containers, and
- related labor costs.

Commissions

The customs service considers, as part of the selling price, commission the buyer paid the seller's agent. The Customs Service considers money the buyer paid to the seller's agent as money the buyer paid to the seller itself. The Customs Service calls commissions paid to the seller's agent selling commissions.

Assists

Assists are goods and services provided to the non-American manufacturer either free of charge or at a reduced rate. The importer must disclose these goods and services because they help the manufacturer lower its costs, and therefore lower its selling price. Manufacturers who receive assists can sell goods to importers at less than the fair market value. Unless the Customs Service adjusts for this assistance, the importer will pay less than the appropriate duty.

Examples of assists include the following.

- Materials, components and similar items built into the final product.

- Manufacturing assistance, such as:
    - moulds, dies and other items used in the manufacturing process,
    - related professional services, such as engineering or design work.

- Goods consumed during the manufacturing process.

Work done in the United States is not an assist, however.

An assist's value is its fair market value. When calculating this value, the Customs Service considers relevant factors such as:

- the cost of transporting the assist to the manufacturer,

- wear and tear,

- modifications,

- appropriate apportionment if the assist could be used with other products in addition to those imported into the United States.

Intellectual property licensing fees

If a non-American manufacturer or seller *requires* its American buyer to also license rights to patents or other forms of intellectual property, as a *condition of sale* of the product itself, then the Customs Service will consider the license or royalty payments to be part of the price of the product itself. The Customs Service will only consider these payments to be part of the price of the product if the buyer could not import the goods into the US if it did not also pay for the intellectual property rights.

(c)   Alternative values

If the Customs Service believes that the actual selling price does not reflect the fair market value of the imported goods, then the Service will use one of several alternative measures of value to determine the fair market value of the imported goods.

The transaction value may not reflect the fair market value for one of the following reasons:

- the seller has imposed restrictions on the use of the imported goods,

- the seller may be entitled to receive subsequent payments, but pursuant to terms which make it very difficult for the Customs Service to determine the fair market value of the goods,

- there are conditions to the sale for which the Customs Service cannot determine a value,

- The buyer and seller are related. The Customs Service determines on a case by case basis whether the transactions involving related parties are based on fair market prices.

Alternative valuation methods

The Customs Service's alternative valuation methods are as follows, in order of priority.

- The value of identical merchandise.

- The value of similar merchandise.

- The so-called deductive value. This deductive value is the resale price in the United States of the imported goods, if the Customs Service can calculate this price. If the Customs Service cannot calculate this resale price, then the Service will first use the resale price of similar goods and then add to or subtract from this price as appropriate, taking into account all relevant factors.

- The so-called computed value. Computed value is the sum of:
  - manufacturing costs,
  - profits,
  - any assists,
  - packing costs.

- A combination of all these valuation methods, if no one method provides an adequate measure of value.

The importer may choose to have the Customs Service use computed value instead of deductive value.

(d) Damaged goods

For all valuation methods, the Customs Service will consider any damage which may have lowered the value of the imported goods.

(vi) Retaining American identity

If a firm brings American goods out of the United States, and then returns the goods back to the United States, the Customs Service will not require the firm to pay duty on goods it is bringing back into the United States. For goods to retain their American identity and therefore be able to come, duty-free, back into the United States it is necessary that while outside the US they must not have been "substantially transformed." For example, cloth cut during a manufacturing process is "substantially transformed." Cut cloth therefore loses its American identity.

An American firm may send goods outside the United States for repairs or alterations, and then reimport the goods back into the United States. In this case the American firm must pay a duty based only on the value of the services performed outside the US.

An importer bringing American goods back into the United States may therefore be able to bring the goods back into the country without paying any duty. An importer should therefore investigate the status of the goods it is importing.

To bring goods back into the United States without paying duty, the importer or other person or firm must have filed the appropriate papers when first exporting the goods from the US. Thus if a firm is exporting from the US goods which it may later import back to the US, then, when exporting the goods it should be sure to file the appropriate papers so it can import the goods without paying import duty.

(vii)   Refund of duty when goods are re-exported out of the US

When an importer re-exports goods out of the United States, the Customs Service will refund whatever duties the importer paid when bringing the goods into the United States. It does this to protect American manufacturers who are competing in foreign markets. If the Customs Service did not refund the duty, then the cost of American exports would be unfairly high.

But, to obtain this refund, the importer must have filed the appropriate papers when it first imported the goods into the United States. Thus, if an importer believes it or another firm may re-export the goods out of the United States, then, when bringing the goods into the United States, it should be sure to file the appropriate papers.

(viii)   Country of origin markings

(a)   General points

Markings must be:

- clear,
- permanent, and
- in English.

Clear

Brand names which contain the name of a place other than the country of origin can mislead consumers. In particular, brand names containing words such as "American," "USA," or the names of locations can create the false impression that they were made in these locations. To solve this problem, manufacturers could inscribe, near the brand name, the country of origin, using words such as: "Made in..." or "Product of..."

If manufacturers commonly combine the product with another product, then they should make clear the country of origin of each product. For example, a manufacturer could mark a bottle: "Bottle made in..."

Permanent

The manufacturer must mark its products at least permanently enough to ensure that the ultimate purchaser knows the country of origin of the product.

If this requirement would force a manufacturer to deface a product, then, as a last resort, the Customs Service will allow the manufacturer to use an alternative form of marking. The Customs Service may, for example, allow the manufacturer of a leather bag to hang a tag on the handle. In this way the ultimate purchaser will know the country of origin of the bag, but the manufacturer will still not have defaced it.

English

The customs service will accept abbreviations, so long as the meaning is clear. Thus an importer may abbreviate Great Britain as "Gt. Britain."

The Customs Service will also accept non-English language names of countries, again so long as the meaning is clear: thus, one may write "Danmark" for Denmark.

(b) Special marking requirements

The United States applies special marking requirements to some products. Manufacturers of battery operated clocks, for example, must individually mark the clock mechanism, the battery, and the face of the clock. If a manager at all suspects that any special marking requirements may apply to his product, he should check. Among others, customs brokers can provide this information. In fact, this is another example of the value of customs brokers. See Customs brokers, Section(x)(a).

(ix)   Regulations of other agencies

All firms considering exporting a product to the United States should examine, in detail, all regulations which may relate to their products. The Customs Service will not allow into the United States goods which fail to meet any of several federal regulations, such as those relating to patents, product safety, and so on. The Customs Service often tests samples of imported goods to see if they satisfy various regulations.

Further, importers should not even try to bring into the United States products which violate regulations. Even if an importer does manage to bring the goods into the United States, it will still not be able to sell the goods. Thus, customs considerations aside, firms exporting to the United States should carefully analyse all laws and regulations relating to products they intend to sell in the United States.

In fact, Customs Service inspection actually helps firms importing goods into the United States. If a firm is trying to import a product which does violate a regulation, it is better for the firm to learn of this problem before it begins to sell the product in the United States.

The Practical appendix to this chapter lists federal agencies whose regulations apply to products which firms commonly import into the United States. If a manager is not sure if an agency's regulations apply to its product, he should find out. Among other things, one could simply telephone the agency. Federal employees are usually quite helpful.

Managers exporting goods to the United States must, however, do more than contact only federal agencies. State, city and local governments and agencies also enforce possibly relevant rules and regulations. Managers must also be careful because all these rules and regulations constantly change.

(x)   Practical aspects of passing goods through customs

(a)   Customs brokers

Customs brokers usually do much of the routine work of importing goods. They file papers, calculate any storage costs which might be due to the Customs Service, and work with those, such as freight forwarders, who will receive the goods after they pass through customs. Brokers can also arrange for appropriate government agencies to inspect the imported goods. Many customs brokers can communicate electronically with the

Customs Service. Thus customs brokers make importing into the United States easier.

Non-American firms importing goods into the United States should hire a customs broker, and they should hire a good one. The broker will speak on behalf of the manager and his firm. He or she will describe the goods to the Customs Service, for example, and will help to decide how much duty the importer should pay. If it later turns out that the broker gave the Customs Service improper information, then the Customs Service will hold the importer liable, not only for any extra duties but possibly also for penalties.

Managers should therefore invest the time necessary to ensure that they hire a good customs broker. Managers should ask friends and colleagues for recommendations. At a minimum they should be sure that the Customs Service, which licenses brokers, has licensed the broker they intend to hire.

(b)   Customs Service officials

Customs Service officials offer free advice to importers. This is particularly true of officials working at the various points of entry throughout the United States. Importers often find these officials' advice very valuable. Managers should therefore not hesitate to ask any Customs Service official any relevant question. See also Customs Service information, Section (xiii).

While examining the imported goods, the Customs Service official will probably ask questions. Common questions concern assists and any payments which the buyer may later make to the seller and which the importer may have inadvertently failed to disclose.

If the Customs Service does begin to investigate a transaction, the non-American manager should be sure to disclose immediately all relevant information. If the manager discloses the information voluntarily, and before the Customs Service has begun a formal investigation, then the Customs Service will limit any penalty it may impose to an amount equal to any duties which the importer failed to pay, and would be very unlikely to impose criminal penalties.

(c)   General points

● Managers should be sure to fill out all customs forms, not only honestly but also completely. The Customs Service will consider an omission just as serious a violation as it would a false statement.

- Managers should keep in mind that while the Customs Service will only consider the value of commissions the buyer pays the seller's agent when determining the duties the importer must pay, the importer must nevertheless report all commissions to the Customs Service. The Customs Service itself will determine whether the commission is a buying or a selling commission.

- Managers should also keep in mind that the Customs Service may make important decisions regarding imported goods long after the importer has brought the goods into the United States. It is possible that, long after goods have entered the distribution chain, the Customs Service may decide, for example, that the goods violate a particular requirement or regulation.

- If the buyer and seller are related, the importer should be sure to tell this to the Customs Service.

- Marking rules cause many problems. Customs Service officials look for clearness and permanence. Permanence means lasting at least until the final user can read the mark.

- Labels made in the United States, but which importers put on goods made outside the United States, often cause problems. Customs Service officials look to see if the importer has included in the label an American patent number, an American address, or some other information which could create the false impression that the manufacturer made the goods themselves in the United States. The Customs Service may also consider such labels to be assists. Regarding assists, see Valuation, Section (v)(b).

- Importers should check whether the manufacturer of the goods they are bringing into the United States used a process patented in the United States. If the manufacturer did use such a patent process, then the importer will need the patent holder's permission to bring the goods into the country. See Commercial intellectual property, Patents, Chapter 4(ii).

(xi)   Programs for lower rates of duty

The United States has entered into numerous agreements, and implemented many programs, which allow goods imported from certain countries to enter the United States at either a reduced duty rate, or duty free. The North American Free Trade Agreement, or NAFTA, is the most widely known of these agreements but there are other such agreements and programs, such as the Generalized System of Preferences, or GSP program. This program allows certain third world countries to import goods into the United States on favorable terms. Managers who believe that they may benefit from such an agreement or program should certainly see if this is true.

(xii)   Restrictions

The United States does not allow all importers to bring all goods into the country. For example, the United States applies quotas to some products, thus limiting the amount of these products which firms may import. Importers should be sure that they can bring into the United States all the goods they intend to bring into the country.

The United States may also apply antidumping and countervailing duties to certain products. These are additional duties that the United States imposes at various times on some products. It does this to counteract the effects of, respectively, firms selling at an unfairly low price or benefiting from an unfair subsidy.

(xiii)   Customs Service information, rulings and appeals

(a)   Information and informal rulings

The Customs Service offers informal, non-binding, information and "suggestions" regarding probable rulings. Customs officials at the port of entry will provide this informal assistance. These officials are generally very helpful. Many importers find the officials' free advice and "suggestions" very valuable.

Importers commonly ask Customs Service officials questions about the value of imported goods, or whether the manufacturer has adequately marked the country of origin of the imported goods. Customs officials can also tell importers if they have prepared their invoices properly. Customs officials may also suggest other federal, state, or local government agencies whose approval the importer may need before selling the goods in the United States.

The Customs Service will also provide information regarding the dutiable status of goods. This information is particularly valuable when a firm is preparing to bring goods into the United States. Importers and other firms may make requests for such information to the district director of the port where the importer intends to enter its goods, or to Customs Service headquarters in Washington.

The informal advice Customs Service officials give does not bind the Service. However, even if an official's advice turns out to be wrong, the Customs Service will almost never impose penalties on any firm which followed an official's incorrect advice.

Some importers, however, may find this informal advice to be of limited value. For example, advice customs officials give after inspecting a small or "test" shipment may not apply to a large shipment of the same type of goods. First, there is no guarantee that the Customs Service will treat any two shipments the same. Secondly, officials may very well treat a small shipment more casually than they would a large shipment.

(b)   Binding rulings

Initial decision

Because the Custom Service's informal advice procedure may not serve all importers' needs, the Service also issues formal, binding rulings. After the Customs Service issues a formal binding ruling, the importer will have no doubt about the rate of duty and other rules relating to the goods it is importing. The Customs Service will issue these binding rulings even before the importer actually brings the goods into the United States.

Customs officials at the port through which the importer intends to bring its goods will issue these binding rulings. The importer may, however, appeal against the ruling.

Appeals

An importer may appeal against valuation and other decisions which Customs Service officials may make at the port of entry but the law requires the importer to appeal very quickly. Thus, if an importer intends to appeal against a binding ruling, it should do so as soon as possible. It should contact its attorney immediately.

The importer's appeal is to Customs Service headquarters. These officials, who typically have many years experience working with the appropriate product and related regulations, will give the importer the opportunity to explain why the Customs Service officials at the port of entry made the wrong decision.

After appealing to Customs Service headquarters, the importer may then appeal to the court system. The Court of International Trade handles trade-related matters and will hear any appeal an importer may make against a decision of the Customs Service. Again, the law requires the importer to appeal very quickly. Thus, again, if the importer intends to appeal, then it should contact its lawyer immediately.

The Court of International Trade may decide an appeal even before the importer brings the goods into the United States. The court will rule this quickly if the importer can show that it would be significantly harmed if the court did not rule until after the importer brought the goods into the United States.

The importer may make appeals against decisions of the Court of International Trade to the United States Court of Appeals. The importer's final appeal is to the United States Supreme Court.

(xiv)   Foreign trade zones

(a)   Final processing before bringing goods into US

Foreign Trade Zones are areas, physically within the United States, where firms can store goods until passing them through customs. For customs purposes, it is as if goods in foreign trade zones are not in the United States. Firms can store goods in foreign trade zones indefinitely. Importers can therefore store goods in the zones, for example, while waiting for their price to rise.

These zones make importing to the United States easier, and non-American managers should consider using these zones to help them do business in the United States. The zones allow firms to physically store their goods close to the market, so the firms can deliver the goods quickly. But the zones also allow firms to delay paying customs duties, and to completely avoid paying duties on goods they will never sell in the US.

Firms can also manufacture in foreign trade zones. Manufacturing in zones is particularly attractive to firms which manufacture by combining both non-American and American-made parts or materials. If the firm manufactures in a zone, then it will not have to incur the expense of transporting the American parts or materials out of the United States. It will also avoid paying duty on the non-American parts or materials until, and unless, it imports the goods into the United States. If the firm sells the goods outside the United States, then it will never have to pay American duty on the foreign parts and materials.

The Customs Service will permanently fix the rate of duty for goods when the importer first brings the goods into a foreign trade zone. Thus, when quoting prices to potential American customers, the importer or other seller will be sure that it has included the proper duty rate into its cost calculations.

Further, it is particularly attractive, for firms which combine non-American parts and materials with American parts and materials as they manufacture in zones, that the Customs Service will have permanently fixed the duty of the non-American parts and material before the firm begins to manufacture. After the firm manufactures, the Customs Service will have great difficulty determining the extent to which the product contains imported parts and materials, and therefore how much duty the importer must pay.

Some importers bring goods into foreign trade zones for final processing. These firms, for example, remove broken bottles and damaged merchandise before passing the shipment through customs. This lowers the total duty they must pay. While the goods are in the zones firms can also make necessary adjustments so their goods satisfy appropriate laws and regulations. They can also put proper labels or marks on their goods.

Finally, firms can establish showrooms in foreign trade zones. Firms can exhibit goods in foreign trade zones indefinitely and without paying duty on these goods.

(b) Bonded warehouse

A bonded warehouse is similar to a foreign trade zone. A bonded warehouse is physically within the United States, but in it importers can store goods, or finally prepare goods, before passing them through customs. In a bonded warehouse an importer may, for example, put the appropriate label on its goods.

Practical Appendix
Federal agencies whose regulations commonly apply to imported goods

1. Federal Trade Commission

2. Food and Drug Administration

3. Consumer Product Safety Commission

4. Federal Communications Commission

5. Department of Agriculture

6. Department of Commerce

7. Department of Justice

8. Department of the Treasury

9. Department of Energy

10. US Department of Transportation

11. Fish and Wildlife Service

12. Animal and Plant Health Inspection Service

13. Drug Enforcement Administration

14. Environmental Protection Agency

15. Library of Congress (regarding copyright)

16. International Trade Commission

PART II   Establishing a Presence in the US Market

3. CORPORATIONS, PARTNERSHIPS AND JOINT VENTURES
Establishing a business in the United States

3. CORPORATIONS, PARTNERSHIPS AND JOINT VENTURES
Establishing a business in the United States

(i) Introduction

(a) Corporations are separate entities

Shareholder not liable for corporate debts

Corporations and their shareholders are separate entities. The law does not hold shareholders personally liable for corporate debts. In fact, so it can distinguish corporations from shareholders and other "natural persons," the law even calls corporations "legal persons."

Thus while one who successfully sues a corporation may collect all the corporation's money he can usually collect no more than the corporation's assets. A court will not order a shareholder to pay money the corporation owes. Thus, if a court awards $100,000.00 and the corporation has only $50,000.00, then the victor in court will receive only half his money. Even if the corporation has only one shareholder and he is a millionaire, the court will not order the shareholder to pay the corporation's debts.

Protect assets with corporation

To protect its non-American assets, a non-American firm entering the American market is therefore overwhelmingly likely to form a new American *corporation*. In fact, when managers talk of a "joint venture," they are almost always actually talking about a corporation two firms have formed together. And managers often incorrectly refer to the shareholders of this corporation as "partners."

Easy to form

A non-American can easily form a corporation in the United States. Unlike some other countries, the US imposes minimal rules of corporate organization. Within broad limits, the shareholders can structure their corporation in any manner they choose. Two or more shareholders, for example, can divide ownership and authority in any number of ways.

Furthermore, American law does not require the corporation to have or keep a particular amount of money in the bank. Some states require a nominal capitalization, such as $100.00, and others do not even require this amount.

(b)   Partnerships

A group of individuals may form a partnership to do business together but these individuals, when forming their partnership, do not create a new entity. A partnership is not an entity separate and distinct from its owners. Just as an individual is liable for his own debts, so too are all the individuals working together in a partnership jointly liable for their joint partnership debts. Unlike a corporation, a partnership does not protect is owners' assets. One who sues a partnership may therefore collect not only all the partnership's money, but also all the money each partner has.

(ii)   How to incorporate

(a)   Minimal formalities

No meaningful capital requirements

Anyone can easily create an American corporation. The rules of corporate organization are very flexible. The law imposes no meaningful capital requirements. A few states require corporations to have a minimal level of capital, such as $100.00, but most do not require even this. A manager can usually create a corporation in less than two weeks.

File documents

The person forming the corporation must only send a few documents to the appropriate state official. Lawyers and incorporation services already have these documents in their computers, and can very quickly make the appropriate changes to their standard documents. Most states charge a few hundred dollars filing fee. Thus, anyone who needs to can quickly form a simple American corporation.

Of the documents one must file to form a corporation, the most important are the by-laws and articles of incorporation. These documents regulate corporate management. Since these documents are, in effect, the constitution and laws of the corporation, those forming all but the most simple corporations should draft these documents with care.

State of incorporation

Each of the 50 states can create a corporation. One can therefore choose to create a corporation under the laws of Nebraska, Ohio, New York, or any of the other states. With a few exceptions such as banks, state law controls how the shareholders may manage their corporation. Some states, for example, require that the shareholders use a cumulative voting system to elect the board of directors. See Shareholders, Election of directors, Section (iv)(b).

Managers usually do not have difficulty choosing the state in which they will incorporate. They usually do not find this to be a major decision. A corporation incorporated under the laws of any state may do business in any other state. All states' corporate laws are generally the same. The different specific corporate management rules of the different states typically affect only the largest corporations.

Many managers believe they should incorporate in Delaware. The state does offer some, perhaps minor, advantages. It imposes flexible rules regarding such matters as board of directors elections and the creation of different classes of stock. Its courts have decided many corporate law cases, and therefore lawyers can research and answer Delaware corporate law questions relatively easily. If a non-American corporation is creating a subsidiary which may later become a joint venture corporation, incorporating in Delaware will help it turn the subsidiary corporation into a joint venture corporation. The joint venture partner's lawyers will most likely be familiar with Delaware corporate law.

But a manager should not overestimate the importance of these advantages. Courts of all the industrial states have decided many corporate law cases. These industrial states also have modern corporate laws, and these modern corporate laws give most managers all the flexibility they need to structure their corporations as they wish.

Furthermore, shareholders who incorporate in one state, such as Delaware, and do business in another state increase their costs. While any state will allow any corporation to do business within its borders, a corporation must first qualify to do business in any state in which it does business. To qualify to do business in a state, a corporation must meet the same tax and other regulatory requirements which the state imposes on corporations created under the laws of that state. A corporation incorporated in one state but doing business in another state must therefore pay two state income, franchise and other taxes. It must also file annual and periodic financial reports to two state authorities.

Thus, usually, firms incorporate in the state in which they are doing business. This is particularly true of firms doing business in a major industrial state. Usually the benefits of incorporating in another state do not outweigh the costs.

However, the usual rule does not apply in all cases. The shareholders may want to structure their corporation's management system, or hire personnel, in a manner which the state in which the corporation is doing business does not allow. Contrary to the shareholders' wishes, for example, the state may not allow the corporation to appoint non-American directors. In such cases the benefits of incorporating in another state may outweigh the costs.

Corporate name

Shareholders may not create a new corporation which has a name "deceptively similar" to that of an already existing corporation. Before incorporating or allowing a corporation to do business in a state, officials of that state will compare the proposed corporate name to names of other corporations already doing business in that state. The officials will only grant the corporation permission to do business in that state if its name is not "deceptively similar" to other corporate names.

Incorporating improperly

A person forming a corporation can easily fail to file one document, or pay one fee. The person will nevertheless have created a corporation. So long as the person honestly thought he had created a corporation, then a court will probably find that he has done so.

If a person doing business with another thought this person represented a corporation, then a court will find that this person did in fact represent a corporation. If the third party thought he was dealing with a corporate representative, then he expected to hold the corporation liable for any debt which grew out of their transaction. He did not expect to hold the corporate representative personally liable. Courts will hold these third parties to their expectations. Therefore a court will hold the corporation liable, and not the corporate representative individually. As with agents, the reasonable impressions of third parties control. See The law of agency, Chapter 1(iv).

(iii) Documents of corporate management

(a) Introduction

Articles of incorporation and by-laws

The by-laws and articles of incorporation describe how the shareholders will manage their corporation. The articles of incorporation contain broad, general rules and are analogous to the constitution of a country. The by-laws contain the specific, detailed rules of corporate management and are analogous to the laws of a country. These documents are important because the shareholders must do what they require. If the shareholders ignore these documents, then a court may find that the shareholders ignored the existence of the corporation. The court may therefore find that no corporation exists, and will therefore hold the shareholders personally liable for the corporation's debts. Share-holders must therefore draft these documents with care.

An American subsidiary of a non-American parent firm should have no difficulty following these rules. The parent will appoint all the members of the board of directors, for example, and the board will therefore vote as the parent instructs. The parent will appoint the managers of the subsidiary, and will then draft by-laws giving these managers the powers it believes are appropriate. In fact, the parent can follow these rules so easily that it may believe that doing so is a useless formality. The parent should resist the temptation to think this way. If the parent does not do as the articles of incorporation and by-laws instruct, then a court may find that the subsidiary corporation does not suit. The court will then hold the parent liable for its subsidiary's debts. See Shareholders liable if corporation does not exist, Section (vi)(a).

If the corporation has more than one shareholder, then these documents will be crucially important. They will determine how the different shareholders run their joint business. In fact, the rules of these documents will be so important that the shareholders should first agree to these rules in a separate shareholders' agreement.

The shareholders' agreement

If two firms or individuals go into business together, then they should of course first negotiate the appropriate contract. If they will create a corporation they should negotiate a shareholders' agreement. In this one agreement they would discuss how they will run their new corporation. They would then draft by-laws, articles of incorporation, and other documents to conform to this agreement.

Structure of this chapter

This chapter's discussion of corporate management is structured around the shareholders' agreement. This section describes the various possible terms shareholders may include in their by-laws and articles of incorporation. The next section, The structure of corporate authority, describes the roles of the shareholders, board of directors, and top corporate managers. The following section, Shareholders' agreements, analyzes the various possible terms of the by-laws and articles of incorporation, the roles of the various corporate officials, and relates all these to the decisions shareholders must make when deciding to form a corporation and go into business. This shareholders' agreement discussion therefore illustrates the issues shareholders must resolve when establishing their corporation. Accordingly, even those who will not draft a shareholders' agreement should read this section.

(b)   Articles of incorporation

The articles of incorporation are, in effect, the constitution of the corporation. Similar to a national constitution, the articles establish the fundamental principles that the parties must follow as they run their corporation. The person forming the corporation must file the articles of incorporation with the state. The public can therefore inspect the articles of incorporation.

The most important provisions in the articles of incorporation discuss the following matters.

- The classes of stock.

- The shareholders' voting procedure, such as cumulative voting. See Shareholders, Election of directors, Section (iv)(b).

- The restrictions, if any, on the sale and transfer of shares.

- Whether the shareholders have the right to purchase additional shares of stock the corporation may later issue, so as to maintain their proportional ownership of the corporation. These are called pre-emptive rights, See Shareholders' agreements, Section (v).

- Corporate dividend policy.

- The rights of shareholders who dissent from major corporate decisions.

- Procedures for removing directors.

- Procedures if the board of directors cannot reach a decision.

- Procedures if the shareholders cannot reach a decision.

- Rules giving shareholders authority which usually resides with the board of directors such as the authority to declare dividends.

- Rules protecting directors from personal liability. These include:
  - automatically approving transactions a director, as an individual, may enter into with the corporation,
  - agreeing that the corporation will pay any award that a court may order a director to pay because he performed his duties unreasonably,
  - requiring the corporation to purchase the appropriate insurance to cover this obligation.

- More narrow rules of corporate management, which are usually in the by-laws.

- Procedures for amending the articles of corporation.

(c)   By-laws

By-law and articles of incorporation may contain same rules

In theory the articles of incorporation establish the broad principles of corporate management and the by-laws establish the specific, day-to-day rules which implement these broad principles. In practice one cannot make a clear distinction between broad principles and day-to-day rules. Share-holders may therefore choose to put many rules in either the by-laws or the articles of incorporation.

Usually it makes no difference whether the shareholders include a particular rule in the by-laws or articles of incorporation but sometimes the distinction does matter. The distinction may matter because:

● the by-laws, not filed with the state, are not open to public inspection

● it is usually easier to amend the by-laws. While usually only the shareholders may amend the articles of incorporation, the board of directors can usually amend the by-laws.

Since shareholders include in their by-laws what they believe to be the more specific, day-to-day, rules, by-laws tend to be longer than articles of incorporation. Typical by-law provisions discuss the following.

● Procedures for shareholders' meetings:
  – when and where meetings will be held,
  – notice of meetings.

● The board of directors:
  – the number and qualifications of directors,
  – how long they will serve
  – meeting procedures, and
  – the authority of the board of directors (the board's most important powers are usually to enter into contracts, borrow and spend money, and hire and fire the top corporate managers, who are called officers),
  – how shareholders may remove directors (this is a good example of a term which may be in the articles of incorporation).

● Top corporate managers, the corporate officers. For example,

- what positions shall exist (usually there are four positions: president, vice-president, secretary and treasurer)
- the duties of each position,
- officer salaries. The board of directors usually sets these salaries.

- Procedures regarding corporate stock, such as:
  - the contents of the certificates of stock
  - whether the shareholders or board of directors may decide if the corporation will issue new stock
  - the vote required for such approval, such as a supermajority of two-thirds.

- Financial matters, such as:
  - corporate dividend policy
  - issuance of the annual report.

(iv) The structure of corporate authority: shareholders, directors, and managers

(a) Introduction

Unlike the law of some other countries, American law creates a very simple corporate structure. The law establishes only three levels of authority: the shareholders, the board of directors, and the top corporate managers, which the law calls officers.

Shareholders, naturally, run the corporation. But the law defines how the shareholders may run their corporation quite narrowly. Most importantly, it does not allow the shareholders to manage the corporation's day-to-day affairs. Normally, the law only allows the shareholders to elect the board of directors and vote on very significant corporate actions. The shareholders can, however, agree to give themselves additional powers.

The board of directors sets general corporate policy. To implement its policy the board hires corporate officers. These officers manage the day-to-day affairs of the corporation. While the law generally prohibits the board from interfering in these managers' work, the board can fire them and hire replacements. The law also allows the shareholders to alter this traditional structure.

(b)   Shareholders

Rights of shareholders

Although shareholders own the corporation, they law nevertheless limits
their authority. Shareholders elect the board of directors, which then sets
corporate policy and hires managers to implement this policy. Shareholders also approve major corporate acts, such as a merger of the corporation. However, shareholders traditionally do not manage the day-to-day
affairs of the corporation.

Shareholders traditional powers include the right:

- to elect the board of directors, and remove directors (usually shareholders can only remove directors who have acted illegally or otherwise
  improperly)

- to approve major corporate decisions, such as:
  - the sale or lease of a significant portion of corporate assets
  - a merger of the corporation
  - the dissolution of the corporation

- to dissent from their fellow shareholders' decisions regarding major
  corporate decisions; in most states these shareholders have the power
  to require the corporation to purchase their stock

- to amend the by-laws and articles of incorporation

- to sue others on behalf of the corporation (a so-called derivative
  action). See Shareholder lawsuits, below.

Change traditional structure in shareholders' agreement

Shareholders can give themselves additional powers. Some shareholders
do so informally. They simply ignore the distinction between shareholders, the board of directors and corporate officers or employees.
Shareholders who disregard the different levels of corporate authority
should do so with care. A court may find that because the shareholders
did not follow proper corporate procedures, no corporation exists. In this
case a court will hold the shareholders personally liable for the
corporation's debts. See Shareholders Liable If Corporation Does Not
Exist, Section (vi)(a).

Thus the shareholders should formally recognize the existence of each of the three levels of corporate authority. At the same time, the shareholders could agree to give themselves more than the shareholders' traditional authority. They may, for example, allow themselves to declare dividends, which is a traditional function of the board of directors. Shareholders who agree to alter the normal division of corporate authority should do so in a shareholders' agreement. See Shareholders' Agreements, Section (v).

Classes of stock

In some cases the shareholders may wish to increase the power of only some shareholders. An easy way for shareholders to distribute authority among themselves unevenly is to create different classes of stock. Each class of stock would give its owner different authority and the shareholders would then distribute the stock as they thought appropriate.

There are two basic classes of stock.

Common stock

- Holders of common stock typically have the right to elect a certain number of members of the board of directors.
    - There can be more than one class of common stock. Each class would then have different rights, such as the right to elect different members of the board of directors.
    - Almost all states allow corporations to issue common stock with restricted or no voting rights.
- Note that in contrast to preferred stock, the board of directors usually sets the dividend payable to holders of common stock.

Preferred stock

- All preferred stock has two basic features.
    - Its dividends are fixed. As with bondholders, the corporation must pay holders of preferred stock a certain sum at fixed times.
    - The corporation must pay preferred stockholders their dividends, in full, before it can pay common stockholders their own dividends.
- Preferred stock could be "cumulative," which would entitle its owner to past years' unpaid dividends. If the stock is not cumulative, then its owner will forfeit any unpaid dividends.

- The preferred stock could also be "participating," which would also entitle its owner to receive any dividends the board of directors may vote in favour of common stockholders.

- Corporations may limit the voting rights of preferred stockholders. Preferred stockholders usually have the right to vote only in special circumstances. A typical special circumstance is if the corporation fails to pay preferred stock dividends.

Preferred stock is actually a mixture: it has some features of common stock but also some features of a corporate bond.

Election of directors

Shareholders often want to ensure that the board of directors represents all groups of shareholders. For example, two firms may create a joint subsidiary corporation in which one parent corporation holds more than half the shares. The shareholders will probably want to ensure that the board of directors adequately represents both firms which are investing in the subsidiary including, in particular, the parent corporation which owns less than half the shares.

The shareholders can use a number of different voting methods, each of which will ensure that the board of directors represents different shareholders, or groups of shareholders. Common voting methods include the following.

Creating classes of stock

This is the simplest method. Owners of each class of stock may elect a certain number of members of the board of directors. Thus, if the parties give the minority and majority shareholders separate classes of stock, and agree that each class of stock may elect a certain number of directors, then they will have ensured minority representation on the board of directors.

Cumulative voting

Under this method of voting each stockholder may cast all his votes for only a few board of director candidates, or even for only one candidate. For example, if a board of directors has 7 members, then each share would entitle its owner to seven votes, one for each seat. The shareholder may, however, vote for one candidate 7 times. Because this method of voting is so effective at ensuring minority representation on the board of directors, some states require it.

Rights of minority shareholders

The law requires majority shareholders to respect the rights of minority shareholders. The law will not allow a majority shareholder who controls the corporation to do whatever he wants. The law requires the majority shareholder to act deal "fairly, honestly, and openly" towards minority shareholders. The majority shareholder must disclose to the minority all relevant information. The law applies this duty not only to majority shareholders themselves but also to the directors they elect.

If a corporation has two or only a few shareholders, then this rule requires the shareholders to act as if they were partners. Each shareholder may argue for what it believes is the best business strategy, but cannot ignore the wishes of his or her fellow shareholders. The rule requires all shareholders to work together.

Courts apply this general rule protecting minority shareholders in many different ways. For example, they do not let majority shareholders sell goods to the corporation at unfairly high prices. They also prohibit majority shareholders from selling their stock to third parties who the shareholders know will either raid the corporate treasury, or in some other way ruin the corporation's business.

Shareholder lawsuits

Shareholders can sue third parties on behalf of the corporation. Minority shareholders commonly use this right to sue majority shareholders. In such lawsuits the minority claims that the majority's acts have injured the corporation itself, and the minority is therefore suing the majority on behalf of the corporation. For example, if the majority shareholder were to improperly take corporate assets, then the minority shareholders could sue, on behalf of the corporation, for return of the assets. Shareholders can also bring an action, on behalf of the corporation, against the corporate managers who have acted improperly, such as signing a contract on behalf of the corporation without revealing a conflict of interest. Because shareholders derive these actions from the corporation, the law calls these derivative actions. Along with derivative actions, shareholders may also sue on their own behalf.

(c)   The board of directors

Sets general corporate policy

The board of directors sets general corporate policy. It hires the top corporate managers, called officers, who implement this policy. The corporate officers, not the board of directors, manage the day-to-day operations of the corporation. But, while the board of directors cannot manage the day-to-day affairs of the corporation, it can fire those who do, and it can then hire new corporate officers.

Owes high duty of loyalty to corporation

The board of directors must do what it believes is in the best interest of the *corporation*. Its owes its duty of loyalty to the corporation itself, not to the shareholders.

This duty of loyalty which the board of directors owes the corporation is a complete, uncompromising duty of loyalty. The law calls this a fiduciary duty and it is the highest duty of loyalty the law can impose. This is the same duty of loyalty the law imposes on one who manages another's money (a trustee).

Most people can serve

Most states impose no restrictions on members of the board of directors. A minority of states require that directors be either citizens of the United States or residents of the state. In most states, therefore, members of the board of directors can be non-Americans living outside the United States.

Authority

The law cannot precisely allocate authority between the shareholders, the board of directors, and corporate officers. It cannot clearly distinguish, for example, between the board of directors' authority to set overall corporate policy and the officers' authority to implement this policy. In fact, in recent years many have criticised American boards of directors for allowing corporate officers to assume too much of the board's traditional authority. In response, boards of directors are increasingly asserting their authority, and are generally supervising corporate officers more closely.

The board of directors traditional powers are:

- setting general business policy

- amending the by-laws

- declaring dividends

- selecting, supervising and firing corporate officers

- calling shareholders' meetings

- selling or purchasing corporate stock

- submiting appropriate important matters for shareholder approval (see Rights of shareholders, Section (iv)(b) above)

- paying corporate taxes

- approving corporate loans

- making political and charitable contributions.

Personal liability of directors

Must not violate duty of loyalty

If a director violates the duty of loyalty which he owes the corporation, then a court will hold him personally liable for the losses the corporation incurred because of this violation. Courts expect directors to do what is in their corporation's interest, not in their own interest. See Shareholders', directors', and managers' personal liability, Section (vi).

Business judgement rule

Courts have developed the business judgement rule to explain how directors must act towards their corporation. As the name implies, the rule requires directors to exercise reasonably good business judgement. The rule requires a director to be more than a disinterested, casual participant in corporate affairs. Rather, the rule requires the directors to adequately involve themselves in corporate affairs so they can make decisions based on a reasonable, good faith belief that they are acting in the corporation's best interest. The rule does not require that the directors make the correct decision. The rule allows a director to make a wrong decision, so long as he made it with reasonable, good faith that it was correct. Thus, the law does not impose a great burden on directors.

Suggested rules of conduct

Even under the business judgement rule, a court may still hold a director personally liable. Directors should therefore exercise appropriate care. To protect themselves from personal liability, and to ensure that they do their jobs properly, directors should do the following.

- Attend all meetings.
  - If a director cannot attend a board of directors' meeting, he should read the records of that meeting, and should talk to other directors. He should be sure to find out what happened at that meeting.
  - A director who cannot attend board of director meetings on a regular basis should consider resigning. A disgruntled shareholder could claim that this repeated failure to attend meetings was unreasonable, and that a court should therefore hold the director personally liable for the board's mistakes. See Shareholder lawsuits, Section (iv)(b).

- Take personal notes of meetings.
  - Should a director or shareholder later claim otherwise, it will be very helpful to have taken notes, at the time, showing that what the director claims happened at the meeting is in fact what happened.

- Check the accuracy of records of meetings the director did attend. This applies in particular to voting records.

- Read all corporate financial reports and legal opinions. Do not rely on someone else's recollection or summary explanation of their contents. These recollections can be inaccurate, and again a disgruntled shareholder may claim that relying on recollections or summaries was unreasonable.

- Avoid voting on matters in which there is even the appearance of a conflict of interest. The director should, in particular, be careful of agreements he may have entered into with the corporation while acting in a capacity other than that of corporate director, for example as an officer of another corporation. These agree-ments could create, at a minimum, the appearance of a conflict of interest.

(d) Managers

Corporate officers manage the day-to-day business of the corporation. The managers implement the board of directors' strategic and other decisions. Most states allow non-Americans living outside the United States to be corporate officers.

There are typically four corporate officers:

- president,

- vice-president,

- secretary, and

- treasurer.

The law generally allows the same person to hold more than one officer position. The same person may also be on the board of directors and be a corporate officer. The same person may have positions in both a parent and subsidiary corporation. Persons serving in more than one position must be careful, however. They must clearly separate the responsibilities of each position. If they do not, then they run the risk that either:

- a court finds that they have a conflict of interest (a court may find that they violated the duty of loyalty they owe their corporations)

- one corporate entity does not exist. (If the person mixed his corporate responsibilities in such a way that he acted as if one corporation did not exist, then a court may find that the corporation does not exist. The court would then hold the corporation's shareholders personally liable for the corporation's debts.)

(v) Shareholders' agreements

(a) Introduction

Helps parties agree to all issues

Before actually starting their new business, the shareholders should think through all the interrelated aspects, all the details, of their new business.

The shareholders should negotiate one comprehensive agreement discussing all aspects of their business. During the process of negotiating this agreement each shareholder will develop a deeper understanding of the others' expectations, intentions, and plans. The shareholders will discover potential disputes before they become real disputes. If the shareholders discuss all the interrelated aspects of their business at the same time, and write the resulting compromises and new ideas down in one compre-hensive agreement, then they will have significantly increased the chances that their new business will succeed. This is as true for corporate shareholders as it is for individuals.

Negotiating a shareholders' agreement is the easiest way for the share-holders to enter into such a comprehensive agreement. In this one document the shareholders can agree on both their business strategy and the structure of the corporation which will carry out this strategy. The shareholders will be able to decide who will manage their corporation, and how much authority each manager will have. They will be able to agree upon both corporate dividend policy and which body will have the authority to declare dividends. They could then later draft conforming by-laws and articles of incorporation.

Shareholders' agreements also allow shareholders to protect minority interests. Unlike the by-laws or articles of incorporation, the parties can easily draft a shareholders agreement which only a supermajority (more than 50%) of shareholders could amend. The agreement may even require unanimous approval for amendments. These procedures would allow a minority of shareholders to veto any corporate policy change to which they objected.

Even shareholders who will not enter into a shareholders' agreement should review the terms of a typical agreement. These terms relate to corporate management, and all shareholders must agree upon their corporation's management structure. If the shareholders cannot agree upon this structure, then they will not be able to manage their corporation jointly. Thus by reviewing the terms of the shareholders' agreement, and the related analysis, all shareholders and potential shareholders' will understand the corporate management issues on which they must agree.

"Joint venture" agreements are shareholder agreements

When two parent corporations form a subsidiary corporation to carry out their new joint business, they commonly enter into an agreement which managers commonly call a joint venture agreement. Managers commonly call the entity they create a joint venture but actually these managers are almost always creating a corporation, not a joint venture, and they therefore almost always enter into a shareholders' agreement, not a joint venture agreement. See Joint ventures, Section (vii)(d).

Comprehensive document of corporate management

All the terms of the shareholder agreement are related, and the shareholders must draft each term so it is consistent with the others. How these terms relate will vary from situation to situation. If two firms jointly create a new corporation, for example, they would probably accept a powerful board of directors. The shareholders will be able to control even powerful directors because these directors will also be their employees. Individual shareholders, on the other hand, may choose not to create a powerful board of directors, but instead to give themselves more than the shareholders' traditional powers.

The relationships among the shareholders will also influence how the shareholders structure their agreement. The shareholders may, for example, agree to give a majority shareholder more power than would be appropriate given the size of its investment. Or the shareholders may agree that although they have made unequal investments all shareholders will nevertheless have an equal say in corporate management. Similarly, the nature of the shareholders' relationships will determine how they structure rules designed to protect the rights of minority shareholders.

(b) Terms

Shareholders' agreements commonly include terms relating to the following issues.

Electing and removing members of the board of directors

- Each shareholder may agree to vote for a particular director, or
- the shareholders may agree on the procedures for choosing directors. For example:
  - each shareholder, or holders of one class of stock, may have the authority to fill one or more seats on the board of directors, or

- elections may be by cumulative voting, or
- outgoing directors may choose new directors.

- The shareholders should agree on how they may remove a director before his term expires. Possibilities include:
  - a supermajority, such as two-thirds or three-quarters of those voting
  - the majority of holders of the same class of stock which elected the director may remove that director (or, instead of the same majority, only a greater majority of the holders of the class of stock that elected a director that may remove that director)
  - a director may be removed, according to the above procedures, but only if he or she acted illegally or improperly.

Control of major management decisions

- The shareholders can give themselves the right to make or approve any corporate decisions they wish. Possibilities include:
  - major capital expenditures
  - basic strategic decisions
  - the election or removal of directors
  - the employment of key employees
  - the transfer of stock (see below).

- Approval could require:
  - a simple majority, or
  - a supermajority, such as two-thirds or three-quarters
  - approval of different classes of stock (under this common method of sharing authority, a majority of each class of stock must approve the corporate act)
  - unanimous approval. In other words, each shareholder, or class of stock, can veto the decision.
    - i.   In some circumstances a provision requiring unanimous approval to amend the shareholders' agreement serves the same purpose as one giving a veto over corporate management decisions to all shareholders. The shareholders' agreement may require the corporation to follow a certain policy. If the agreement requires unanimous approval to change this provision then the agreement in effect requires unanimous approval to change the corporate policy.

ii. Provisions requiring unanimous approval are dangerous. They give one shareholder, who may hold just a few shares, the power to stop all the other shareholders from implementing their business strategy. Further, over time a person or firm, not participating in corporate affairs on a regular basis, may obtain even a very small number of shares. Such an outsider will then be able to disrupt the corporation's business.

iii. On the other hand, veto powers protect minority shareholders. In particular they protect the minority from the majority's possible attempt to reduce or eliminate the minority's power and influence. Majority shareholders sometimes try to "freeze out" the minority by merging the corporation with another corporation it controls, or by improperly selling or transferring corporate assets. If the minority can veto such actions, then the majority will not be able to "freeze out" the minority.

The duty of care majority shareholders owe minority shareholders should, in theory, protect minority shareholders from such tactics. To use this duty of care to protect their rights, however, minority shareholders would have to institute at least an arbitration proceeding, and possibly even a lawsuit. Minority sharedholers who brought such an action would have to invest considerable time and money, while the outcome would be uncertain. As a practical matter, veto powers give minority shareholders much more protection.

- Some states require all stockholders, even those holding nominally non-voting stock, to vote on at least some of these major corporate decisions, such as dissolution of the corporation.

Hiring corporate officers (managers)

The board of directors normally hires and fires the president, vice president and other corporate officers. The shareholders' agreement could change this. Possibilities include:

- delegating authority to some or all shareholders to hire corporate officers, or
- giving some or all of the shareholders the authority to fire some or all corporate officers.

Dividends

Most corporations face two primary issues regarding dividends.

- Timing. When dividends:
  - may be declared
  - must be declared
  - may not be declared.

- Which body has the power to declare dividends:
  - the board of directors, which is the usual case, or
  - the shareholders.

Shareholders' agreements rarely set the amount of dividends. Business success must determine the amount of dividends. To protect holders of non-voting stock, the shareholders' agreement should spell out the corporation's dividend policy regarding non-voting stock.

Restrictions on stock transfer

In corporations with only a few shareholders, these shareholders must be able to work together. These shareholders are, in a practical sense, partners. When deciding to go into business together, all the shareholders chose to work with one another. Each shareholder will want to be sure that it will continue to work with these shareholders. Each shareholder will therefore want to prohibit the other shareholders from selling their shares to another person or firm which it either does not care to work with or does not know.

The law, however, does not allow shareholders to completely restrict the sale of their stock. The free market demands that shareholders be able to sell their stock. Courts therefore only enforce reasonable restrictions on the sale or transfer of stock. Reasonable restrictions are those the shareholders must impose so they can operate their business.

Reasonable restrictions shareholders normally impose include the following.

- Requiring consent before being able to transfer stock. The agreement could require consent from either:
  - the board of directors, or
  - the shareholders.

- Granting the corporation the right to purchase the stock at the price for which the shareholder had agreed to sell it. If the corporation buys the stock, the other shareholders will maintain their proportionate ownership of the corporation. Thus shareholders' agreements usually give the corporation the first right to purchase the stock. Shareholders usually have the right to purchase stock which the corporation has declined to purchase.

- Prohibiting the transfer of stock to certain parties, such as competitors.

- Purchasing the stock as required in a buy-out proposal. (See Buy-out provision, below.)

Right to maintain proportional ownership (pre-emptive right)

Protects current shareholders

If the corporation sells new stock to new shareholders, then, after the sale, those who had owned stock before the sale will own a proportionally smaller percentage of the corporation's total outstanding stock. The pie will have grown, and each shareholder will therefore own a smaller percentage of the larger pie. For example, before the sale a shareholder may own shares representing 50% of all corporate stock. After the sale this same number of shares may represent only 40% of all corporate stock. For this 50% shareholder to maintain its 50% ownership, it must purchase the appropriate portion of newly issued shares.

Most shareholder agreements give the shareholders the right to buy this appropriate portion of newly issued shares. Thus most shareholder agreements allow the shareholders to maintain their proportional ownership. The right to buy these additional shares is called a pre-emptive right, because the shareholder can pre-empt other stock purchasers, and buy some of the newly issued shares first.

This right protects both minority and majority shareholders. For a majority shareholder, its right to buy additional shares is in reality its right to maintain control. For a minority shareholder, its right to buy additional shares helps it preserve whatever degree of corporate control it may have. This right also helps the minority shareholders preserve the value of their corporate interest.

In particular it protects minority shareholders of corporations with only a few shareholders

This right to preserve the value of its corporate interest is particularly important for minority shareholders of corporations with only a few shareholders. These minority shareholders, be they individuals or firms, also often do work for the corporation. The value of their corporate stock therefore often reflects their skill and hard work in building up the corporation's business. The market often has difficulty valuing the stock of such firms and, in any case, the majority shareholders usually set the price for which the corporation will sell its stock. Without the right to buy additional shares, the majority shareholders could sell the corporation's stock, which the minority shareholders' work has made valuable, to outsiders, possibly even friends or affiliated firms of the majority shareholders, at unfairly low prices. But if the minority can buy the appropriate percentage of this stock which the majority is selling at an unfairly low price, then the minority shareholders will be able to preserve their interest in the corporation.

Required by many states

Because the right to buy additional shares goes to the heart of corporate control and reward, almost all states regulate this right. Because the right protects both majority and minority shareholders, most states encourage shareholders to give themselves the right. The laws of most states automatically gives the shareholders this right. In most states, if the shareholders do not want the right to purchase the appropriate portion of any newly issued stock, then they must affirmatively act to take this right away from themselves.

Balance minority and majority rights

Shareholders should not rely on such state laws, however. These laws are often unclear and, in any case, the state could always change them. Shareholders should deal with this subject openly, as part of their agreement. They should structure these rights to suit their particular needs.

When deciding how to structure these rights the shareholders have to strike a balance. On the one hand, as explained above, granting these rights protects both majority and minority shareholders. On the other hand, granting such rights may unfairly benefit minority shareholders who have not helped to build the corporate business. One way shareholders can strike a balance is to issue different classes of stock, and to grant pre-emptive rights to only some classes.

Procedure for issuance of new stock

Shareholders or board of directors could issue new stock

In their agreement the shareholders should also develop procedures for exercising the rights to buy additional stock. The shareholders should agree on the method of payment, the necessity of notice and similar details. Most importantly, they should decide whether the shareholders or board of directors has the authority to issue new stock. They should also develop voting procedures for the issuance of new stock.

Whether the shareholders give themselves or the board of directors authority to issue new stock is often critically important. Often some shareholders, particularly minority shareholders, cannot afford to purchase some or all of their allotted portion of newly issued stock. Thus, in many cases, the minority can only protect itself if it can influence or control the decision to issue new stock. Whether the board of directors or shareholders has the authority to issue new stock may determine whether the minority has sufficient influence to protect itself.

Majority which must approve

The shareholder must also decide how large a majority must approve the sale of new stock. The agreement may require a mere majority of those voting, or it may require a supermajority, such as two thirds, or even unanimity. To protect the influence of minority shareholders, the shareholders usually require the approval of at least a supermajority.

When forming the corporation shareholders are sometimes not able to decide if they should grant themselves the right to buy additional shares. In this case the shareholders should grant themselves the right. They can always remove the right later. But if shareholders, particularly minority shareholders, should later decide they need the right, it will often be too late by then.

Dispute resolution, or corporate dissolution

Disagreements among shareholders can cause corporate deadlock. The shareholders squabble, and the corporation's business stagnates. The risk of deadlock is greater the greater the majority needed to approve shareholder decisions. Thus, supermajority or unanimous voting requirements protect minority shareholders, they also increase the risk that a minority will stop the corporation from functioning properly. The minority may cause corporate deadlock.

Common ways of dealing with the problem of corporate deadlock include the following.

Requiring the corporation, or the other shareholders, to purchase the stock of the dissatisfied shareholder

These provisions raise two difficult and related issues:

- determining the price the corporation or shareholders should pay for the stock, and

- deciding which shareholder should buy the other's stock. This is a particular problem if there are only two or a limited number of shareholders. Common solutions to these problems include the following:
  - Each party making a sealed bid, and the low bidder has to sell his shares to the high bidder. Further, the high bidder must pay for the stock the price it said the stock was worth. This is an interesting solution. The shareholder who believes the corporation has the greater value is the one who maintains ownership of the corporation. But to maintain this ownership it has to buy its fellow shareholder's stock at the higher price that it said the stock was worth. The shareholder that believes the corporation has lesser value loses ownership, but receives for its shares more money than it said they were worth.
  - Another solution is for prices to be fixed by agreement or by agreed formula. For example, the price of each share could be the value of the portion of corporate assets which it represents (the so-called "book value").
  - An independent third party may value the shares.

Arbitration and mediation

- If at all possible, the shareholders should resolve their differences without resorting to arbitration. Arbitrators choose winners and losers, they do not devise business strategy. In addition, the distrust generated during the arbitration process may linger long after the arbitrator has issued a ruling. It may be difficult for shareholders who have arbitrated their dispute to work together later.

- Some shareholders therefore opt for the appointment of an outside business expert. He could become a new and deciding member of the board of directors. This provision has the advantage of avoiding arbitration. It allows the parties to work together with the help of the outsider. The outsider's job will be not to choose a winning side but to calm emotions and develop a coherent business strategy. This outside expert is very similar to a mediator. See Court system: law-suits and arbitration, Chapter 9.

Requiring dissolution of the corporation

- Even if the shareholders' agreement does not call for dissolution, if the deadlock persists a court will dissolve the corporation.

- The agreement would require shareholders to dissolve the corporation. Agreements which make it easy for the shareholders to dissolve the corporation actually tend to increase the leverage of minority shareholders. Usually no shareholder wants to dissolve the corporation, and particularly not the majority shareholder, who, after all, owns most of the corporation. Thus, the more the minority shareholders' threat to dissolve the corporation is credible, the more powerful a weapon they have.

Buy-out provision

The agreement may give shareholders who dissent from major corporate actions the right to have the corporation buy their stock.

- Such major corporate actions could include:
  - mergers,
  - sale of at least a substantial part of the corporation's assets, or
  - amendments to the shareholders' agreement which substantially harms the rights of the shareholder.
- If there is no free market price for the dissenting shareholders' stock, then an outside expert would usually determine the price of the stock.

Relative powers of shareholders and the board of directors

The law requires the shareholders to elect the board of directors. The law expects the board of directors to set corporate policy and hire corporate officers. The shareholders could, however, give themselves some or all of the board of directors' traditional authority.

Amendments

Amending agreement is re-writing it

Shareholders must decide how they may amend their agreement. This is a crucially important power because the shareholders who can amend the agreement can rewrite it. Thus shareholders usually require that at least a supermajority approve any changes to their agreement. They may even require unanimity.

Unanimity requirements give minority shareholders great power

Shareholders should think carefully, however, before requiring all shareholders to agree to any change to their agreement. Such unanimity requirements may give any one shareholder too much power. This one shareholder will be able to veto decisions to which every other shareholder agrees.

Balance – different provision, different requirements

Thus when drafting the amendment procedures, shareholders face conflicting pressures. On the one hand, they do not want only a limited number of shareholders to rewrite their agreement. On the other hand, they do not want one shareholder to derail the plans of all the other shareholders. One way the shareholders can balance these conflicting pressures is to require different voting majorities to approve amendments to different parts of the agreement. For example, the shareholder could agree that while a supermajority may be able to amend some provisions, all the shareholders must agree to amendments relating to each shareholder's right to buy newly issued stock. The shareholders may also allow a shareholder dissenting from a decision to amend the agreement to sell its stock to the corporation. See Buy-out provision, above.

If the shareholder agreement requires supermajority or unanimous approval for a certain decision, then the shareholders should also agree that only the same majority may amend that provision. If the shareholders do not agree to this, then a smaller minority could amend the provision requiring the greater majority. The provision would therefore not offer minority shareholders the protection they may think it does.

(vi) Shareholders', directors' and managers' personal liability

(a) Shareholders liable if corporation does not exist

Corporation's existence depends on shareholder's actions

To ensure that a court will not hold them personally liable for corporate debts, the shareholders must ensure that their corporation exists, and continues to exist. If a court finds that no corporation exists, then it will hold the shareholders personally liable for the corporation's debts. If the shareholders want a court to find that a corporation exists, then the shareholders must themselves *always* act as if the corporation does in fact exist.

The shareholders, directors, and officers must therefore always manage the corporation as if it is the separate entity they want it to be. Shareholders must always separate corporate finances from their own. The shareholders and directors must ensure that the corporation pays its taxes. The Corporation must have enough money to exist on its own.

Must follow corporate procedures

All those involved in the corporation must also always follow proper corporate procedures. They must take all the formal steps of corporate management which the by-laws, articles of incorporation and shareholders' agreement require. They must, for example, hold formal shareholders' and board of directors' meetings, and must hold these meetings at the appropriate times. To prove that they held these meetings, they must record what they did at these meetings.

Some managers do not bother with these corporate formalities. Shareholders who are also directors and officers of their corporation, for example, may not bother to hold formal corporate meetings. These shareholders, who work together every day, may feel that holding formal shareholders' or board of directors' meetings, complete with records, is unnecessary, excessively legalistic, and inconvenient. However, the law requires them to treat the corporation as a separate entity. These shareholders will find being held personally liable for all corporate debts a far greater inconvenience than holding occasional meetings.

Many states allow shareholders or directors to sign a memorandum recording their decisions. In these states the memorandum can substitute for a formal meeting. While shareholders can rely on such memoranda, the shareholders or directors must be sure to actually draft and sign the appropriate memoranda and to do so in the manner the law requires.

Impressions of third parties control corporate existence

Furthermore, all corporate representatives must *always* present themselves to third parties as representatives of the corporation. Corporate letterheads, business cards and similar items must always identify shareholders, directors, or employees as representatives of the corporation. Most importantly, officers and employees must always clearly sign documents as corporate representatives, not as individuals. Mr. Hansen, for example, must sign as: "John Hansen, president of XYZ Corp."

To protect themselves from personal liability corporate representatives must tell the persons they are doing business with that they represent the corporation. They must tell the third parties that they are the corporation's agent. As explained in The law of agency, Chapter 1(iv), the reasonable impression of third parties determines the agent's authority. Corporate representatives are the corporation's agents. Thus if a corporate representative acts so that third parties reasonably believe that the representative has the authority to act on behalf of the corporation, then a court will find that the corporate representative is in fact acting on behalf of the corporation. The third parties will know they are dealing with a corporation, and cannot expect the corporate representative to personally pay any debt which may arise from the transaction.

The crucial factor is a third party's reasonable expectations. The law expects a third party to investigate the corporation before signing a contract with it. If this third party does not believe the corporation is creditworthy, then it could, among other things, seek the personal guarantee of a shareholder, or decline to do business with the corporation. But the law only expects the third party to make this investigation if it knows that the corporate representative is in fact acting on behalf of a corporation. If, on the other hand, the third party reasonably believes that it is dealing with the representative as an individual, then a court will hold the corporate representative personally liable for any debt which may grow out of the transaction.

(b) Minimum corporate assets

No required minimum

As mentioned above, the law expects everyone to investigate those with whom they do business. Thus the law does not require corporations to have a certain minimum amount of money. If a party doing business with a corporation believes the corporation does not have sufficient assets, and is therefore not creditworthy, it should take whatever steps it believes are appropriate. It could, for example, seek the personal guarantee of a shareholder, or decline to do business with the corporation.

Cannot use corporation to commit fraud

One the other hand, the law will not allow shareholders to use the corporation to commit fraud. The law will not allow shareholders to give third parties the impression that the corporation has more assets than it in fact has, sign a contract on behalf of the corporation, and then claim that the undercapitalized corporation is liable for the ensuing debt. Shareholders who do this commit fraud. See Warranties and fraud, Chapter 8.

A court may also hold the shareholders of an undercapitalized corporation liable for corporate debts because it found that no corporation ever existed. A court could reason that because the corporation did not have sufficient funds to exist as a separate entity, it was not in fact a separate entity. The court would then hold the shareholders personally liable for the corporation's debts.

(c) Unreasonable acts

The law requires all persons to act reasonably. If someone acts unreasonably, the law will hold him responsible for the consequences of his unreasonable act. Thus poor drivers must pay for the accidents they cause. The law calls acting unreasonably "acting negligently". See Negligence and the ordinary standard of care, Chapter 6(ii).

Managers and other corporate representatives must therefore be sure always to act reasonably. If a corporate director, officer, or employee, performs his job unreasonably, a court may hold him liable for the consequences of his unreasonable act. For example, if, because a manager acted unreasonably, corporate assets are stolen, a court may hold the manager liable for the theft. As another example, if a director failed to examine corporate books and records to a reasonable degree, and by acting unreasonably caused the corporation to lose money, a court could require the director to reimburse the corporation.

If a court did hold a director liable for his unreasonable acts, it would probably do so because a disgruntled shareholder brought a lawsuit. This shareholder could bring an action, either on his own behalf, or on behalf of the corporation. See Shareholder lawsuits, Section (iv)(b) above.

(d) Violate duty of care

Directors, officers, and other employees owe a duty of uncompromising loyalty to their corporation. This is the fiduciary duty described above. The law requires corporate representatives to further the corporation's, not their own, interest. See Board of directors, Section (iv)(c).

All corporate officials, even shareholders, can violate this duty. They do so most commonly by taking for themselves a business opportunity which rightfully belongs to the corporation. A court can order an official who takes the opportunity for himself to pay the corporation the money the corporation would have earned if it had exploited the opportunity.

(e) Removing corporate assets

Removing corporate assets is a form of fraud. While the law allows, and expects, corporate officials to spend and transfer the corporation's assets as part of the corporation's legitimate business activities, the law requires them to act in good faith when doing so. The law certainly does not allow them to transfer assets out of the corporation, declare bankruptcy, and then fail to pay the corporation's debts. Doing so would defraud creditors. If corporate officials did this, then a court would at least order the beneficiaries of the scheme, the shareholders, to transfer the assets back into the bankrupt corporation.

Courts and creditors therefore closely examine business transactions corporations enter into with friends and relatives of corporate officials, and with corporations these officials control. A shareholder can easily remove corporate assets, for example, by selling corporate assets to his brother at a fraction of their true price. The shareholder could then leave a bankrupt corporation unable to pay its debts.

(f)   Dealing with corporation in different capacities

Courts and others are often suspicious of corporate officials who do business with the corporation. A 50% owner of a corporation, for example, may improperly take corporate funds when selling goods to the corporation. By overpricing these goods the shareholder can easily take for itself corporate assets which rightfully belong to all the shareholders.

To avoid even the appearance of acting improperly, a corporate official doing business with the corporation should ask another official, or the board of directors, to approve all significant transactions. This person should also be sure to charge the corporation no more than the market price for his or her goods and services.

(vii)   Partnerships and joint ventures

(a)   Introduction

Partnership not separate entity

Unlike a corporation, a partnership is not an entity separate and distinct from its owners. A court will hold partners liable for partnership debts. Thus, to protect shareholders' personal assets, managers usually establish a corporation rather than a partnership.

To carry out its business in the United States, a non-American firm is therefore far more likely to form a corporation than a partnership. In fact, when managers talk of two firms being "partners," they are usually actually referring to co-shareholders of a corporation.

Reasons for partnerships

Sometimes, of course, managers actually do establish partnerships. Many do so for tax reasons. Others do so to avoid financial reporting requirements which apply only to corporations. Others do so inadvertently. In some states groups of professionals, such as lawyers or architects, may only carry on business as a partnership. A growing number of states, however, now allow professionals to form limited liability companies as well as partnerships.

Managers sometimes create a special form of partnership, a limited partnership. As the name implies, limited partners have only limited rights. But limited partners also enjoy limited liability protection very similar to the protection shareholders enjoy.

Misuse of term "joint venture"

Managers also often misuse the term "joint venture." A "joint venture" is a separate and distinct form of business. It is not a corporation. It is very similar to, but different from, a partnership. When managers talk of a joint venture, however, they usually actually mean a corporation with two or more corporate shareholders.

(b) Creating and managing partnerships

Partners' full liability

Courts hold partners fully liable for all partnerships debts. A partnership is merely an association of individuals who join together to do business. When partners work together they create a partnership. They can create a partnership without filing any papers. The law gives each partner his proportionate share of partnership profits and also holds him liable for his proportionate share of partnership debts. Because a partnership is merely a group of people working together, the law does not create a separate partnership entity. Therefore, unlike a corporation, a partnership does not protect its owners' personal assets.

Some may see a partnership as a separate entity. Superficially, this is correct. The partnership can do business, and sue and be sued, in its own name. It can own property in its own name. But these conventions do not change the nature of partnerships – partnerships are not corporations. Even if one sues a partnership, a court can still hold the partners personally liable for any resulting court award.

Partners liable for debts partners and employees incur

Because the law holds each partner personally liable for all partnership debts, it holds each partner liable for his fellow partners' acts. Each partner can act as the partnership's agent, and can therefore incur debts on the partnership's behalf. Since the law holds all the partners personally liable for all partnership debts, it will hold all partners personally liable for the partnership debts any one partner incurs.

The law also holds each partner liable for the debts the partnership's employees incur on behalf of the partnership. The partnership's employees can also act as the partnership's agents, and can therefore also incur partnership debts. Courts will hold each partner fully liable for these partnership debts. Thus partners must be sure to limit their employees' authority. See The Law of Agency, Chapter 1(iv).

Partners owe high duty of care

Because the law holds each partner liable for the acts of all partners, it also imposes on each partner a high duty of care. The law imposes on partners the same fiduciary duty that it imposes on trustees and corporate directors. This is the highest level of duty the law can impose. Partners must therefore use care to only incur reasonable debts on behalf of the partnership. The other partners can hold a partner personably liable for any unreasonable partnership debts he may incur.

While a court will order a partner who unreasonably incurs a partnership debt to reimburse his fellow partners, the court will still order all the partners to pay this debt. Thus courts still hold each partner liable to third parties even for partnership debts which a partner incurred unreasonably. Since the partner who unreasonably incurred the debt can only reimburse his partners if he has sufficient funds, all the partners retain the risk that they will pay even unreasonably incurred partnership debts.

Partners liable for other's unreasonable acts

Further, since courts hold partners liable for all partnership debts, they also hold partners personally liable for the unreasonable acts partners and employees commit while working for the partnership. While a court may order the partner or employee who acted unreasonably to reimburse the partnership, this person can only do so if he or she has sufficient assets.

This expansion of liability has led some to argue that the partnership is a separate entity. To the extent this is true, the partnership's entity status increases, rather than decreases, each partners' potential liability.

Corporation as partner

The law allows corporations to be partners. Thus one could work in a partnership, have the same authority as a partner, yet create a business structure which would stop a court from ordering one pay the partnership's debts. This individual could be a shareholder in a corporation which is itself a partner. This corporation must, however, legitimately be a partner. The partners cannot create a corporation as part of a fraudulent scheme to defraud creditors of the partnership. If they do, a court will simply ignore the corporation and hold the partners personally liable. See, Shareholders', Directors' and Managers' Personal Liability, Section (vi).

Accidentally create partnership

Managers must be careful not to create a partnership inadvertently. If two or more individuals or firms act in such a way that a third party reasonably believes that they are partners, then, regarding that third party, a court will treat those working together as partners. Thus, just as a third party's reasonable expectations determines whether a court will recognize the existence of a corporation, so too do these expectations determine whether a court will recognize the existence of a partnership. This possibility illustrates, yet again, why managers should be sure to give third parties the correct impression regarding their authority, and regarding their employees' and agents' authority. See Shareholders', directors' and managers' personal liability, Section (vi)(a), and The law of agency, Chapter 1(iv).

Tax advantages of partnerships

Many managers create partnerships for tax purposes. Since partnerships are not separate entities, partnerships do not pay income tax. Thus partnership income passes directly to the partners, free of any tax. By contrast, corporations pay corporate income tax. Only after corporations have paid income tax can they distribute their income to shareholders.

Partnership agreements

Partners often negotiate a partnership agreement. A partnership agreement is analogous to a shareholders' agreement. Just as negotiating a shareholders' agreement forces the shareholders to think through all aspects of their corporation's business, so too does negotiating a partnership agreement force the partners to think through all aspects of their partnership's business. Thus, just as shareholders should enter into a shareholders' agreement, so too should partners enter into a partnership agreement.

Uniform Partnership principles

The Uniform Partnership Act regulates partnerships in all states but Louisiana. A few states have enacted their own partnership acts, which differ slightly from the Uniform Act. Other states have never adopted the Act, but the courts of these states nevertheless use the Act to help them decide partnership matters. Thus 49 of the 50 states apply the same general principles of partnership law.

(c) Limited partnerships

Limited partners enjoy limited liability

Limited partnerships allow certain partners to invest in a partnership without becoming liable for all partnership debts. A limited partnership must have at least one general partner, and may then have several limited partners. Courts hold general partners as fully liable for partnership debts as they do any partner. Courts do not hold limited partners personally liable for partnership debts.

Limited partners invest in the partnership. They money they invest becomes the partnership's money. A court can order the partnership to use this money to pay its debts, and a limited partner investing in a partnership may therefore lose this money. But a court will not hold the limited partner liable for the partnership's debts, thus the limited partner can lose no more than the money he invests in the partnership.

Limited partner may not be involved In partnership's business

In return for the limited liability protection it provides, the law limits the extent to which a limited partner may involve himself in the partnership's business. If a limited partner involves himself too much, then a court will treat him as a general partner, and will therefore hold him fully liable for all partnership debts.

The law allows limited partners to "consult and advise" general partners. The limited partner may also be an employee of the partnership, but not a manager. Courts interpret these restrictions differently in different business contexts. Limited partners must therefore act with great care. The law is unclear, and limited partners should therefore err on the side of caution and non-involvement in partnership affairs. Limited partners should avoid the risk that a court will hold them liable for partnership debts.

Similar state rules

With the exception once again of Louisiana, the limited partnership laws of all states are similar. About half the states have adopted the Uniform Limited Partnership Act, and about half have adopted its successor, the Revised Uniform Limited Partnership Act.

(d)   Joint ventures

Joint venturers' personally liable

The law creates a type of business entity called a joint venture. Joint venturers are very similar to partnerships. Most importantly, joint ventures, like partnerships, do not protect their owners' personal assets. A court may hold a joint venturer personally liable for the joint venture's debts.

The two most important differences between a partnership and joint ventures are:

- joint ventures, unlike partnerships, must be for a specific purpose, such as constructing a building or producing a play

- a joint venture may be for "commercial gain," while a partnership may only be for profit.

Accidentally create joint venture

While to some this second distinction may seem to be overly technical, it is not. This second distinction can lead a court to hold a manager liable for the acts of another manager with whom he is not in business. Managers may join together, merely for "commercial gain," and, without realizing it, create a joint venture. They may create a joint venture even if they join together for only a short period. In the classic case, two traveling sales representatives agreed to travel together in one car. They joined together for "commercial gain," and thereby created a joint venture.

Managers must therefore be careful when joining together with others. Indeed, in the classic case the court held one joint venturer liable for the other joint venturer's unreasonable, negligent, acts.

Most "joint ventures" are jointly owned corporations

Most managers do not create joint ventures. When managers use the term joint venture they usually mean a corporation they and others create to carry out a joint business. Thus, to be technically accurate, these managers should call the entity they create, not a joint venture, but simply a corporation.

(e)   S corporations

Limited liability and tax advantages

Small businesses have traditionally formed S corporations. Just as with other shareholders, courts will not hold shareholders of S corporations personally liable for corporate debts. But the Internal Revenue Service (IRS), the federal agency responsible for collecting taxes, does not require S corporations to pay corporate income tax. Shareholders of S corporations therefore enjoy the limited liability protection of corporations and the tax advantages of partnerships.

Must meet definition of small business

The IRS created S corporations to allow small business owners to avoid the double taxation the corporate structure creates. The IRS will therefore only give S corporation status to businesses which meet its definition of a small business. Most importantly, the IRS defines a small business as having only a limited number of shareholders, and only one class of stock.

(f) Limited Liability Companies

Limited liability and tax advantages

In recent years the majority of states have created a new form of business entity, the limited liability company. Limited liability companies combine aspects of partnerships and aspects of corporations. As with shareholders, courts cannot hold owners of limited liability companies personally liable for the debts of the limited liability company. But unlike corporations, the IRS does not require limited liability companies to pay income tax. Owners of limited liability companies, like owners of S corporations, therefore enjoy the limited liability protection of corporations and the tax advantages of partnerships. To take advantage of this limited liability protection, many former partnerships have turned themselves into limited liability companies.

Cannot sell stock

An owner of a limited liability company may only sell his shares if all the other owners agree to the sale. Owners of limited liability companies cannot freely sell their shares. This is the main disadvantage of limited liability companies.

Advantages

Limited liability companies offer the following advantages.

- In comparison with **partnerships**, limited liability companies provide their owners with limited liability. Courts will not hold limited liability company owners personally liable for the company's debts.

- In comparison with **limited partnerships**, limited liability companies provide this protection to all owners. By contrast, owners of a limited partnership must designate a general partner, who will be personally liable for the partnership's debts.

- In comparison with **S corporations**, owners of just about any business can form a limited liability company. They do not have to satisfy the IRS's definition of a small business.

(viii) Practical Appendix Establishing a sales office

(a) Introduction

The following is an overview of the most important legal and practical requirements a manager must satisfy to open a simple sales office in the United States. These requirements are not so demanding that they should, by themselves, stop a non-American firm from opening an American sales office.

(b) General items

Corporate formalities

To create a corporation, a manager must file the corporation's:

● articles of incorporation

● by-laws

● other miscellaneous documents such as:
  – a fictitious name statement, and
  – a certificate qualifying it to do business in the appropriate state.

Local business licenses

Nearly all cities, towns and other localities require those doing business within their borders to obtain a license. So long as the new business does not wait so long to obtain the license that it has to pay a penalty, it will pay only a nominal license fee.

State and federal business licenses

Most states require at least some types of businesses to obtain the appropriate license. The requirements vary from state to state.
On the other hand, most businesses do not need federal licenses. Only

those selling highly regulated products such as alcohol and tobacco need a federal license.

Insurance

Workers' compensation

The law requires firms to purchase workers' compensation insurance for their employees. Workers must make claims against their employers for job-related injuries through the workers' compensation system rather than through the traditional court system. To ensure that workers receive whatever workers' compensation they may be due, employers must purchase the appropriate insurance.

Other insurance

All business should, as a practical matter, also purchase the following insurance:

- general liability,
- fire and similar disasters,
- theft,
- interruption of business, and
- product liability. See Strict Products Liability, Chapter 6 (iii).

(c) Tax

A new business must comply with the following tax requirements.

Employer identification number

To obtain an employer identification number a firm need only mail the appropriate form to the IRS. The IRS is the agency responsible for federal taxes.

Obtaining this form will allow the new business to:

- withhold its employees' income and social security (FICA) taxes, and

– pay its employer's social security tax.

Unemployment insurance

The firm must pay unemployment insurance taxes to both:

– the federal government, and

– the appropriate state government.

Seller's permit

A firm making retail sales must obtain a seller's permit, which will allow it to collect sales tax. State sales tax agencies issue these permits.

(d) Employee benefits

Not required

The law does not require employers to pay fringe benefits. Some American employers nevertheless provide some or all of the following benefits.

- Pension benefits
- Health insurance
- Long-term disability insurance
- Life Insurance

Employers must report the nature of its fringe benefits to the federal government. These reporting requirements are quite extensive.

PART III   Selling Ideas

4. COMMERCIAL INTELLECTUAL PROPERTY
Protecting valuable ideas

4. COMMERCIAL INTELLECTUAL PROPERTY
Protecting valuable ideas

(i) Introduction

(a) General points

A firm's intellectual property is the heart of the firm. A firm's intellectual property is everything the firm knows, all the knowledge the firm has developed over the years. If the firm has managed to stay in business, if the firm has managed to stay one step ahead of the competition, then it has done so only because it has developed valuable ideas, valuable intellectual property. In fact, today, a firm's intellectual property is almost always its most important asset. Firms with more valuable intellectual property earn more money.

A firm's intellectual property is all the knowledge the firm controls. It includes the firm's patents and trademarks, but it also includes much more. It includes the firm's right to copyright its manuals and other printed material, and also its right to copyright other valuable materials such as software. Finally, it includes the firm's know-how. Know-how, which the firm can control as a trade secret, is the firm's more general knowledge. Know-how can relate to technologies, processes, business organizations, and so on, and how these all interrelate. Many firms find know-how very valuable.

Intellectual property is important to the non-American manager for two reasons. First, quite simply, intellectual property is very important. If a non-American manager intends to do business in the United States, he must know how to use and protect his firm's intellectual property in the United States. Second, licensing is one common way to enter the American market. By licensing, a firm can earn money from the American market while avoiding many of the risks of doing business in the United States. The following chapter therefore analyzes a licensing agreement in depth. When a firm licenses, it is selling intellectual property. To understand licensing, therefore, a manager must understand intellectual property law.

(b)   Types of intellectual property

The law protects ideas in many different ways. Patent, trademark, trade secret, and copyright law all protect ideas and knowledge. These different areas of the law protect all ideas and knowledge which satisfy their criteria for protection. Because ideas are intangible and so varied, several of these areas of the law may each protect the same idea. An idea may be a trade secret, for example, but also be part of a written manual and therefore copyrightable.

This overlap often confuses managers, and lawyers. Managers are often unsure whether, for example, trade secret or copyright law protects an industrial process. The answer may very well be both.

The key to understanding intellectual property law, therefore, is to see each area of intellectual property as a separate body of law. Each is independent of the others, and each has its own concepts and rules. Below is a description of these different areas of law.

(ii)   Patents

(a)   Introduction

Patent protection is strong, and therefore difficult to obtain

Patent protection is the strongest the law offers to protect ideas. The law will provide patent protection only to specific, practical ideas. One cannot patent general concepts. An inventor can patent only practical technology which will help a firm either make a new product or make an existing product more efficiently.

Patent law offers very strong protection. It gives inventors more control over their ideas than does any of the other areas of intellectual property law. A patent holder can stop a third party from using his patented technology. This is true even if the third party has developed the technology completely on his own and with no help whatsoever from the patent holder. Patent law offers this protection for 20 years. By contrast, owners of trade secrets cannot stop those who have independently developed the trade secret from using the technology they have developed on their own.

To qualify for this very strong protection, an inventor must meet very demanding requirements. Patent law demands more from those who seek its protection than does any other area of intellectual property law. The US Patent and Trademark Office (PTO), which issues patents, rejects many patent applications. Further, courts invalidate many patents which the PTO had previously issued. For inventors, patent law therefore offers a two-edged sword: on the one hand it offers strong protection, but on the other hand, this protection is difficult to obtain.

Hard to value

Managers have great difficulty determining the value of patents. Some managers overestimate the value of a patent. These managers tend not to realize that inventors must invest a great deal of time and money to obtain a patent. Some managers also fail to realize that even after the PTO issues a patent, a court may later invalidate the patent.

Other managers underestimate the value of patents. They believe that American courts are quick to invalidate patents. While this may once have been true, the American court system now protects patents rather strongly.

(b) Requirements

General points

Inventors can patent an invention which is:

- new,
- non-obvious, and
- useful.

Each of these three requirements is very demanding. Inventors must satisfy all three. The law makes these requirements demanding because it provides so much protection to those who satisfy them.

New

The law cannot define "new." The best it can do is describe what is *not* new. An invention is *not* new if:

a. it is known in the US or

b. a printed publication or patent application anywhere in the world describes the invention, or

c. someone has already used the technology in the US for one year before the inventor filed his patent application, or

d. another inventor has already developed and used the technology, and has filed or will file a patent application.

Not only can the law not define "new," but even its definitions of "*not* new" are unclear.

Known in the US

The law cannot adequately define what others "know." In one sense all inventors manipulate processes and techniques which someone else already "knows." To solve this problem, when deciding whether to issue a patent, the PTO considers factors such as how important the invention is, how valuable it is to customers, and therefore how much of it customers will demand. If the invention has value, then the PTO will decide that no one other than the inventor "knows" of the invention. Practitioners in the field have a good sense of how the PTO decides what others "know."

Publication and patent applications

The PTO will not issue a patent if the applicant has disclosed his technology as part of a patent application he has made in another country. This certainly applies to any public disclosures a patent holder may make when a country actually grants a patent. But it also applies to countries, such as Germany and Japan, which require all persons simply applying for a patent to disclose the technology they want to patent.

The PTO will also not issue patents for inventions which any printed publication describes. A "printed publication" is more than a magazine or book. Some courts consider photocopies or typewritten manuscripts "printed" publications. Since, for example, a dusty back shelf of a university library may be hiding a typewritten doctoral thesis describing the inventor's new process, the inventor will always have to worry that, even years after the PTO granted his patent, an obscure researcher may successfully overturn his patent. The obscure researcher may have "published" the invention before the PTO granted the patent.

Used for one year in the US

If, before the inventor applies for a patent, someone has already been using the invention for one year in the US, then the inventor may face two separate difficulties. First, the PTO may find that someone already "knew" of the technology. (See above.) Second, the PTO may reject the application because the invention is already in "use."

The law defines "use" as "nonconcealed use." But even this definition is ambiguous. A firm may use an invention, but, depending on how it uses the invention, its use may or may not be "concealed."

Developed by another

Before the inventor applied for his patent another inventor may have developed the same invention. This first inventor may challenge the second inventor's right to the patent. The first inventor may claim that because he had already developed the invention, it was already "known." (See above) The first inventor may also try to patent the invention himself. The law gives him one year after he develops the invention to file his patent application. See Patent goes to first to invent, below.

Non-obvious

One cannot patent an obvious invention. What is obvious, however, is not always obvious. The general rule is that the PTO will not give a patent to an inventor who has merely extended an existing device or technique, or combined two existing devices or techniques. Doing so, the PTO usually claims, is obvious.

But this general rule is not always appropriate. An inventor could, for example, combine two known techniques in a new and original way, a way which is far from obvious. In all fields, advances seem obvious when their developer later explains them, but these can nevertheless be profound, valuable, advances. To determine what is obvious, therefore, the PTO also often considers factors such as whether the improvement gives a product unique abilities. The PTO will also consider whether the new product is commercially successful, and therefore presumably something others would have done if they had thought to do it. In short, the PTO will try to see if the improvement is one of kind rather than degree. Experienced practitioners have a "feel" for what the PTO will consider obvious.

Useful

The PTO will only grant patents for specific, useful technology. One may not patent general concepts, such as a mathematical formula.

The law has particular difficulty defining useful when an inventor combines his technology with other technologies, processes, etc. In general, the PTO will consider the inventor's technology useful if, when used in combination with other technologies, the invention produces a useful result.

Combined use – define in license agreement

If a licensee will use the licensed technology in combination with other technologies, then the parties must be careful to draft an agreement which carefully describes what the licensed technology can do. If the agreement does not describe the properties of just the licensed technology, then, if the technology cannot do what the licensor said it could do, the licensee will not be able to prove this. (The licensor is the firm selling the technology and the licensee is the firm buying the technology.)

(c)   Patent goes to first to invent

First to invent

The United States awards patents to the first to develop an invention, not the first to apply for a patent for the invention. Thus a first inventor may successfully challenge a second inventor's patent if the first inventor can show that he developed the invention first.

File within one year

To enjoy this protection the first inventor must file his patent application during the first year within which he uses, or sells, his invention.

The inventor must be very careful not to inadvertently start the one year clock ticking. The law will allow the inventor to experiment and perfect his invention. But the law also draws a very thin line between "perfecting" and "using" an invention. An inventor could easily and inadvertently cross the line, "use" the invention, and start the one-year clock ticking.

File as soon as possible

Other practical considerations also behoove the inventor to file his application patent as soon as possible. While one inventor waits, adjusting and perfecting his invention, another inventor may apply for a patent for the same technology. The two inventors could find themselves involved in an expensive, time consuming lawsuit. The inventors may not even settle their lawsuit until the technology has lost much of its value. This is particularly true if the market for the technology is developing rapidly. Thus, while in theory the law may allow an inventor as much time as he wants to perfect his invention, an inventor should, as a practical matter, apply for his patent as soon as possible.

Inventors should keep records

In theory the PTO will issue the patent to the first to invent the technology. But it is perhaps more accurate to say that the PTO will issue the patent to the inventor who it believes was the first to invent. Inventors should therefore keep careful records of all their work. It is these records which will convince the PTO that they were the first to invent.

International priority

An inventor must apply for his American patent within 12 months of having applied for his non-American patent. American law gives those who first apply for a foreign patent 12 months to apply for an American patent. If an inventor does not apply for his American patent within those 12 months, then the PTO will never grant him a patent. American law will thereafter never allow the inventor to receive a patent for his invention.

Provisional application

The provisional application allows the inventor to preserve his claim while he is preparing a complete and proper patent application. The PTO will not examine a provisional application, which is very simple and need not even be in English. Within one year of filing this application the inventor must file a standard application, which the PTO will examine.

(d) Patent lawsuits

Courts can overturn patents

PTO does not bind courts

Initially, the PTO issues patents. But even if the PTO does issue a patent, a court may later invalidate the patent. The PTO is not a court, and the PTO's decisions do not bind courts. Any third party could, at any time, bring a lawsuit claiming that the PTO should not have issued a patent.

Numerous challenges possible

If challenged, the patent holder will of course defend his patent by claiming that the PTO issued his patent correctly. But even if the patent holder should successfully defend his patent in one case, another third party could then bring another case challenging the patent yet again. A patent holder could face an infinite number of such challenges. And if a patent holder loses just once case, then, by definition, a court will have ruled that he is not entitled to his patent. He will therefore lose his patent rights. Thus patent holders always face the risk of losing their patent. This risk lowers the value of the patent itself.

Grounds for challenging patents

Three grounds on which parties often challenge the validity of patents are that the patent holder:

- failed to meet the formal patent requirements, such as novelty,
- misstated information during the application process,
- improperly used the patent to monopolize a market.

The law limits the ways in which a patent holder may use his patent. A patent holder may not, for example, use his patent to monopolize markets related to the market of the patented goods. For example, as a condition for licensing the patent, a patent holder may not require a licensee to buy from him other, unpatented, goods. If a patent holder tries to monopolize markets related to his patent, then a court may strip the patent holder of his patent rights. See Preliminary note on antitrust law, in Licensing, Chapter 5 (i)(c).

American courts protect patents

American courts are relatively vigilant in protecting patent rights. There was a time when courts believed that patents gave patent holders monopoly powers, and, because courts instinctively disliked monopolies, they were rather quick to invalidate patents. To remedy this Congress directed that appeals for all patent lawsuits must go to one court, the Court of Appeals for the Federal Circuit. This court tends to see patents as property rights, not monopolies, and therefore it is not quick to invalidate patents. This court has therefore increased the value of American patents.

Licensing – anticipate future claims

Potential licensees should investigate the possibility that a court will invalidate the patent it is considering licensing. Potential licensors should anticipate that potential licensees will make this investigation. Before offering to license a technology, therefore, potential licensors should themselves analyze the likelihood of a successful challenge to their patent. By doing this analysis beforehand they will both be able to answer potential licensees' questions, and, perhaps more importantly, prepare for potential challenges to their patents.

Patent holder's claim against infringers

Use of invention while lawsuit pending

In almost all patent infringement lawsuits, when the patent holder begins the case he will ask the court to order the alleged infringer to stop using the patented technology immediately. Courts are, however, generally reluctant to issue such orders, called injunctions, which, before the trial, give the patent holder the outcome he seeks.

A court will only order an alleged infringer to stop using the technology if the patent holder can prove that he is very likely to win the patent infringement lawsuit. Since patent lawsuits are complex, at the outset a patent holder will usually have difficulty showing that he is very likely to win the lawsuit.

Nevertheless, at times, even before trial, courts do order alleged infringers to stop using the technology. If the patent holder has won similar cases, then he will probably be able to convince the court that he will win this case too. Further, the Court of Appeals for the Federal Circuit, reflecting its relatively pro-patent attitude, is surprisingly willing to order alleged infringers to stop using technology.

A patent holder who licenses his technology will have great difficulty persuading a court to order an alleged infringer to stop using technology. The patent holder will have to show the court that if it fails to issue the order, then the patent holder will suffer damage which a later award of money would not correct. But if the patent holder licenses his technology, then the court will probably reason that if it should later find that the alleged infringer did in fact use the technology improperly, then the court would order him to pay the royalties he should have paid to license the technology.

Patent infringer must pay money

A court will order the infringer to pay the patent holder the amount of money the infringement cost the patent holder. A court may, for example, order an infringer to compensate a patent holder because the infringer's excessive competition forced the patent holder to charge an unfairly low price. As another possibility, a court may order the infringer to pay a sum based on the number of products he sold containing the patented technology, and the extent to which the technology increased the value of the product.

Many patent holders have difficulty calculating how much an infringement cost them. The law therefore allows them to recover, as an alternative, a reasonable royalty. The court would order the infringer to pay what he would have paid if he had licensed the patent.

Punitive damages and attorney's fees

Courts have the authority to order an infringing party to pay punitive damages and attorney's fees. While courts are generally reluctant to order infringers to make these payments, they will make the appropriate award in the appropriate case. For example, a court would probably order a patent infringer who blatantly ignored a patent, or who abused the lawsuit process, to pay punitive damages, attorneys' fees, or both.

Use license agreements to avoid expensive lawsuits

If two parties dispute the ownership of a patent, they should try to resolve their dispute. Parties commonly settle a patent dispute by entering into a license agreement. The parties should try to enter into this license agreement before suing each other. Lawsuits force parties to harden their positions. They are expensive. If a patent holder resolves a dispute by licensing his patent, then he will avoid the risk of losing his patent rights completely. And if a patent infringer licenses the patent, then he will avoid the risk that the court may order him to pay punitive damages and attorneys' fees.

If the parties cannot resolve their dispute, then they should arbitrate, or, better yet, mediate. By arbitrating the parties will save time and money, and will be able to keep their dispute confidential. A mediator may help the parties reach a license agreement which makes business sense for both parties, but which neither an arbitrator, nor certainly a judge, could impose. A good license agreement will allow both parties to make money instead of wasting it fighting each other. See Court system: lawsuits and arbitration, Chapter 9.

Employee's personal liability for corporate infringement

As a general rule, if a corporation infringes a patent, then a court will only order the corporation to pay the patent holder. Courts will generally not hold corporate officers and employees personally liable for the actions they take while acting on behalf of their corporate employers. However, if a corporate officer or employee personally knows of a patent and chooses to ignore it, then, along with the corporation, a court may also order the officer or employee personally to pay the patent holder.

(e) Imported goods made with US patented process

Must get patent holder's permission

If an importer is bringing into the United States goods which were manufactured by a process patented in the United States, then the importer must get the patent holder's permission to bring the goods into the country. In other words, the law will not allow a firm to avoid an American process patent by simply using the patented process outside the United States, and then importing the goods into the country.

Only firms intending to improperly bring in goods are liable

Courts will hold liable under this rule the firm which actually imported the goods. Thus if a non-American manufacturer simply sold its goods to another non-American firm, then the American courts will not hold the non-American manufacturer liable. The courts will only hold liable the firm bringing the goods into the United States improperly.

(f)   Length of patent

Patents last for 20 years from the date the inventor filed his patent application.

(g)   Application time and costs

The American patent system is not notably efficient. The PTO can take up to 5 years to act on a patent application.

On the other hand, inventors do not pay particularly high fees to patent their inventions in the United States. While an applicant's total costs will vary depending on the complexity of his invention, an inventor should expect to pay no more than several thousand dollars for the study which he will need to show that his patent application is valid, and a further few thousand dollars to actually apply for the patent. The United States also charges a relatively modest patent maintenance fee.

(h)   Design patents

General points

Most designers do not find design patents valuable. To obtain a design patent the designer must show that his design is new, non-obvious, and *ornamental*. New and non-obvious are the same requirements as described above. Ornamental, the third requirement, is specific to design patents. And ornamental, to paraphrase, is in the eye of the beholder. Most PTO officials, and most judges, have difficulty seeing the ornamental value of designs. They are therefore reluctant to award or uphold design patents.

Design patents and trademarks

If, over time, consumers come to associate a distinctive design with a particular product, this will allow the designer to trademark the design

(See Trademarks, Section (iv) below). Some designers therefore seek design patents despite the weakness of design patent protection. These designers hope the design patent will protect their design only until consumers have come to associate the design with the product. At that time they will trademark their design. Since a designer can obtain a design patent for up to 14 years, the design patent may very well offer the designer this more limited, but still very valuable, protection.

(i)   Patents and product liability

Patent licensors must be sure that they give full and accurate information to their licensees. If they give incorrect information, a court may later hold them liable, under product liability law, for the damages the resulting defective products caused. See Strict products liability, Chapter 6 (iii)(f).

(iii)   Trade secrets

(a)   Introduction

Broad protection

Trade secret law protects a firm's valuable business information. It does not protect ideas as strongly as does patent law but firms can much more easily obtain trade secret protection. Trade secret law also covers a much wider array of ideas than does patent law.

Both patent and trade secret law may protect the same technology. Thus, in many cases, firms must choose whether to use trade secret or patent law to protect their technology. In a surprising number of cases firms will choose to use trade secret rather than patent law. Finally, a firm may devise a strategy to enjoy both patent and trade secret protection.

Uniform Trade Secrets Act

Trade secret law is state law. Therefore to some extent trade secret law varies from state to state. However, most states base their trade secret law on the Uniform Trade Secrets Act. Thus the general principles of trade secret law are fairly uniform throughout the United States.

(b) Requirements

General points

The law automatically applies trade secret protection to qualifying information. To qualify:

- the firm must use the information in its business,

- the information must help give the firm a competitive advantage,

- the firm must try to keep the information secret, and

- the information must also in fact be secret.

A firm must use the information

To be a *trade* secret, the firm must *use* the information in its trade or business. Thus:

- a *trade* secret must relate to a firm's *trade* or business and,

- the firm must actually *use* the information in its trade or business. Trade secrets are therefore practical, concrete ideas or information – ideas firms use. Since abstract plans or mere proposals are not concrete ideas firms can use, the law does not protect abstract plans or mere proposals as trade secrets.

Trade secrets provide competitive advantage

To be a trade secret, the information must have value, it must give its owner a competitive advantage. If, over time, the information has come to lose its value, then at some point the law will no longer protect it as a trade secret.

The law will protect just about any idea which gives a firm a competitive advantage. It will protect both complex and simple ideas. Common forms of trade secrets include the following.

Product characteristics and specifications

Only subtle, hidden, product characteristics, which reverse engineering (see below) will not reveal, qualify as trade secrets.

Manufacturing processes

In many cases trade secret law offers owners of sophisticated manufacturing process better protection than does patent law. Patent law requires disclosure of the patented technology, and the patent will eventually expire. Trade secret law does not require the owner to disclose the technology it is protecting, and trade secret protection could last indefinitely. Thus if the valuable knowledge relates to a manufacturing process, and if a competitor cannot reverse engineer the end-product to learn the manufacturing process, then trade secret law may provide longer, and more easily obtainable, protection than does patent law.

Formulas

Formulas which firms use to manufacture products are usually valuable information, and the law will protect this information as a trade secret.

Know-how

Know-how is techniques and ways of doing things. Its owner has often developed it over a long period of time, and it therefore often includes much experience and practical knowledge. Firms find know-how very valuable. When licensing patents, licensors also usually license related know-how. Licensees pay for know-how because it usually allows them to use the patented technology, and run their businesses, better, faster and cheaper.

Cost information

Trade secret law protects information relating to a firm's costs, and which competitors cannot readily obtain. This includes not only manufacturing related costs, but also suppliers' special discounts and similar non-public information.

Customer lists

Customer lists which a competitor could not develop from public sources are trade secrets.

Firms must try to keep the information secret

Since the law protects trade *secrets*, it only protects information which its owner intends to keep secret. Therefore if a firm wants to protect information as a trade secret, it must try to keep the information secret. The firm must implement procedures to keep secret information which it wants the law to protect as a trade secret.

The law does not list any specific steps which a firm must take to keep information secret. A firm must simply take reasonable steps. These reasonable steps could include the following.

- Including in employment contracts provisions forbidding:
  - employees from disclosing trade secrets, particularly after they stop working for the firm
  - employees from working for competing firms. See below.

- Controlling outsiders' access to areas containing trade secrets. A prudent firm will also restrict employees' access to areas containing trade secrets.

- Controlling circulation within the firm of documents containing trade secrets.

- Identifying documents containing trade secrets. This will:
  - warn employees of the importance of the information, so they will keep the information confidential, and
  - show the firm's intent to keep the information secret.

- Keeping to a minimum trade secrets which the firm reveals to supporting firms such as suppliers. The firm should also require supporting firms and other third parties, to whom it tells its trade secrets, to agree to keep the information confidential.

The owner must actually keep the information secret

Since the law protects trade secrets, it will only protect information which a firm has in fact kept secret. In this context, however, managers should keep in mind that the law is protecting commercial information, not military information. Accordingly, the law requires firms to maintain commercial secrecy, not military secrecy. A few firms may each know the same trade secret. But the industry generally must not know the information.

Reverse engineering

Since competitors can and do examine each others' products, many firms cannot protect information they incorporate into their products. Almost all competitors have developed the fine art of reverse engineering, carefully dismantling and examining their competitors' products. The law therefore considers public, and not a trade secret, any information any competitor could obtain through reverse engineering.

Protect through lease

To stop reverse engineering, a firm may lease rather than sell its product. It would only lease its products to those who agreed not to reverse engineer. The firm may even forbid its customers from repairing its product. If its market were small enough, and it could do business this way, then a firm using this technique could protect as a trade secret information contained within its product.

(c)   Maintenance costs

Directly, trade secret law imposes no maintenance costs. However, because trade secret law only protects information which a firm keeps secret, the firm's cost to keep the information secret is in reality the firm's trade secret maintenance cost. Given the value of trade secrets, many firms actually find this cost to be a wise investment.

(d)   Rights of a trade secret owner

Control disclosure

The owner of a trade secret has the right to selectively disclose its trade secret. The owner can tell it to some employees, or can license it. And, most importantly, a trade secret owner can stop these and other persons from disclosing its trade secret.

Independent developers may use the trade secret

Most emphatically, and unlike a patent holder, a trade secret owner has no right to stop someone who has developed the trade secret information completely on his own from also using the trade secret. The law only gives the trade secret owner the right to control the disclosure of its secret. If another firm should independently develop the same secret, the first trade secret owner has no right to stop this independent developer from using the information which it developed on its own. By contrast, patent law allows patent holders to stop all persons from using the patented technology, including persons who have independently developed the patented technology.

Restrictions on employment of former employees

To protect trade secrets, some firms try to limit their employees' right to work for competitors. Courts are generally reluctant to enforce these provisions. Courts generally believe that employees should be free to work for any employer they choose. Courts will, however, enforce reasonable restrictions on an employee's subsequent employment. A court will, for example, probably enforce a restriction on an employee's right to take a job with a competitor if this new job were likely to require the employee to disclose the employer's trade secrets.

Restrictions on licensee's employees

A licensor may require a licensee to restrict the licensee's employee's subsequent employment. Courts will enforce such requirements, again so long as they are reasonable. In fact, a licensor should try to restrict its licensees' employee's subsequent employment. This will not only actually help it keep its trade secrets confidential, it will also help to show its intent to keep its trade secrets confidential, and thus help the secrets qualify as trade secrets.

Employees who develop trade secrets

Firms should be sure that they, and not their employees, become the owner of any valuable information which their employees develop while working for the firm. Employers often require employees to acknowledge that the employer will own any *patentable* technology the employee may develop on the job. But employers should go further: this acknowledgment should apply not only to patents, but also to unpatented valuable information such as trade secrets.

Trade secret protection lasts indefinitely

Unlike patent protection, the law does not terminate trade secret protection at any predetermined time. The protection will last as long as the information stays secret and stays valuable. This period could be infinite.

The law will not protect information which is no longer secret

Since the law requires trade secrets to be secret, when the information is no longer secret the law will not longer protect it as a trade secret. The law considers information which is widely known within an industry to no longer be a secret. Information will become widely known if, for example, an academic were to publish the information, or if the manufacturer were to sell a product which competitors could reverse engineer.

On the other hand, no one event may cause the information to lose its trade secret status. Over time many competitors may independently develop the trade secret technology. The information may spread gradually through the industry, so that after a while it is no longer secret. In this case the trade secret owner, and its licensees, may not even realize that the information is no longer secret.

Licensing royalties can be forever

Since a trade secret could in theory last forever, a firm licensing trade secrets could, in theory, collect royalties forever. By contrast, after a patent expires, a patent licensor may no longer collect royalties. After a patent expires anyone may use the now-unpatented technology.

Parties to an agreement licensing both patents and trade secrets must decide how to allocate royalty payments. The licensee will stop paying royalties for the patent when the patent expires. But, even after the patent expires, the licensee will still have to pay royalties for trade secrets. How the parties will allocate royalty payments is certainly an issue they must negotiate.

The parties must also decide when the licensee must stop paying royalties for the trade secrets. The licensee will hesitate to agree to pay royalties for a long period because soon after it signs the agreement the information may lose its trade secret status. However, the licensor may worry that if it agrees that the licensee may stop paying royalties as soon as the information loses its trade secret status, then, if the information loses its status quickly, the licensor will not receive full compensation for having disclosed its trade secret.

Parties often solve this problem by agreeing that the licensee will pay royalties so long as the information remains a trade secret, but will also pay a minimum royalty. This minimum payment may be an initial lump-sum payment, may be a fixed minimum payment over a set period of time such as five years, or it may be a combination of these.

License trade secrets while patent pending

Before an inventor patents his technology, he will be able to protect it as a trade secret, and therefore will be able to license it. When the PTO grants the inventor his patent it will require the inventor to reveal his technology but until the PTO grants the patent the inventor may keep the technology secret, and thereby protect it as a trade secret. Further, if the PTO declines to grant the patent, then the inventor will, for the long-term, still be able to protect his technology as a trade secret.

(e)   Trade secrets outside the US are licensable in the US

American law recognizes trade secrets developed anywhere in the world. Unlike patent law, trade secret law does not require owners to register their rights. A firm's information may therefore qualify for trade secret protection even if it is outside the US. Since an American court will protect trade secrets located outside the US, the owner of such trade secrets can license them inside the US in the same way that an American trade secret owner may license its trade secrets.

(f)   Arbitration

Courts do not allow arbitrators to decide important issues of public policy. If a case involves important public policy issues, then a court will not allow the case to proceed in arbitration. Instead, the court will decide the case itself. This is true even the parties agreed to arbitrate their dispute.

Since a defendant will usually prefer the slower traditional lawsuit to the faster arbitration hearing, defendants in arbitration often raise issues of important public policy. In this way they hope that the court will remove the case from arbitration. To remove cases involving intellectual property, licensing, and similar issues from arbitration, defendants often raise issues relating to restrictions on an employee's right to subsequent employment, or relating to antitrust policies. Courts, however, are becoming increasingly suspicious of defendants' motives when they raise such issues. Courts resist allowing defendants to use these issues simply to avoid arbitration.

(g) Penalties for violating trade secrets

Preliminary order to stop using secret

American courts prefer to order a liable party to pay money. They are, by contrast, hesitant to order a party to take some specific action. Despite this general rule, if a trade secret owner believes that a firm is improperly using its trade secret, then it will almost always ask a court to immediately order the other firm to stop using its trade secret. It will then bring a lawsuit against the alleged infringer.

In the case of alleged trade secret infringement, courts are more inclined than usual to order an alleged trade secret infringer to take an a specific action, in this case to immediately stop using the trade secret. This may seem surprising: not only would the court be ordering the firm to take a specific action, but it would be making this order at the beginning of the lawsuit, before it found that the firm had in fact used the trade secret improperly.

Courts take this very aggressive position regarding trade secrets because the infringer's continued improper use of the trade secret would almost certainly undermine the value of the trade secret. If the alleged infringer continues to use the trade secret, then the trade secret will probably not continue to be secret for very long.

Nevertheless, a court will still not issue such an order, called an injunction, lightly. It will first require the trade secret owner to show that it is likely to win the lawsuit. And if the trade secret owner ultimately loses the lawsuit, then the court will order the trade secret owner to pay the alleged infringer the costs the firm incurred because the court ordered it to stop using information which, it turns out, it was always perfectly entitled to use.

Money

If a firm uses a trade secret improperly, then a court will of course order that firm to give to the trade secret owner the profits it improperly earned because it used the trade secret. The court will also order the infringer to compensate the trade secret owner for any losses the infringement cost the trade secret owner. These losses may, for example, include the trade secret owner's lost profits. In this area courts look to patent law for guidance. In fact, in this area of calculating losses, there is little if any difference between patent and trade secret law.

(h)   Patent protection v. trade secret protection

Inventors must usually decide whether to use patent law or trade secret law to protect their inventions. Many inventors initially prefer patent protection. But some inventors should consider protecting their inventions as trade secrets rather than as patents.

Forced disclosure

Patent law requires inventors to reveal the technology they have patented. Trade secret law, on the other hand, allows inventors to keep their technology secret. Thus all inventors have to decide whether they want to disclose their invention in order to obtain a patent. Some inventors may want to keep their invention secret. These inventors can do so and still use trade secret law to protect their inventions.

Further, an inventor who applies for a patent runs the risk that after the PTO grants his patent, and he discloses his technology, a court will then invalidate his patent. If this happens the inventor will have incurred significant legal expenses and will have disclosed his technology. He will have lost his patent, and will not be able to protect his technology as a trade secret. Competitors and potential licensees will have free access to his invention. To avoid this possibility many inventors play it safe and settle for trade secret protection.

Compare with process patents

This is particularly true if the inventor would otherwise apply for a process patent. Patent holders find process patents notoriously difficult to protect. Since manufacturers can use patented processes to make standard products, holders of process patents have great difficulty determining if manufacturers used their patented processes to make these standard products. Since, after disclosing the invention, policing costs are so high, many inventors of unique processes choose not to disclose their invention in order to obtain a patent. Instead they protect their processes as trade secrets.

Enjoying both patent and trade secret protection

An inventor may be able to enjoy both patent and trade secret protection. If the nature of his invention makes this possible, an inventor may disclose just enough of his technology so the PTO will issue a patent. The inventor would therefore have kept secret other information which potential infringers, or licensees, will need to successfully exploit the technology. The inventor will then protect this information as a trade secret.

An inventor using this strategy will enjoy the greater rights patent law gives him, and still be able to protect the valuable trade secret information indefinitely. This strategy will allow the inventor to both protect his patent from independent developers and collect license royalties after his patent expires.

Trade secrets are also easy to establish outside the United States

Many countries recognize trade secrets. A trade secret owner may therefore be able to bring lawsuits in many different countries to stop infringers in those countries. Thus, because inventors do not have to formally apply for trade secret protection, they can very easily and quickly enforce their trade secret rights in many countries.

Patent law, by contrast, requires inventors to make separate expensive, time consuming, applications in many different countries. Thus the inventor may choose to protect his technology as a trade secret because he can enforce his trade secret rights much more easily throughout the world.

(iv) Trademarks and other marks

(a) Introduction

Distinguish products

Trademarks distinguish products. Trademarks include words, names, symbols and so on, which distinguish one product, or family of products, from others. Trademarks can be very valuable. This is particularly so because over time well-managed trademarks increase in value.

Types of marks

Managers and lawyers often incorrectly refer to service marks, collective marks and other marks as trademarks. The law in fact recognizes many different types of marks.

- **Trademarks** identify actual, tangible, products.

- **Service marks**, by contrast, identify services.

- **Collective marks** identify organizations. A product's label, for example, might identify the union of the workers who made the product.

- **Certification marks** are marks organizations give to products or services that meet certain standards. Examples of certification marks include the "Union Label," which certifies that union labor made the product, and "Roquefort" cheese, which certifies regional origin.

- Finally, one should not confuse trademarks with **corporate names**. A corporate name identifies an entire corporation. A corporation cannot register its name as a trademark. On the other hand, the corporate registration system prevents others from improperly using a corporation's name. See Corporations, partnerships, and joint ventures, Chapter 3.

(b)   Firms can trademark words, styles and designs

Distinctive words

Since a trademark identifies a particular product, it follows that the word which is or becomes the trademark must clearly identify only that particular product. The word cannot cause confusion among consumers. A firm cannot trademark a word which merely describes a product. A firm cannot market "Excellent" computers. No firm will ever be able to trademark these so called generic words.

On the other hand, firms can trademark descriptive words, words which consumers have over time come to associate with a particular product. Thus while the law will not allow a soft drink manufacturer to trademark the generic word "soda," it did allow one manufacturer to trademark the descriptive, and at one time meaningless, word "Coca-Cola."

If consumers have come to associate a word with a particular product, then the word has developed what the law calls a secondary meaning.

Writing style

A firm can register as a mark not only a word, but also the style with which it writes the word. Part of the Coca-Cola trademark is certainly the descriptive style with which the firm writes the name of its famous soft drink.

Designs

Along with words, a firm can also register a design as a mark. In fact, many firms successfully combine words and designs to develop a truly distinctive mark.

Slogans

Firms can also register slogans, so long as consumers associate the slogan with the appropriate product. As any marketing executive knows, slogans can be powerful compliments to trademarked product names.

Product shape

A firm can also protect the distinctive shape of its product. The firm must have given the product a distinctive shape, and the shape's only purpose must be to help consumers identify that product. Consumers must have come to associate that shape with that particular product. By contrast, a firm cannot register as a mark any design which is in any way useful or functional.

Packaging

Just as a firm can trademark a product's shape, so too can it trademark a product's packaging. Once again, the law will only protect those parts of the package which have no practical purpose, but which the firm merely uses to distinguish its product, and which consumers have come to associate with the product.

(c)   Obtaining rights to mark – use and registration

Use creates ownership – not registration

Use of a mark creates ownership. Registration does not. Firms earn their rights to their marks by using them. Firms register their marks because registration provides several advantages, not because they need to register to gain ownership of the mark.

Use of mark

Use creates ownership

A firm can easily earn ownership of a mark. So long as another firm is not using the mark, the firm need only "use" the mark. It must merely put the mark on the goods or services with which it wants consumers to associate the mark. Further, courts have been defining "use" in an increasingly liberal fashion. Thus, in general, courts do not require the firm to actually attach the mark to the good or service. The firm need only use the mark in some way, such as advertising, which will lead consumers to associate the mark with its product or service.

Despite this general rule, however, firms should usually physically attach their marks to their products. From a legal point of view, the closer the connection between the goods and the mark, and stronger is the firm's claim to the mark. From a marketing point of view, the stronger the consumer's association between the goods and the mark, the more valuable the mark.

Investigate before using

Before using a mark a firm should be sure that no other firm is using that mark. Several firms specialize in researching the use of marks. These research firms generally charge modest fees, and are usually well worth their price. But their services are not foolproof. Computers cannot appreciate all the different ways artists draw and write marks, nor can they always appreciate how two different words, spelled very differently, can nevertheless sound alike. The human supplement to these computer searches, though necessary, is also not foolproof.

Registration of mark

Although registration does not create ownership of a mark, it does provide many advantages. Registration offers only advantages, and no disadvantages. All firms should therefore register their marks.

Registration requirement

Firms can register marks with federal and state authorities. Federal registration is the most important. Firms may only register marks:

- which meet the substantive mark ownership requirements, and

- which they are either actually using, or intend to use.

Advantages of federal registration

Firms should register their marks with the federal agency which manages federal mark registration, the PTO. They should also include with their marks the ® symbol, which indicates that they have registered their marks. Firms that register their marks enjoy the following advantages.

- They may bring infringement lawsuits throughout the United States.

- They may bring these infringement actions in federal court. A number of attorneys prefer federal to state court. See Court System, Chapter 9.

- If they sue another firm for mark infringement, the firm they sue cannot claim that it did not realize that the registering firm claimed ownership of the mark.

- The Customs Service will not allow infringing goods to pass through customs. See Import procedures, Chapter 2 (iv).

- If they win an infringement action, then the court will be able to increase the amount of money it awards them, if it needs to, to ensure that these firms are fully and fairly compensated, and the court may also award them attorney's fees.

Firms will suffer no disadvantages from registering their marks with the PTO. Because firms suffer no disadvantages from registering their marks, but do enjoy several advantages, all firms should register their marks. The remainder of this chapter assumes that all mark owners have registered, or intend to register, their marks.

Registration before use

A firm can register a mark by either using the mark or by telling the PTO that it intends to use the mark. If a firm registers its mark by telling the PTO of its intent to use the mark, then it must thereafter use the mark. In theory, the firm must use the mark within six months of registering it.

However, the PTO may extend this six-month period. In total a firm may wait up to two years before using the mark. To receive the first six-month extension, and thus be able to wait one year before using the mark, the firm must simply tell the PTO that it intends to use the mark within the second six-month period. The PTO will also grant the first six-month extension if the firm tells it that a related corporation, such as a subsidiary or licensee, will use the mark within the six-month period. The PTO then has the discretion to extend the period for an additional two six-month periods, for a total of two years from the initial filing date. The PTO will only grant these extensions if the firm has a good reason for waiting to use its mark.

This intent to use procedure gives firms marketing flexibility. For example, firms can register their intention to expand the class of goods on which they will later put their mark. Thus a firm could, initially, use a mark for one type of good, but also register its intent to later use the mark on other types of goods. In this way a firm can develop an entire marketing program based on its marks. This program could include licensing the mark, or licensing the mark along with patents and know-how.

International registration and priority

International treaties which the US has signed, such as the Paris Convention for the Protection of Industrial Property, provide rights which may help non-Americans. For example, these treaties may give non-Americans, who have registered their marks outside the United States, the right to stop others from using their marks inside the United States.

(d)   Rights of mark owner

Mark owner can stop possibly confusing use

A mark owner may stop anyone from using the mark in any way which *may* cause consumers to confuse the marked goods with other goods. This simple statement has broad implications.

This right only relates to goods of the marked goods' class

Since the law seeks to ensure that consumers do not confuse the marked goods with other goods, the law will only allow the mark owner to stop others from using the mark with goods of the same class as the marked goods. Courts reason that consumers will not confuse goods of two different classes.

Courts, however, often have difficulty defining goods of a different "class." Consumers could confuse, for example, the names of an outdoor magazine and sporting equipment. Relatedly, over time mark owners commonly expand the number of products on which they put their increasingly well known and valuable mark. The law provides no clear rule as to when dissimilar goods are of the same "class." Courts decide on a case by case basis.

Third parties may not refer to the mark

The law not only forbids competitors from putting the mark on other goods of the same class, but it also forbids competitors from using the mark when they advertise or promote their competing products. Such use could certainly cause confusion among consumers.

A competitor may not engage in activity which merely may cause confusion

To stop a third party from using his mark, a mark owner does not have to prove that the third party's use will in fact cause confusion among consumers. The mark owner need only show that the third party's use *may* cause confusion among consumers. If the third party's act simply *may* cause confusion among consumers, if confusion is possible, then a court will stop the third party from engaging in the possibly confusing activity.

In some cases third parties, particularly competitors, attempt to use marks, or aspects of marks, in ways which *may* cause confusion among consumers. A competitor could, for example, use as a mark a completely different word, but write it in a style which is very similar to the registered mark. This may cause confusion, and the law will not allow it.

In short, the law does not put a great burden on the mark owner. With relative ease the mark owner can stop others from using its mark. In fact, it is because mark owners can so easily stop others from using their mark that the right to a mark is so valuable.

Lawsuits

Seizure of counterfeit goods

A firm which, without permission, puts another's mark on its products is creating counterfeit goods. Courts will order the immediate seizure of counterfeit goods, even before a trial. A mark owner asking for such immediate seizure must, however, proceed with caution. If, based on its request, a court does order that the goods be seized, and it later turns out the goods were not counterfeit, then the firm requesting the order will have pay the other firm its lost profits, and possibly also its attorneys fees.

Compensation and punitive damages

A court will order a firm which improperly used another's mark to give the rightful mark owner at least all the profits the firm earned from its improper use of the mark. If the improper use of the mark caused the mark owner to lose more than this amount of money, then a court will order the mark infringer to reimburse the trademark owner for these losses as well. If the infringer has acted maliciously, then the court may also award punitive damages.

(e)   Infinite duration

Manage properly

Firms can in theory use their marks forever, so long as they manage their marks properly. Firms must manage the legal aspects of the mark properly, by periodically renewing their registration. Firms must manage the marketing aspects of their mark properly, by maintaining the appropriate product and mark image.

Firms should see their ability to use marks indefinitely in sharp contrast to the limited time in which they can use patents and trade secrets. Patents expire after 20 years. Time decreases the value of trade secrets, either as other firms come to learn the trade secret, or as new technologies make the trade secret less valuable. A well-managed mark, however, could remain valuable indefinitely. In fact, as over time more and more consumers come to recognize a mark, the mark may increase in value.

Licensing royalties

Due to a mark's perpetual duration and possibly increasing value, a firm may very well license its mark. If a firm licenses a technological package containing a patent, related know-how, and a trademark, the more this licensor allocates royalties to the trademark, the greater the royalties the licensor will earn in the long run. This is so because the licensor's trademark rights will probably remain enforceable longer than will its trade secret or patent rights. In fact, licensors commonly allocate royalties to marks so they can, in reality, extend the life of their patents. See Licensing, Chapter 5.

(f)   Loss of rights to mark

Introduction

A mark owner can lose its rights to its mark in several ways. These include:

- altering the mark substantially from its original form,

- using the mark on products of an unrelated class,

- substantially altering the quality of the products associated with the mark,

- failing to actually use the mark.

Maintain mark form, class of product, and product quality

Mark owners must be sure to:
- use the mark in the form in which they have registered it,

- use the mark only on goods of the registered class (the mark owner may also use the mark on goods of a related class),

- maintain the quality of the marked goods. In fact, most firms will find that the cost of maintaining quality is actually a good investment. Not only will it help the firm preserve its rights to its mark, it will also help to increase the long-term value of the mark.

Finally, if a firm licenses its mark, then it must be sure that its licensees also take these precautions. However, licensors must be careful not to supervise their licensees so closely that a court considers them to be their licensees' co- manufacturer, and therefore liable under product liability law. See Strict products liability, Chapter 6 (iii).

Use mark

The law will not allow the mark owner to make perfunctory use of its mark simply so it can claim that it is using its mark. After registering the mark the mark owner must actually use its mark.

(g)   Costs to enforce

Firms can acquire and maintain marks for only a modest cost. The PTO's initial filing fees are minimal. Should the PTO require a mark applicant to take further steps to show the PTO that it should issue the mark, the costs of this further proceeding are rarely more than several thousand dollars. And trademark lawsuits, while hardly inexpensive, are usually less costly than patent lawsuits.

(h)   Combining mark and other areas of intellectual property increases protection

Supplement to design patent

A firm can both trademark a product's shape and patent the product's design. Trademark and patent law are two separate areas of intellectual property law. Each protects ideas and concepts which satisfy its requirements. The same concept may therefore enjoy both types of protection. As discussed in the patent section, these two areas of intellectual property, working together, may provide greater protection than would each area by itself. For example, the design patent may protect a product's shape just long enough for consumers to associate that shape with that product. Once consumers make this association, then the design patent owner will register the product shape as a trademark. See Design patents, Section (ii)(h).

Supplement to copyright

If a firm can copyright its marks, then copyright law can provide trade-mark owners with valuable additional rights.

- Copyright law may protect a word while it is developing the association with the product which it needs to qualify for trademark protection.

- A court may order a copyright infringer to pay a substantial, fixed, money award. Courts can order infringers to pay these sums even if the copyright owner cannot prove that the infringement hurt it financially. If a firm has both trademark and copyright rights, then if it does bring an infringement action, the mere possibility that a court will order the infringer to pay this fixed substantial sum will give the firm additional bargaining leverage during the inevitable settlement negotiations. See Court system, Chapter 9.

Trade secrets and patents v. marks

Marks can provide valuable supplementary protection to inventors who rely mainly on trade secret and patent protection. An inventor can obtain mark protection for any distinctive feature, or name, of his product and this mark protection could last indefinitely. This additional, indefinite, protection has many advantages, such as allowing the inventor to collect royalties long after his patent has expired. However, marks do not protect *useful* features and so an inventor should therefore be careful not to rely too heavily on mark protection.

(v) Copyright

(a) Introduction

This section analyzes copyright law from the perspective of a firm doing business in the United States. It examines issues such as a firm's ability to copyright the packaging of its products, or use copyright law when licensing technology. Within society copyright law of course plays a much broader role than this. This broader perspective is, however, beyond the scope of this book.

The fundamental principle of copyright law is that it protects the author's form of expression, but not the author's ideas. It protects the exact words the author uses to explain the principles of physics, or law, for example, but it does not protect those ideas of physics or law. No one can copyright a field of knowledge. Everyone has the right to use ideas.

This distinction is not as clear in practice as it is in theory. In some cases courts have difficulty distinguishing form of expression from idea. Further, judges and legislators have developed copyright law mostly with the printed word in mind. Thus while courts have some difficulty applying the form/idea distinction to books and magazines, they often have great difficulty applying it to software, the internet and other modern methods of recording information.

Further, while copyright law does not protect ideas, other areas of intellectual property law do. In particular, patent law and trade secret law protect ideas. In fact, to allow authors to use copyright law to protect their form of expression, while still using trade secret law to protect their ideas, Congress created a special procedure for authors to register and copyright, but still keep confidential, material containing trade secrets.

Copyright law's main impact on business transactions relates to the amount of money an injured party may collect in a lawsuit. If the injured firm qualifies as an infringed author, then copyright law may allow the firm to collect the sum of money the law requires copyright infringers to pay. Many managers do not appreciate this important role. They do not realize the extent to which a court would favor their firm if the court saw the firm as a wronged author. For example, many managers do not realize that they can copyright the manuals they supply to their licensees. If these managers register their firm's copyright in these manuals, then, if the licensee breaches the license agreement, a court may hold the licensee liable, not only for breaching the license agreement, but also for infringing the licensor's copyright.

(b)   Copyright protects the form of original works

Requirements

Authors may copyright "original works of authorship that are fixed in a tangible medium." Thus to qualify for copyright protection the work must be:

- original, and

- recorded in a tangible medium.

Original works

The law protects only original works, not copies. Thus so long as an author has actually created a work, he owns its copyright. Courts do not evaluate the artistic merit of copyrighted material, they merely ask whether the author in fact created it. Copyrightable works must therefore reflect some degree of originality. Authors cannot copyright shapes, words, or standard phrases. Creative writing could not flourish if authors could copyright common phrases such as: "He looked deeply into her eyes..."

Techniques to prove originality

Every author should be able to prove that he created his work. Authors should take steps so that, if someone does copy their work, they will be able to prove that the copy is in fact a copy. This is particularly true regarding works, such as software, which authors record on new electronic media. To help them identify copies, authors, among other things, include in their works superfluous or decorative material, or hide in their works small, inconsequential, errors. Once authors begin to think of ways of ways to catch copiers, they usually develop appropriate, and sometimes ingenious, techniques. The key is that authors should think of ways to catch copiers.

License agreements

Some licensors require their licensees to recognize the "originality," and therefore the copyrightablity, of the software, documents, and other materials related to the licensed technology, which these licensors provide their licensees. After recognizing these works' originality, licensees have difficulty later claiming that the licensor could not copyright the material because it was not original.

Firms can copyright many types of works

Manuals and technical writings

Manuals and technical writings are original works. Firms can register their copyright in them, and licensors should do so. Licensors should then allocate some of their royalties to these copyrights. In this way, if a court should later invalidate, for example, the licensor's patent, the licensor could still collect some royalties. This is particularly important because licensors typically have more difficulty establishing their patent rights than they do their copyright rights.

Firm records and materials

Since an employee wrote the business records of every firm. They are original works and every firm can therefore copyright its business records. A firm can also copyright its instruction manuals, engineering designs, advertising brochures, even the writing on its product's packaging.

In most cases, however, firms will find this protection to be of limited practical value. Copyright does not protect the ideas these documents contain, merely the form of expression. Thus even if a firm has copyrighted a document, without further protection a competitor could still use the ideas the document contains.

Drawings and pictures

A firm may copyright not only writings, but also drawings and designs. A firm could copyright, for example, a written design of a lamp, even if it could not copyright the lamp itself. By contrast, if the firm were able to protect the idea of the lamp itself, it would do so using a design patent. See Patents, Section (ii) above.

Tangible medium

A tangible medium is not only a traditional medium such as paper, but also other media, such as computer disks, which also store information. Thus a firm can copyright not only the records it records on paper, but also those it records on computer disks and CD-ROMs.

Software

Computer software is becoming increasingly valuable. Unfortunately, in this area technology is far outracing the law. While courts have some difficulty applying copyright law's distinction between the expression of an idea and the idea itself to traditional printed material, they have great difficulty applying the distinction to computer software. Software is at the same time both an expression of an idea and the idea itself. The courts are therefore struggling to appropriately classify and protect computer software. In general, copyright law only partially protects software.

Machines

Since a firm can copyright a design, it follows that a firm can copyright a model based on that design. But since copyright law protects only the expression of ideas, and not objects themselves, a firm cannot copyright an object, such as a machine. Thus a firm can copyright a model of a machine, but not the machine itself.

Unpublished works protected

Unpublished works are just as entitled to copyright protection as are published works. Unpublished works enjoy the same protection as published works. This is particularly relevant for firms, which usually do not publish their copyrightable works.

(c) Only the copyright owner has the right to copy the work

General points

The law has few more appropriate terms than "copyright." A copyright gives its owner the right to copy. Only the copyright owner can copy the work. The owner can therefore stop others from copying the work.

Business applications

This seemingly simple idea has many business applications. A firm could, for example, use its copyright rights to control how others copy documents containing the firm's trade secrets.

Relatedly, licensees should maintain reference copies of all copyrighted material their licensors provide to them. This will help the licensees distinguish their works, such as their own manuals, from the licensor's copyrighted manuals. This prudent step could help avoid later disputes.

What is "copying"?

If an impartial casual observer were to believe that two works were the same, then a court would find that the author of the second work copied it. Courts tend to have difficulty applying this test in cases involving technical subjects such as software development. In these cases the parties typically ask expert witnesses to testify on their behalf.

Fair use

The fair use doctrine allows the general public to copy a small portion of a copyrighted work. Courts have developed this exception to the prohibition on copying to encourage the free exchange of ideas. However, courts also recognize that, to protect commercial value, they must limit the "fair use" of copyrighted material.

License agreements

In their license agreements, licensors may be able to limit their licensees' right to the fair use of the licensors' copyrighted material. Since licensors should try to control their documents and related material as much as possible, they should see if their licensees will waive their rights to the "fair use" of the licensors' materials. Licensees, of course, may resist waiving their rights.

(d)   Copyright ownership

Employees

The law gives employers, not employees, the copyright to works employees create on the job. Nevertheless, to eliminate any possible employee copyright claim, if an employee will write manuals or similar documents then the employer should ask the employee to sign an employment contract in which the employee acknowledges that the employer owns the copyright to the employee's work.

Consultants

The law gives the consultant the copyright to all works he creates for his client. Therefore, firms hiring consultants should be sure that their agreement with the consultant gives the firm the copyright to any works the consultant produces on behalf of the firm. In fact, if a firm hires a firm of consultants, then the hiring firm should be sure that its consulting agreement transfers to it not only the copyright of the consulting firm, but also the copyright of each individual consultant.

Finally, firms now commonly hire what they believe to be employees for short periods. Many firms also decline to give many of these "employees" health and other fringe benefits. The law may therefore see these "employees" as outside consultants rather than employees. To avoid even the chance that the law will give these "consultants" the copyright to any work they may write for the firm, the firm should require all relevant employees to sign an employment agreement in which they acknowledge that the firm owns the copyright to any work they may create on behalf of the firm.

Licensors and licensees

Licensees should be sure that their licensors, and not third parties, own the copyright to any materials for which they are paying the license fee. In this way the licensee will be sure that, to continue to use the technology, it will not have to later pay a third party.

To help maintain control of its technology, the licensor should ask the licensee to transfer back to the licensor the copyright to any materials the licensee may write, and which relates to the licensed technology. The licensor should also make sure that the licensee, and not a third party related to the licensee, owns the copyright to any material the licensee writes relating to the licensed technology. If the licensor is not careful, then a subsidiary of the licensee, or an outside expert, may own, and be able to retain, the copyright.

(e)　International protection

American copyright law protects most works copyrighted outside the United States. The US has ratified the Universal Copyright Convention, the Buenos Aires Convention, the Berne Convention, and other treaties and international agreements relating to copyright. Because the US is a party to these agreements, US copyright law protects works written in many other countries.

In the US, as in other Berne signatory countries, copyright attaches instantly to a work. To ratify the Berne Convention, Congress had to repeal the law's previous requirements that authors attach a copyright notice, such as the © symbol, to their works, and that they deposit a copy of their work with the Library of Congress. However, while Congress wanted to ratify the Convention, it also wanted authors to continue to take these steps. Congress therefore created incentives, described in the next section, to encourage authors to continue to attach a copyright notice to their works, and to continue to deposit their works with the Library of Congress.

(f) Deposit and registration

General points

Before the United States ratified the Berne Convention, to copyright a work an author had to deposit a copy of his work with the Library of Congress. This requirement allowed the Library of Congress to collect copies of almost all books and related material circulating in the United States. Since the Berne Convention prohibits countries from establishing any formalities which may hinder the creation of the copyright, when ratifying the Convention Congress had to eliminate this requirement.

However, Congress wanted authors to continue to deposit a copy of their works with the Library of Congress. Furthermore, Congress believed that, to discourage unauthorized copying, authors should continue to include with their works the © copyright notice. Therefore, when ratifying the Berne Convention, Congress created incentives to encourage authors to both continue to attach a copyright notice to their works, and to continue to deposit a copy of their works with the Library of Congress. These incentives are as follows.

- If an author has included the © copyright notice on his work, then a court will not allow a copyright infringer to claim that he did not know that the author claimed the copyright to the work.

- An author cannot sue someone for copyright infringement until he has deposited a copy of his work at the Library of Congress.

- If an author deposits a copy of his work with the Library of Congress before a third party improperly copies the work, then a court *may* order the infringer to pay the author both:

- the author's attorney's fees, or
- a substantial, fixed, money award, which could be more than the actual cost to the author of the infringement. If the author has not deposited the work, then the court can only award the author the actual cost of the infringement.

Publication inside and outside the United States

The first two of these limitations on the rights of authors who do not deposit a copy of their work with the Library of Congress apply only to works published in the United States. Thus, for example, if an author publishes his work in another Berne signatory country, then he will be able to sue an infringer in the US even if he has not deposited a copy of his work with the Library of Congress. Congress considers an author to have published his work "in the US" if he has published it both in the US and a third country at the same time, or if an American author publishes it in a non-Berne signatory country.

The third limitation applies to all works, regardless of where their authors have published them. Thus, for this reason alone, almost all authors, including many who have published their works outside the US, should deposit their works with the Library of Congress. Authors should protect their rights as much as possible.

Deposit of trade secrets

Generally, anyone can read any copyrighted work any author deposits with the Library of Congress. Thus, if the Library of Congress did not make appropriate provisions, no individual or firm could deposit a work containing a trade secret and still preserve the secrecy of that information. To solve this problem, the Library of Congress has developed a procedure whereby it will accept for deposit, but not allow others to read, works containing trade secrets. The Library of Congress will protect in this way not only manuals and other printed material but also works such as software.

(g) Duration

General points

While the length of a copyright can vary, the copyright will usually last for longer than the commercial value of the work.. If a corporation is the author of the work the copyright will last for a minimum of 75 years, which is certainly long enough to protect the commercial value of just about any corporate information or technical development.

Revocation of sold rights

Individuals, but not corporations, retain the right to withdraw whatever copyright rights they have sold or licensed. While the time period after which authors may exercise this right varies, in general the period is 35 years. Thus after 35 years individual authors may demand that their publishers return to them all their copyright rights. Individual authors retain this right despite what any relevant contract or license may say. Thus any firm buying or leasing any copyright rights must be sure that it is not paying for rights which an author may soon be able to reclaim.

(h)   Moral rights

The US does not recognize moral rights. Moral rights are rights some countries give authors, which are very related to copyrights, and which authors cannot sell. Countries granting moral rights forbid copyright purchasers from, for example, altering or modifying a work. Although the Berne Convention recognizes moral rights, Congress ratified the Convention in such a way that Berne Convention moral rights do not apply in the US.

(i)   Lawsuits

Federal claim

Since copyright law is federal law, parties bringing a lawsuit which includes copyright claims may be able to bring their lawsuit in federal court. For example, because trade secret law is state law, a firm must bring a trade secret lawsuit in state court. However, if the firm includes a copyright claim in its lawsuit then it may be able to bring its lawsuit, and therefore its trade secret claim, in federal court. As some attorneys prefer to bring lawsuits in federal court, these attorneys believe that one advantage of including copyright provisions in license and other agreements is that they may allow a firm to bring its lawsuit in federal court. See Court System, Chapter 9, Section (ii)(b).

Whether a federal court will hear a case involving copyright, trade secret, contract, and other related claims would depend on the nature of that dispute. The mere possibility that a plaintiff may be able to bring the action in federal court will increase his bargaining leverage during at least early lawsuit settlement negotiations.

Arbitration

Courts will not allow arbitrators to decide issues of important public policy. Freedom of speech, antitrust, and copyright infringement are important public policy issues which defendants often raise to avoid arbitration. However, overworked courts are becoming increasingly reluctant to allow defendants to use these issues to avoid arbitration. This is particularly true if the parties' underlying dispute relates to a commercial transaction. See Court System, Chapter 9.

Court orders to stop infringement

Before trial

Until the plaintiff has proven his case at trial, a court will usually be very reluctant to order the defendant to stop doing what the plaintiff claims he has no right to do. The court will reason that the defendant may be perfectly entitled to do what he is doing, and if he is not, then after trial the court can order the defendant to pay the appropriate sum of money to the plaintiff. In the case of alleged copyright infringement courts are not as reluctant to order the alleged wrongdoer, the defendant, to stop doing what the plaintiff alleges he has no right to do. Courts take this aggressive attitude because they realize that money usually will not adequately compensate victims of copyright infringement.

The author asking a court to order an alleged infringer to stop his activities must take care. The court will not issue the order unless the author has deposited his work with the Library of Congress. And if the author eventually loses his lawsuit, he will have to compensate the person he incorrectly accused of infringing his work. The author will have to pay the costs the other person incurred because the court ordered him to stop doing what, it turns out, he was perfectly entitled to do.

An author's ability to have a court order another party to stop his alleged copyright infringement, such as distributing possibly infringing material, is a very powerful tool. This is particularly true in the commercial context. Commercially valuable information usually loses its value long before any trial would begin. The author's ability to stop the alleged infringer from distributing information which will only be valuable for a limited period therefore puts the author in a strong bargaining position during the inevitable settlement negotiations.

After trial

After a trial a court will certainly order an infringer to stop his illegal activities. An author may enforce this order throughout the US. By contrast, an author may not be able to enforce an order protecting its trade secrets quite so easily. Trade secrets law is state law, and, unlike copyright law, trade secret law contains no mechanism for quick nationwide enforcement. This is yet another reason why, when possible, firms should use copyright law to supplement the other areas of intellectual property law.

Penalties for infringement

Money award

General points

A court will order a copyright infringer to pay the author whatever the infringement cost the author. The court will also order the infringer to pay the author whatever profits his infringing acts earned.

However, authors usually cannot prove these costs and profits. The law therefore allows courts to order copyright infringers to pay an alternative money award. The law has developed alternative fixed sums which a court may award to an author instead of awarding him his lost profits and similar amounts. These alternative sums can be quite substantial.

Employee's personal liability for corporate infringement

As with patent infringement, if a corporate employee has personal knowledge of a copyright, and chooses to ignore the copyright, then, along with the corporation, a court may also order the employee to pay the author.

Punitive damages

While a court cannot order a copyright infringer to pay punitive damages, it can order the infringer to pay an alternative money award. Since this alternative award will probably be quite substantial, it is very similar to a punitive damage award.

Attorney's fees

In some copyright cases courts award attorney's fees. If the infringer knowingly violated the author's rights, a court may order the infringer to pay the author's attorney's fees. A court can only award attorney's fees if the author had deposited a copy of his work with the Library of Congress before the infringer made his improper copies.

Seizure of counterfeit goods

A court may order the seizure of counterfeit and other goods manufactured in violation of copyright law. A court may also order the seizure of the machines the infringer used to make the counterfeit goods.

Criminal liability

Copyright infringement is a criminal offense. Criminal charges are very serious. The law imposes many rules and restrictions regarding criminal charges which it does not apply to commercial lawsuits. For example, an author cannot use the threat of a criminal charge as bargaining leverage during commercial lawsuit settlement negotiations. Thus, while the commercial plaintiff must be very careful not to use criminal charges to further his private interests, the possibility remains that the authorities may charge a copyright infringer with a crime. With minor exceptions, the authorities cannot bring criminal charges against those who violate the other intellectual property laws. This threat of criminal charges is yet another reason why, when they can, businesses should use copyright law as an additional source of protection for their intellectual property.

(j) Copyrights and other areas of intellectual property law

Copyright v. patent and trade secrets

Copyright protects only the decorative features of a product. Inventors should therefore not rely on copyright law to protect the *useful* features of their inventions. Inventors should probably use patent or trade secret law to protect the useful features of their inventions.

Copyright v. trademark

A firm may be able to copyright a design, such as the style with which it writes its logo. The firm may be able to copyright this as a pictorial or graphic work. If it can copyright its design, then the firm could sue an infringer for violations of both trademark and copyright law, and could obtain whatever money awards and other court orders both these areas of law offer injured parties.

5. LICENSING
The technology transfer agreement

5. LICENSING
The technology transfer agreement

(i) Introduction

(a) Enter the US market by licensing

Licensing technology is a potentially lucrative strategy. Through licensing firms can earn profits quickly. This strategy is particularly attractive to firms which would not otherwise be able to enter a given market. Many firms, notably smaller firms lacking resources, choose to enter the large, competitive American market through licensing. They sell their technology to an American licensee, who has greater knowledge of the American market and is able to successfully exploit the technology in the United States.*

Licensing also carries risks. First, after the license agreement expires the former licensee may become a competitor. Secondly, the licensor can easily lose control of technology it has sold. Technical and business knowledge, once released, can spread quickly. This risk is more than just that of the licensee releasing information knowingly and improperly. Licensees' employees can leak technological secrets in less direct ways–through idle comments, inadvertently while later working for a competitor, and so on. While there is no iron-clad protection against these risks, a good license agreement will lower the risks.

(b) Types of licensable knowledge

In a license agreement the parties buy and sell intellectual property. The typical license agreement transfers rights to several different types of intellectual property. A patent license agreement, for example, will usually also transfer trade secrets which relate to the patent. It may also transfer the licensor's trademark or copyright rights.

The previous chapter on intellectual property described each of these areas of intellectual property law. But, as the previous chapter also explained, ideas are too fluid to fit neatly into legal categories. Therefore,

---

* For a further discussion of licensing, see my 'International Marketing Strategy' in L. Lyck and V.I. Boyko (eds) (1990) *Management, Technology and Human Resources Policy in the Arctic* Kluwer Academic Publishers pp 85–102.

patent, trade secret, trademark, and copyright law may, may to varying degrees, all protect the same technology.

This overlap often causes confusion. Managers are often unsure whether, for example, patent or trade secret law protects an industrial process. The answer may be that both do, or that each protects part of the process.

(c)   Preliminary note on antitrust law

Introduction

The law generally allows parties to enter into any license agreement they wish. The parties do not need the United States government's approval to enter into a license agreement. However, the law does impose some restraints on the parties' freedom to contract. In the area of license agreements, antitrust law imposes the most serious restraints.

Antitrust law protects the free market. To ensure that the free market operates, antitrust law prohibits practices which restrain trade. Competitors agreeing to fix prices is the classic example of a practice which restrains trade and which is therefore illegal.

Many commercial practices are legal in some contexts but illegal in others. Market conditions vary greatly. To determine whether a particular commercial practice restrains trade a court must usually perform a very complex analysis, and the result of this analysis usually applies only to that one case. The number of competitors, the market power of each company, and numerous other relevant factors, all vary greatly from situation to situation.

This chapter points out commercial practices and license agreement terms which may violate the antitrust laws but cannot definitively say whether a provision is legal or illegal. The same practice may, in one context, violate the antitrust laws, but in another context be perfectly legal.

Challenge licensor's patent

A licensor may not forbid a licensee from challenging the validity of the licensor's patent. To do so is itself a violation of the antitrust laws. The law does, however, allow a licensor to forbid its licensees from challenging the validity of its trademarks.

Penalties

Violating the antitrust laws is serious. A firm which violates the antitrust laws must pay the wronged party three times the loss its antitrust violation caused, and pay the wronged party's attorney's fees. Further, courts will not allow patent holders to exercise their patent rights during periods in which they used their patents in ways which the antitrust laws prohibit. Patent holders who violate the antitrust laws could therefore lose substantial royalties.

Antitrust law and dispute settlement

In the context of patent licensing, the licensee usually raises the antitrust issues. Typically, the licensee claims that the licensor, as the monopoly owner of valuable technology, has in some manner abused its market power in violation of the antitrust laws. The licensee may claim, for example, that the licensor has improperly used its market power to gain control of technology which its patent does not cover. In other words the licensee will claim that the licensor has improperly expanded the scope of its patent.

Also typically, the licensee raises this claim when its true, underlying, dispute relates to another matter. The licensee's ability to make this credible antitrust claim against the licensor, or merely its ability to threaten to do so, gives it additional bargaining power when the parties negotiate to settle the underlying dispute. Licensors must therefore be careful not to include in their agreements provisions which will give their licensees bargaining leverage, should the parties later have a dispute regarding any part of the license agreement.

(d) A word about selling technology

In many firms, technical staff will not value an advance they did not develop. Thus, if a patent holder is trying to license technology he should first contact the potential licensee's business and marketing executives rather than its technical personnel. Business and marketing executives tend not to be so prejudiced against technology "not invented here."

(ii)   Pre-agreement negotiations

(a)   Confidentiality

Issue

How can the licensor protect the confidentiality of its technology and its trade secrets while negotiating with a potential licensee?

Commentary

General points

While the parties are negotiating a possible license agreement, one of the licensor's primary aims will be to maintain the confidentiality of its technology and trade secrets. This can be difficult. Before agreeing to pay for the technology, the potential licensee will ask to examine the technology. As soon as the potential licensee examines the technology, it will know it. It will thereafter not need to pay the potential licensor to learn what it already knows.

Only partial solutions exist for this problem. Here are three examples.

● The potential licensee could visit a factory using the technology which is the subject of the negotiations. In this way it can see the benefits of the technology while still not examining the technology, or at least not examining it in depth.

● The potential licensor could release the technology step-by-step. After each step the potential licensor will assure itself that the potential licensee is indeed seriously considering licensing the technology, and has no ulterior motive.

● The prospective licensee should also sign a confidentiality agreement.

Confidentiality agreement

The parties typically enter into a confidentiality agreement while negotiating a possible license agreement. This agreement is usually a simple letter in which the potential licensee agrees to keep confidential the information the potential licensor will give it. The licensor will be able to enforce the confidentiality agreement, not only while the parties negotiate a possible license agreement, but also after the parties conclude their negotiations, particularly if the parties never reach an agreement. Thus the confidentiality agreement will always bind the potential licensee, even if the parties never enter into a license agreement.

These confidentiality agreements have teeth. American courts are usually sympathetic to licensors trying to keep commercially valuable information secret. Using emergency procedures, licensors are usually able to quickly obtain a court order, called an injunction, requiring the licensee to stop releasing or using the confidential information. At first, the court will usually only apply this order for a short period. But during this period the licensor will ask the court to extend the period. The court could apply the order for a long period of time.

(b) Memorandum of understanding

A memorandum of understanding is a non-binding document which outlines the main terms of a possible license agreement. Often one or both the parties are themselves not sure exactly which rights they wish to sell or buy. By forcing the parties to write down the main issues, areas of agreement and areas of disagreement, these memorandums help the parties clarify the issues. They also help the parties see potential disputes sooner rather than later.

In fact, a potential licensor will usually draft its memorandum of understanding before even negotiating with a potential licensee. As the negotiating process is starting, it will give this draft to the potential licensee. The draft will then be the foundation for further negotiation. It will get the process going.

A memorandum of understanding will also help the potential licensor judge the potential licensee's level of interest. If, after sufficient negotiating time, the potential licensee is not willing to sign a mere non-binding memorandum, then it is not very likely to sign a binding contract.

(iii) The license agreement

(a) Introduction

The following discussion lists the major issues which the parties to a license agreement must resolve. It provides an overview of the major issues relating to licensing technology. A technology license typically includes a patent, related know-how and trade secrets and, sometimes, also a trademark or copyright rights. Not all the issues the discussion identifies are relevant to all the different possible types of technology licensing agreements. Franchise agreements and license agreements which include trademarks, for example, will raise other, related, issues. Nevertheless, the chapter provides a good overview of the issues parties negotiating a license agreement must resolve.

(b) Parties to the agreement – subsidiaries and the transfer of rights

Issues

- May the licensee:
  - sublicense, or
  - sell its rights?

- Which persons or corporations are parties to the agreement? Are any subsidiary corporations parties to the agreement?

- If new persons or groups take control of a corporation which is a party to the agreement, or to a related corporation such as a parent corporation, will this affect the agreement?

Commentary

The agreement may or may not allow the licensee to transfer the technology itself. The agreement could allow the licensee to transfer the technology to:

a. all firms, or

b. to the licensee's subsidiaries and other corporations or firms related to it.

Forms of reselling

The licensee could resell the licensed knowledge in either of two different ways.

Sublicensing

A licensee that sublicenses enters into a second license agreement. As the diagram shows in this second agreement the original licensee is now the licensor, and is called the sublicensor. The firm paying for the right to the technology in this second agreement is the sublicensee. In this case the original licensee would still be a party to the original license agreement, and would still have obligations to the original licensor.

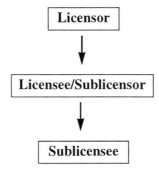

Selling its rights

By contrast, the licensee could sell the rights it bought from the original licensor. The law calls this assigning the license. In this case the licensee would transfer all its rights and obligations to the party which is buying its rights. This transaction would completely remove the former licensee from the original licensing arrangement. The original licensee would have no obligations to the licensor. The firm buying the rights would assume all the rights and obligations of the original licensee. The licensor would have a direct relationship with the party assuming the rights and obligations, which would become the new licensee.

Licensor's conflicting interests

Make technology more valuable to licensee

The licensor is often not sure whether to allow the licensee to transfer the licensed technology. On the one hand, allowing the licensee to transfer rights would allow it to reach more markets, earn more money, and therefore pay more royalties.

Lose control of technology

On the other hand, if the licensor allows the licensee to transfer its technology, it further risks losing control of its technology. The licensor could lose each of three different types of control.

- Control over the quality of the products all the licensees and sublicensees make using the licensed technology. (See Quality control, Section (1) below.)

- Control over the financial aspects of the transaction. This itself raises two separate issues.
  – Which party, the licensee or sublicensee, must pay royalties to the licensor? The licensor will want the licensee to retain this obligation. It will not want a third party, which whom it has not negotiated, and whose creditworthiness it has not investigated, to instead assume financial responsibility.
  – Will the licensor be able to examine the records of those who pay royalties? As the number of firms which may owe the licensor money increases, so too does the difficulty of policing all the different transactions which may create royalty obligations.

- Control over the technology itself. The more firms, and the more employees, know the technology the more likely it is that the technology will one way or another, inadvertently or not, leak to competitors.

Subsidiaries

At issue is not only the transfer of rights to independent third parties, but also to corporations and firms related to the licensee. These related firms, such as subsidiaries, pose a number of questions and risks.

- A subsidiary is not necessarily a wholly owned subsidiary. Technology, particularly know-how, can easily leak to other part-owners of the original licensee's partially owned subsidiaries.

- An incorporated subsidiary is, legally, a completely separate entity from its parent. The subsidiary may be assuming financial responsibilities to the licensor which it may not be able to meet. Furthermore, unless the licensor drafts the contract appropriately, then if, for example, an original licensee were to transfer its rights to its subsidiary, the licensor may lose its right to bring a lawsuit against the original licensee, the parent corporation. Parent corporations usually have more money to pay court awards than do subsidiaries.

Change of ownership

The parties may agree that if one party, or its parent corporation, changes ownership, then either party may terminate the contract. Such a provision would allow both parties to avoid doing business with other firms or persons, who they either may not approve of, or may not know.

(c) The technology which is the subject of the contract

Issues

The licensor should:

- describe and define the technology it is licensing,

- state how it has come to own the technology it is licensing, and

- list any limits on the uses to which the licensee may put the technology.

The parties should also discuss each party's rights to any technical developments the other party may develop while the agreement is in force.

Commentary

Defining technology

A licensor can easily cite any patents it may be licensing. However, the licensor may have difficulty defining unpatented trade secrets and know-how. In almost all cases, despite the attorneys' best efforts, the license agreement will at some level be ambiguous. The non-lawyer has to appreciate the limits of written language.

This fact that the parties will probably not be able to accurately define the unpatented technology, highlights the importance of arbitration. Parties' differing beliefs about exactly what technology they have licensed is a common cause of disputes. If the parties have agreed to arbitrate then, if they do later have a dispute, they will at least be able to limit the costs of their dispute. See Court system, Chapter 9.

Combined with other technologies

If the licensee is to combine the technology with other technologies, then the licensee should be sure that the licensor clearly defines the licensed technology, and describes the properties and abilities of just the licensed technology. Such a description will make it much easier for the licensee, should it have to, to later prove that the technology cannot do what the licensor said it could.

Source of technology

Along with defining the technology, the licensor should state how it has come to own the technology. If, for example, the licensor has obtained the patent it is licensing from another firm, including a subsidiary or other affiliated company, then the licensee must be sure that the licensor does in fact own the patent.

If the licensor is licensing know-how and other trade secrets, then the licensee has to be particularly careful to ensure that the licensor does in fact own and control the relevant know-how and trade secrets. The licensor may have obtained this valuable information from another firm, and may not actually own the information. Alternatively, it may have hired outside consultants to help it develop the technology, and the consultants, not the licensor, may in fact own the rights to the technology.

Limits on use

The licensor may want to limit the uses to which the licensee may put the technology. For example, as part of its overall licensing strategy, the licensor may plan to license the technology to different firms in different markets. Or it may plan to license the technology only to non-competing firms. These non-competing firms could either be firms which make products different from those of the licensor, or which sell in geographical areas in which the licensor does not expect to compete.

There are several ways in which the licensor can limit the uses to which the licensee may put the technology. The limitations can be by, amongst other criteria:

- scope, (how the licensee may use the technology),

- quantity, (how many products the licensee may sell), and

- geography.

Antitrust concerns

A court may find that these restrictions are a restraint of trade in violation of the antitrust laws. A court's decision in this area will depend on the particular competitive structure of the relevant market at that time. The court's analysis will probably also depend on whether the licensor has given the licensee exclusive rights. See Exclusivity, Section (d) below.

Further technological developments

Each party usually agrees to share with the other any improvements to the licensed technology which it may make while the agreement is in force. See Further developments, cross-licensing and grantbacks, Section (f) below.

(d)   Exclusivity

Issues

- The parties should decide if the licensor may also license the same technology to other firms. If the agreement does restrict the licensor's ability to further license, in other words if it does give the licensee some degree of exclusive rights, then the agreement should carefully describe this degree of exclusivity.

- Even if the licensor gives the licensee exclusive rights to the technology, it may retain for itself the right to also use the technology.

Commentary

Exclusive or non-exclusive

The licensor must decide if it will earn more money from one exclusive license or from several non-exclusive licenses. Licensors often have difficulty deciding which of these options is more profitable. As it turns out, most license agreements relating to patented technology are non-exclusive.

Degrees of exclusivity

The issue is more complex than simply whether the licensor will give the licensee exclusive rights. There are different degrees of exclusivity. The licensee could, for example, have the exclusive right to use the technology only within the United States or only within a part of the United States. The licensor could also retain the right to use the technology itself.

The licensor could also give the licensee exclusive use the technology, but only for certain limited uses. In general, the licensor may limit the uses to which the licensee may put the technology, and this is true even for exclusive licenses. See Subject of the contract, Section (c) above.

Antitrust concerns

In this area of exclusivity licensors must be very careful not to violate the antitrust laws. A licensor may, for example, enter into several exclusive agreements. Each agreement may give the licensee the exclusive right to use the technology in only one market. A court may interpret such a series of contracts as an agreement among the licensor and all its licensees to divide the larger market. Thus, at least in the court's opinion, the parties will have agreed to restrain trade and this would be illegal. Whether a court would interpret a series of exclusive licenses as an attempt to divide the larger market would depend on the nature of that specific technology and market. See Preliminary note on antitrust law, Section (i)(c) above.

(e)   Non-exclusivity – most favorable terms

Parties to non-exclusive agreements sometimes agree that if a licensor should later license the same technology to a second licensee, and if it should give the second licensee more favorable terms, then those more favorable license terms will also apply to the agreement between the licensor and the original licensee.

If the licensor will agree to such a term, then it will usually also require the licensee to accept not only any additional benefits which the second license agreement may give the licensee but also any additional burdens which the second agreement may impose on the licensee.

(f) Further developments, cross-licensing and grantbacks

Issues

- The license agreement may require the licensor to share with the licensee any further developments to its technology which the licensor may make after it signs the license agreement.

- The parties could enter into a cross-license. In a cross-license each party provides technology to the other. Thus, to pay for the technology it is receiving, each party agrees to provide technology to the other.

- The parties could include in their contract a grantback, which is similar to a cross-license. A grantback requires a licensee who improves the licensed technology to give the improvement to the licensor.

Commentary

Further developments

If the licensor has a well-developed, continuous, research and development (R&D) program, then its promise to provide continuous improvements may be at least as valuable as the technology in the original license agreement. On the other hand, if the licensor has such a well-developed R&D program, then it will probably want to limit its obligation to provide future improvements. To resolve this issue, the parties often compromise. For example, the parties may agree that the licensor will share the fruits of its R&D efforts with the licensee free of charge, but will do so for only one year.

Cross-licensing

Cross-licenses may violate the antitrust laws. The risk of violating the antitrust laws is greater the more the agreement is among competitors, and the more it allows the parties to the agreement to control the relevant market. The agreement may, for example restrict other firms' access to the relevant market, control prices in the relevant market, allocate customers, or allocate geographic submarkets.

Grantbacks

Parties often include a grantback provision in their license agreement. Grantbacks too can violate the antitrust laws. The law's concern in this context is that through the grantback the licensor may have abused the monopoly power of its patent. Arguably, by forcing its licensee to give it any improvements the licensee may make to the technology, the licensor has improperly used its patent to obtain control over the additional technology. The more the grantback gives the licensor the exclusive right to the improvement, the more likely a court is to find that the licensor has used its patent to obtain control of additional technology.

(g) Royalty payments

Issues

- Should the licensor require a minimum royalty?

- Should the agreement require the licensee to sell a minimum number of products? A minimum sales requirement is very similar to a minimum royalty requirement. A minimum sales requirement requires the licensee to make a certain minimum amount of sales. If the licensee fails to sell this minimum quota, then it will suffer a penalty. The typical penalty is that the licensor will lose some of its rights to the technology, such as its exclusive right to the technology. This allows the licensor to seek better, more aggressive, licensees. Minimum sales requirements therefore serve the same purpose as minimum royalties: both help to assure the licensor that it will receive at least some minimum adequate compensation for its technology. See Minimum sales requirements, Section (h) below

- How should the parties calculate royalties?

- When must the licensee pay royalties?

- How should the parties structure the other financial aspects of the transaction? For example:
  - Which currency should the parties use?
  - How should they set and periodically adjust the exchange rate?
  - How should they adjust for inflation?

- Does the licensor have the right to examine the licensee's books?

Commentary

Research other party's cost structure

While negotiating the liccnse agreement, each party should research the other's cost structure, market position, expected sales, and so forth. This is standard market research, and is usually well worth the expense. The lost, or excessive, royalties the uninformed party will either pay or not receive is, over the long term, usually greater than the cost of this market research. Both parties should do their homework before agreeing to a royalty structure.

Minimum royalties

Agreements often call for a minimum royalty payment, which the licensee must pay regardless of its success in exploiting the licensed technology. This is particularly true if the licensee will receive the benefits of the license, such as information regarding how to manufacture the product, as soon as the parties sign the agreement. This minimum payment could be a one-time payment or a periodic, typically yearly, minimum payment. A related, but different, provision is a minimum sales requirement. See Minimum sales requirements, Section (h) below.

Calculating royalties

The parties can calculate royalties in numerous ways. They could agree to a fixed royalty, they could base the royalty on the licensee's business performance, or they could devise a combination royalty structure.

If the parties base the royalty at least partially on the licensee's business performance, then they must measure this performance. They could base the royalties on, among other things, a percentage of the licensee's:

- profits,
- selling price, or
- manufacturing costs.

The licensee's business practices and market position will determine which of these options is most appropriate. The parties must choose the most logical option, given the licensee's entire business. For example, if the parties base the royalty on the licensee's selling price, then they must do so with the licensee's distribution system in mind. The licensee may sell directly to customers, or may sell to distributors at lower prices.

Define "selling price"

If the parties decide to base the royalties on the licensee's selling price then they must precisely define this "selling price." Selling price could include:

- commissions to salespersons,

- sales to subsidiaries and other parties with which the seller has a close relationship.

The potential problem here is that the licensee could adjust the price to artificially lower the royalties it must pay. There are many examples of licensees going to great lengths to lower royalty payments. In one case the licensee sold each part of the product separately, thus lowering the price of the product sold "under license." Of course after each "sale" of the separate parts the licensee's customer assembled the parts into one product. To avoid royalty payments other firms have "leased" rather than "sold" their products, thus avoiding "sales."

Appropriate contract terms make it more difficult for the licensee to use these and other royalty-avoidance techniques. Exactly how the licensor should draft the contract so the licensee at least has great difficulty employing these royalty-avoidance techniques will depend on the characteristics of the technology the parties are licensing, the structure of the relevant market, and the licensee's corporate structure and corporate relations. However, no contract will ever be able to completely stop the determinedly dishonest licensee from employing some trick or technique to improperly avoid or lower its royalty payments.

Selling price and antitrust law

When defining "selling price" the parties must, once again, be careful not to violate the antitrust laws. The licensor cannot, for example, set the licensee's selling price. That is price fixing, and it violates the antitrust laws. Further, a patent licensor cannot base royalty payments on the licensee's total sales, in contrast to sales of products made with or by its patented technology. The law would see such a royalty structure as an improper attempt by the licensor to expand the market power of its patent.

The licensor may not collect royalties relating to patented technology after the patent has expired. A patent gives the patent holder the exclusive right to use the technology only so long as the patent is in force. When that period ends, and the patent is no longer valid, anyone can use the now unpatented technology. If the patent holder were to collect royalties for the period after the patent expired, then it would in reality be extending the length of its patent. The law will not allow it to do this.

However, in the license agreement the licensor could apportion its total royalties. It could allocate some of its royalties as payment for use of its patented technology, and some as payment for use of its unpatented trade secret, trademark, or copyright rights. The law allows the licensor to collect royalties for the use of its unpatented intellectual property indefinitely.

Timing of royalty payments

The parties usually co-ordinate the minimum payment and the timing of royalty payments. For example, the agreement may call for an initial payment, when the parties sign the agreement (a front-ended fee). The parties usually make this fee non-refundable. The fee will therefore serve at the same time as both an advance royalty payment and a minimum royalty.

Licensee agreements typically require the licensee to make quarterly royalty payments, and to include with its payments the appropriate financial reports. The parties may of course devise any royalty payment procedure they wish. Licensees at times make monthly or semi-annual payments, and some make yearly minimum royalty payments.

Sublicense royalties

If the licensee may sublicense, then the parties must also agree to a method of calculating royalties due the licensor for the sublicensee sales . The licensor usually receives a percentage of the royalties the licensee/ sublicensor collects. In this way the licensor and licensee/sublicensor share the sublicensing revenue.

Financial adjustments

The parties will have to choose a currency in which the licensee must pay royalties. Although agreements with Americans tend to use the US dollar, the parties can certainly base royalty payments on another currency. The parties will also have to adjust the royalty as appropriate to control for exchange rate and inflation fluctuations, which are of course related. The parties should be particularly sure to adjust for inflation if the royalty is to be a periodic flat fee. To make this adjustment in the United States parties often use the US Dept. of Commerce's Monthly All-Commodity Index of Wholesale Prices, which is a useful guide to wholesale price inflation in the US.

Examine books and records

In most cases the licensor may inspect the licensee's books and records. If the licensor were not able to inspect these records, and thereby assure itself that it was receiving all the royalties it was due, then it would have great difficulty enforcing its right to royalties.

Related to the licensor's right to inspect records is the licensee's obligation to keep records. If the licensor has the right to inspect records which do not exist, then its right is obviously not very valuable. The licensor must therefore be sure that the agreement requires the licensee to keep appropriate records.

(h)   Minimum sales requirements

Issues

● Must the licensee sell a minimum number of goods? If so, what is the minimum?

● What penalties will the licensee suffer if it does not meet the minimum sales requirement?

Commentary

A minimum sales requirement obligates the licensee to sell a certain minimum number of goods. It if does not meet this minimum, then it will suffer some penalty. By contrast, if the licensee agrees to pay a minimum royalty, then it has guaranteed the licensor that it will pay that minimum royalty, regardless of its level of sales.

Licensors usually demand either a minimum sales requirement or a minimum royalty, particularly if they have granted the licensee exclusive rights. Without at least one of these provisions the licensee may never adequately compensate the licensor. The licensor may transfer its technology to the licensee, but the licensee may thereafter not exploit the technology to its fullest commercial potential. If the licensee does not use the technology as much as it could, then it will not pay as much in royalties as it could. Minimum sales requirements and minimum royalties therefore both give the licensor protection against a licensee who does not exploit the licensed technology to its fullest potential.

The appropriate minimum sales requirement varies, of course, from situation to situation. This item invariably leads to hard bargaining.

Penalty

If the licensee does not meet the minimum sales level then, typically, the licensee will:

• lose its right to the technology, or

• lose its *exclusive* right to the technology. Note that under this option the licensee retains a non-exclusive right to the technology. See Termination of the agreement, Section (j) below.

Best efforts

The law includes in all license agreements an implied "best efforts" clause. In theory, this clause ensures that the licensee adequately compensates the licensor. The "best efforts" clause requires the licensee to use its "best efforts" to earn as much money as it reasonably can from the licensed technology. Since, in theory, the licensee will exploit the technology to its fullest commercial potential it will, again in theory, pay the licensor the highest possible royalty. See Agents and distributor agreements, Chapter 1.

Reality often differs from theory. In reality, courts have great difficulty defining "best efforts," and, given the high cost of lawsuits, licensors usually do not find these implied best efforts clauses to be of much value. Licensors should therefore include in their license agreements either a minimum royalty or a minimum sales requirement.

(i) Licensor's assistance to licensee

Issues

• The licensor could help the licensee develop its business. The licensor could provide:
   – technical assistance, or
   – business assistance.

• The licensor's technical assistance could include:

- lending trained personnel,
- developing a training program for the licensee's employees,
- supplying related technical information not included in the contract, or
- supplying parts and materials.

● The licensor's business assistance could include:
  - marketing help – for example, showing the licensee techniques it has found effective
  - management help – for example, helping the licensee implement the appropriate management system, or
  - capital investments or loans.

Commentary

Wide possibilities, therefore common source of disputes

Aside from providing the licensee with the technology itself, the licensor could also provide other forms of assistance to the licensee. The forms of assistance the licensor could provide are almost limitless. To choose one example, the licensor may provide trained personnel who would help the licensee integrate its new technology into its business.

The licensor should clearly define any additional services it may provide. For example, if the licensor is to provide trained personnel, then it should specify:

● the type or types of personnel the licensor will supply,

● the number of each type of personnel,

● the duties of each type of personnel,

● at least the approximate dates on which it will provide the personnel,

● the length of time for which the licensor will provide the personnel,

● any related knowledge or information which it will also supply.

In short, the parties must clearly describe in the agreement the nature and extent of any assistance the licensor may provide – careful, precise, contract drafting is imperative. Because the licensor could provide so many different services, the parties often have disputes over exactly which services the licensor did agree to provide.

Additional fees

Relatedly, the licensor should be sure that it receives full compensation for all the services it provides. The contract should clearly distinguish between the technology for which the licensee must make royalty payments and any additional services the licensor may provide, and for which the licensee must make additional payments. Not infrequently, each party has a different understanding of which technology, know-how, and services the royalty payments buy, and those for which the licensee must pay an additional fee.

Related goods and services

Antitrust laws

The law will not usually allow the licensor to require the licensee to purchase from it related goods and services. Licensors are often eager o sell to licensees spare parts and other materials, supplies and services relating to the licensed technology. These additional sales provide additional income. Providing these additional goods and services also often helps licensors ensure that their licensees' products are of appropriate quality.

Nevertheless, the licensor cannot usually require, as a condition for licensing the technology, that the licensee buys goods or services from the licensor. Such provisions usually violate the antitrust laws. They tend to restrain trade because they hinder the licensee from searching in the free market for the best and least expensive supplier of these additional goods and services.

Many licensees do buy from licensors

Legal restrictions aside, however, the licensee will very often buy goods and services from the licensor. The licensor is often best able to provide the goods and services which allow the licensee to best exploit the licensor's technology. Most licensees also feel that buying from the licensor helps them maintain a strong relationship with the licensor. These licensees are usually right to maintain a good, strong relationship with their licensor.

Import duties

If a non-American licensor is selling goods along with intellectual property rights, then it must be careful that the Customs Service does not include the value of the intellectual property rights in the value of the goods the licensor is exporting to the United States. If the Customs Service believes that the licensor will not sell the goods unless the licensee buys the related intellectual property rights, then the Customs Service will include the value of the intellectual property rights in the value of the imported goods. See Bringing Goods into the United States, Chapter 2.

(j)   Termination of the agreement

Issues

● When will the agreement expire?

● What technology may the licensee use after the agreement expires?

Commentary

Contract length

The licensor usually prefers a short contract. If the licensee is not exploiting the technology to its fullest commercial potential then, if the agreement will expire after a short period the licensor will be able to find a more aggressive licensee sooner rather than later. The licensee, on the other hand, will usually prefer a long contract which will give it security and flexibility.

A short contract therefore has the same effect as a minimum sales requirement and a minimum royalty: they all encourage the licensee to exploit the technology fully. Thus parties usually co-ordinate their minimum sales requirement and the minimum royalty with the length of the contract.

Use of technology after agreement expires

Patent licenses

Patent license agreements usually expire when the patent expires. After the patent expires, the licensee may use the now unpatented technology without paying royalties. If either party terminates the agreement early, then the agreement will almost always require the licensee to stop using the technology until the patent expires.

Non-patent licenses

Unpatented technology such as know-how presents a more difficult problem. Once the licensor has shown the licensee unpatented technology, the licensee will always know the technology, and will almost always be able to use it. Common solutions to this problem include the following.

- Requiring the licensee to make a significant initial royalty payment. See Royalty payments, Section (g) above.

- Requiring the licensee to stop using the licensor's technology.
  - This can be a harsh requirement. For the following reasons, the licensor must limit such a requirement. *First*, the licensor's unpatented know-how may not qualify as a trade secret. If not, then the licensor may not be able to stop the licensee from using the information. The licensee may claim that it could have developed the technology on its own. *Second*, licensors have great difficulty enforcing such requirements. Once engineers and other employees of the licensee learn of know-how and other unpatented technology they will always in some sense "use" the information. *Third*, courts resist enforcing provisions they feel are unduly harsh, and therefore "unfair." See Contracting, Chapter 7.
  - The easiest way for the licensor to make such a requirement reasonable is to limit the time period during which its now former licensee must not use its technology. Generally speaking, the licensor should stop the licensor from using the technology for no more than two years.

(k)   Responsibility to initiate lawsuits

Issue

- Which party is responsible for protecting the patents or related intellectual property in the United States?

Commentary

American firms not necessarily better able to handle American lawsuits

Non-American licensors sometimes ask their American licensees to handle all lawsuits in the United States which relate to the licensed technology.

They do this although the law allows both licensors and licensees to be parties to any lawsuit which may affect their rights to the licensed technology. These non-American firms assume that the American firm is better able to handle an American lawsuit.

While requiring the American licensee to handle the lawsuit does allow the licensor to shift the cost of the lawsuit to the licensee, it also forces the licensor to lose some control over the lawsuit. The licensor must be careful because the lawsuit will determine the licensor's rights to its technology, and if the licensor cannot adequately involve itself in the lawsuit, then no one may adequately represent its interests. To pick an extreme example, if the American licensee were negotiating with a third party who claimed that the licensor's technology violated its patent, the licensee may be tempted to settle with the third party by agreeing that the third party's claim is valid, and that the licensee will thereafter license the technology from the third party. In such a settlement the licensor would be the clear loser.

Thus the non-American licensor must be sure that, even if the license agreement requires the American licensee to bring infringement lawsuits in the United States, the agreement also gives it the right to sufficiently involve itself in the lawsuit. The agreement must, for example, give the licensor the right to approve any lawsuit settlement agreement.

Further, the non-American licensor should not overestimate the value of having an American firm prosecute the lawsuit. If there were a lawsuit, both the American and non-American firm would hire an attorney, and each would manage the lawsuit in the way its attorney recommended. Thus, in reality, no matter which party has responsibility for the lawsuit, an attorney would actually handle the lawsuit, and the outcome would probably be the same.

Solutions

To resolve the issue of which party should assume responsibility for lawsuits, the parties could agree that the American licensee will defend both parties' rights to the technology, but subject to certain limitations. These limitations could include the following.

- Requiring the licensee to manage only one lawsuit at a time.

- Limiting the extent to which the licensee must pay the costs of the lawsuit.
    - The agreement may only require the licensee to pay a certain percentage of the legal fees.

- The licensee may be responsible for the fees only up to a certain maximum, after which the licensor would also be responsible for some or all of the fees.

● Limiting the licensee's authority to settle lawsuits. This authority could be limited by giving the licensor the right to approve settlements. The parties could limit this right so that, for example, the licensor may not "unreasonably withhold" its approval. Regarding 'unreasonably withhold' clauses, see Sale of right to distribute, Chapter 1 (ii)(q).

(l) Quality control

Issues

● Will the license agreement give the licensor the right to ensure that the licensee's goods are of adequate quality?
- If so, then how do the parties define "adequate quality?"
- What penalty will the licensee suffer if its goods are not of adequate quality?

● Will the licensor have any control over the licensee's business?

Commentary

General points

The quality of the licensee's products may affect the licensor's reputation. This is particularly true if the licensee is using the licensor's trademark. If this is the case, then the licensor will want to ensure that its licensee produces goods of adequate quality. Some licensee agreements, particularly those relating to trademarks, therefore require the licensee to manufacturer goods whose specifications show "no significant deviation" from the licensor's specifications.

Licensors concerned about the quality of their licensees' goods also usually ensure that they have the right to inspect their licensees' production processes and goods. Without this right to inspect, the licensor may not be able to ensure that the licensee's goods are of adequate quality. The right to inspect gives force to the licensee's obligation to produce goods of adequate quality.

Penalty

If the licensee does not manufacture goods of adequate quality, then the agreement usually gives the licensee a certain period of time within which it must improve its products' quality. If the licensee does not adequately improve its products' quality, then, typically, the agreement gives the licensor the right to terminate the agreement.

Dispute resolution

The issue of adequate quality generates many lawsuits. The parties usually have great difficulty defining quality. Licensees are usually reluctant to follow their licensors' instructions to improve quality. Doing so increases costs, and may also require them to temporarily stop manufacturing.

  If the parties should have a dispute regarding quality, it is imperative that they resolve the dispute quickly. If goods of poor quality continue to enter the market, this may permanently damage the licensor's reputation. On the other hand, if the dispute forces the licensee to stop manufacturing, then it will lose sales and profits. The parties should not wait for the court system to resolve their dispute. They should either compromise, possibly through mediation, or take the matter to arbitration.

Partial ownership and franchising

To help them ensure that their licensee's goods are of adequate quality some licensors buy a portion of their licensees' shares. These firms feel that they are better able to control the products of firms they partially own. Other licensors use franchising way to control their licensee's business.

Product liability

Licensors must also be careful not to exercise so much control over their licensee's business that a court holds them liable under the product liability laws. The law may also hold patent licensors liable under strict products liability law. See Patents and product liability, Chapter 4 (ii)(i) and Strict products liability, Chapter 6 (iii)(f).

(m) Confidentiality during and after the term of the agreement

Licensor should require confidentiality

The licensor should require the licensee to keep all know-how, trade secrets, and related information confidential. Licensors should impose this requirement not only while the agreement is in force, but also after the agreement expires. Courts will enforce these confidentiality provisions even after the license agreement expires.

Courts helpful

As discussed above, American courts are usually very helpful to licensors trying to keep commercially valuable information confidential. The licensor may be able to obtain a court order, called an injunction, which will require the licensee to maintain secrecy. The licensee may be able to enforce this court order for a long period of time. See Pre-agreement negotiations, Section (ii) above.

Arbitrators must also enforce confidentiality agreements

However, if the license agreement contains an arbitration clause, then a court may not enforce the confidentiality requirement. Many courts feel that an arbitrator should decide all matters relating to a contract which contains an arbitration clause. These courts will therefore refuse to enforce a confidentiality requirement in a contract which also contains an arbitration clause.

Furthermore, arbitrators tend to be hesitant to issue orders requiring the licensee to maintain secrecy. Therefore, the licensor should be sure that the arbitration clause in its license agreement clearly states that the arbitrator has the right to order the licensee to maintain secrecy, particularly after the agreement expires.

PART IV   The Business Environment

6. PRODUCT LIABILITY
Managing Risk

6. PRODUCT LIABILITY
Managing Risk

(i) Introduction

(a) Product liability lawsuits are surprisingly uncommon

Many managers, particularly non-American managers, fear the American product liability system. As soon as they introduce their products in the American market, these managers believe, tens, if not hundreds of consumers will bring products liability lawsuits against their firms, and irrational juries will then award these consumers huge sums. Thus these managers hesitate to enter the American market.

These fears are misplaced. The threat of a product liability lawsuit should not, by itself, stop a firm from doing business in the United States. If this alone were reason not to do business in the United States then no firm, including any American firm, would do business in the United States.

While a few cases make headlines, product liability cases are in fact much less common than most people believe. Firms doing business in the United States do face a good chance of being sued – but the greatest risk comes from their fellow firms, not from injured consumers. Most firms sued in the United States are sued by other firms. Hence the importance of structuring all contracts and transactions with the idea that a lawsuit may later grow out of the transaction. See Court system, Chapter 9.

There is no product liability "explosion" in the United States. Studies show that a typical manufacturer is unlikely to ever have to defend itself in a products liability lawsuit. Studies also show that juries are not irrational and prone to awarding excessive compensation. Studies show that juries make similar awards in similar situations. In other words, they are rational.

(b) The contingency fee

Since there are not as many product liability lawsuits as some managers fear, it follows that product liability lawyers are not as quick to file a lawsuit as some believe. The contingency fee structure has created the impression that lawyers arc quick to file claims. But this is not true.

The contingency fee is less attractive to lawyers than many suppose. Under a contingency fee the lawyer receives as his fee a part of the money the court awards his client, the injured consumer. Therefore, if the court awards the consumer no money, then the lawyer will receive no fee. After doing all the work to bring a case to trial, and then trying the case, under the contingency fee system the lawyer will receive nothing. A lawyer losing a product liability case has therefore wasted a tremendous amount of time and money. The lawyer will not only have invested his own time, but will also have paid his general office expenses and the expenses specific to that case, such as expert witness fees.

If the consumer's lawyer does win at trial, the defendant will probably appeal, further delaying the time when the lawyer receives his fee. Thus even an attorney bringing a successful product liability lawsuit must wait years before receiving his contingency fee. Attorneys will therefore not invest their time and money in cases they are likely to lose. In fact, attorneys who bring products liability cases also want to settle these cases, not only so they will receive their fee quickly, but also so they can avoid the risk of losing the case.

Of course the unscrupulous lawyer will bring improper lawsuits and of course manufacturers should be wary. Managers should see product liability lawsuits within the context of the entire American court system, however. First, the entire court system is slow and expensive. Secondly, plaintiffs' lawyers do not bring product liability lawsuits as quickly as many suppose. Thirdly, a manufacturer will not lose every case brought against it. In short, the products liability system is not the terror some managers imagine.

(c)   Punitive damages

Managers tend to blame punitive (punishment) damages for excessive product liability awards. In response to this fear, many states have either taken steps to lower the frequency and size of punitive damages, or have abolished them completely. Further, even if a court does order a manufacturer to pay punitive damages, the manufacturer is still not likely to actually pay the punitive damages the court awarded. Appeals and further negotiations give manufacturers the opportunity to limit their losses. In less than half the cases does the manufacturer actually pay the punitive damages the court awarded at trial.

(d)   Risks and insurance

While the risk that a court, in a products liability case, will order a manufacturer to pay a large sum is less than some managers fear, it is nevertheless a risk. This is one of many risks facing all firms. To protect themselves against these risks, firms buy insurance. Manufacturers should therefore buy product liability insurance.

Rationales for system

In fact, this idea, that manufacturers should buy insurance, is one rationale for the products liability system. The theory behind this system is that since all competitors face the same risk, they will all buy the same insurance. All competitors must therefore incur the same insurance costs, and no firm will be at a competitive disadvantage. Further, says this theory, all manufacturers will pass this insurance cost on to their customers. Thus manufacturers will increase the price of all their products by a few cents to pay their insurance premiums, and in this way society will spread the cost of product-related injuries.

The second rationale for strict products liability law is that it encourages manufacturers to make ever safer products. If manufacturers must assume the financial risks of the accidents their products cause, then, according to this theory, they will constantly design safer products.

In reality the system is not as perfect as these theories describe. Not all firms are equal competitors. In some fields firms simply cannot buy product liability insurance. Finally, non-American firms trying to enter the American market face a particular problem. When they first enter the American market these firms typically do not sell enough of their product to justify the expense of buying product liability insurance.

(ii) Negligence and the ordinary standard of care

(a) Introduction

In theory strict products liability and negligence impose different standards

Product liability is technically called strict products liability. In theory strict products liability and negligence impose very different standards on manufacturers. Strict products liability law, in theory, holds a firm liable for all the injuries its products cause. Strict products liability law, again in theory, imposes liability whether or not the manufacturer was somehow at fault.

Negligence law, by contrast, only imposes liability on firms which were at fault. General negligence law holds all member of society, individuals as well as firms, liable for the damage they cause because they made a mistake. For example, if a driver hits a pedestrian with his car by mistake, he must reimburse the injured pedestrian for the costs his mistake caused. The law makes him pay because he made a mistake, because he was negligent.

Negligence law also holds manufacturers liable for the mistakes they make. The law expects manufacturers not to make products which are so unreasonably poor that they injure consumers. The law requires manufacturers to use reasonable production methods, reasonable designs and so on, so that they do not make unreasonably poor products. If a manufacturer does make products which are of such unreasonably poor quality that they cause injuries, then the manufacturer will have made a mistake. Negligence law will hold the manufacturer liable for its mistakes.

Thus, strict products liability law seems to favor the injured consumer. While negligence law requires the consumer to prove that he was injured because the firm made a poor quality product, strict liability law seems to allow the injured consumer to collect money simply because the manufacturer's product injured him.

In reality strict products liability and negligence impose similar standards

In reality strict products liability law and negligence law impose on manufacturers a nearly identical standard. And this is in fact inevitable and unavoidable.

Even strict products liability law must limit manufacturer's potential liability. Strict products liability law cannot, and does not, hold manufacturers liable for every injury involving their products. If a consumer hurts himself while sitting on a chair, for example, the law cannot, without more reason, hold the chair manufacturer liable for the consumer's injuries. If the law did hold the manufacturer liable, then it would turn manufacturers into insurance companies. And the law does not want to, and does not, turn manufacturers into insurance companies.

The sole way strict products liability law can limit a manufacturer's liability is to hold it liable only if its products somehow caused the consumer's injury. As is discussed below, this "somehow caused" standard is, unavoidably, the negligence standard. Thus, with one possible exception, strict products liability law and negligence law impose, in reality, the same standard.

Thus strict products liability law does not, in reality, create a standard of liability which injured consumers will find easier to satisfy than the negligence standard. Strict products liability law has therefore not made it easier for injured consumers to win lawsuits. It has not created the liability "explosion" some imagine.

(iii)   Strict products liability

(a)   Introduction

Background of product liability law

Strict products liability law developed from warranty law. Courts developed strict products liability law because consumers traditionally could not sue manufacturers for breach of warranty. The consumer and manufacturer had never entered into a contract with each other. Since there was no contract, the manufacturer had not made any warranty promises to the consumer. Thus the consumer could not sue the manu-facturer for breach of warranty.

Thus, before courts developed product liability law, if a product did not satisfy its warranty, the consumer could only sue the store where he or she bought the product, who could sue the distributor, who could then sue the manufacturer. Courts developed strict products liability to allow the consumer to sue the manufacturer directly.

Applies to all with responsibility

Courts will generally not hold liable firms such as distributors and retailers simply because they helped distribute the product. Courts will only hold liable firms which did more than merely resell a product. If a firm repaired a product, for example, or if it had a duty to inspect a product, then a court may hold the firm liable only if it did not perform these services properly.

Non-American manufacturer

Lawsuits in the United States

An American consumer can only sue a non-American manufacturer if the non-American manufacturer intended to put the product in commerce in the United States. See Court system, Chapter 9. This principle applies to manufacturers of component parts as well. Thus an injured American consumer can only sue a non-American manufacturer in the United States, under strict products liability law, if the non-American manufacturer either sold the product directly to a buyer in the United States, or *knew* that another firm would sell the product in the United States. On the other hand, courts will not hold liable firms whose products *may* enter the American market. Thus courts will only hold liable in strict products liability non-American firms which, as part of their business strategy, directly or indirectly export to the United States.

Lawsuits in the manufacturer's home country

American products liability law may still force a non-American manufacturer to defend itself in a court in its home country. This could happen, for example, if a non-American firm manufactured a component which a second firm used. The non-American manufacturer may not have intended to sell its product in the United States, but the second firm may nevertheless have done so. An injured American consumer may sue the second firm, and the second firm may thereafter sue the non-American component manufacturer, claiming that the component caused the consumer's injuries. This second firm could sue the non-American component manufacturer in the manufacturer's home country.

Leasing is selling

To avoid liability, a manufacturer cannot structure a sale as another type of transaction. Strict products liability law will hold a manufacturer who leases its products just as liable as it would one which sold its products. Similarly, a manufacturer cannot avoid strict products liability by requiring consumers to waive their strict products liability rights. Regarding the ability to disclaim generally, See Disclaiming liability, Section (iii)(e).

(b) "Strict" products liability law is not as "strict" as it seems

Introduction

Strict products liability law is not as "strict" as some believe. As discussed above, with one possible exception, strict products liability law imposes on manufacturers the same standard as does negligence law. This is so because courts must limit manufacturer's liability. They therefore only hold liable manufacturers whose products caused an injury. In other words, with one possible exception, strict products liability law only imposes liability on manufacturers who were at fault.

Four potential types of defective products

Poor products are unreasonably dangerous

All products are, to at least some extent, dangerous. The law does not forbid manufacturers from producing products merely because they are dangerous. Cars are certainly dangerous. Just as certainly, the law does not forbid manufacturers from selling cars. Strict products law only forbids manufacturers from selling products which are so poor that they are *unreasonably* dangerous.

Not all products are unreasonably dangerous. The law considers a product *unreasonably* dangerous if:

- a less dangerous alternative was economically feasible, or

- the product was dangerous beyond the expectations of the ordinary consumer.

Two ways a product can be defective

The law aside, as just a physical reality there are only two ways in which a manufacturer could possibly manufacture a product improperly, or defectively. A product can only be defective if:

- the manufacturer made that particular product improperly, (only that one product is defective), or

- the manufacturer used a defective design (all the products are defective).

Thus there are four different ways to make a defective product

Thus, there are four different ways in which a manufacturer could possibly make a defective product. The manufacturer could produce a product which is defective in one of two ways: either it made one defective product, or it made all defective products.

And strict products liability law has two different definitions of defective. Thus there are four possible ways in which a manufacturer could produce a product which violates strict products liability law. The following grid best illustrates these four possibilities:

	Less Dangerous Alternative Economically Feasible	Dangerous Beyond Expectations of Ordinary Consumer
Production Defect	1	2
Design Defect	3	4

The following discussion analyzes these four possibilities. The discussion shows that for three of the four possibilities strict products liability law imposes on manufacturers the same liability that standard negligence law imposes. Only for the fourth possibility, dangerous beyond expectations of ordinary consumer/design defect, is the strict products liability standard *possibly* more "strict" than negligence law.

The four possibilities

Less dangerous alternative/production defect

Less dangerous alternative

If a manufacturer sells a product when it could have sold a less dangerous product, then the firm has acted unreasonably, and is at fault. Strict products liability law does not expect a manufacturer to sell the *absolutely* safest possible product. It only expects the manufacturer to sell the safest product which was *economically* feasible. To determine what is economically feasible, the manufacturer must perform a cost/ benefit analysis. It must then do what is reasonable, considering the risk of harm and the cost of preventing that harm. If the firm does not do what is *economically* feasible, then it has not done what is reasonable. It acted unreasonably and is at fault. Thus the strict liability standard is not different from the negligence standard. Both require fault.

Production defect

A product with a production defect is different from all the manufacturer's other products. There is something wrong with it. It is defective. While producing it, the manufacturer made a mistake. The manufacturer is at fault. In fact, if a manufacturer sells a defective product, then it is at fault for two reasons: it first made a defective product and it then allowed the defective product to pass inspection. To use the classic example, if Coke sells a bottle with a mouse inside, then it made a mistake. It is at fault.

Thus a manufacturer is at fault either when it sells a dangerous product, and it was economically feasible for the manufacturer to sell a less dangerous product, or when it sells a product with a production defect. Thus, while strict products liability law will hold a manufacturer liable for either of these acts, so too will negligence law. Strict products liability law imposes no higher a standard than does negligence law. Both require fault.

Dangerous beyond expectations/production defect

A product with a production defect is, by definition, dangerous beyond the expectations of ordinary customers. Consumers do not expect a product to have a production defect. Consumers, for example, do not expect a Coke bottle to have a mouse in it. Thus, strict products liability law will hold liable a manufacturer who sold a defective product. However, if a manufacturer sells a defective product, then he has made a mistake. He has acted unreasonably or, in other words, negligently. This strict products liability law will only hold liable a manufacturer who made a mistake. It does not hold a manufacturer to a higher standard than negligence law.

Less dangerous alternative/design defect

In this situation as well, strict liability and negligence law impose the same standard. Again, to determine if a less dangerous alternative design was economically feasible, the manufacturer must first perform a cost/ benefit analysis, and then must use the most economically rational design. A manufacturer violates this standard only if it does not do what is economically rational, in other words only if it is at fault.

When deciding if a less dangerous design was economically feasible, a court will consider the designs of a manufacturer's competitors. If competitors use safer designs, then a court will probably reason that the manufacturer too could have used a safer design. But even if other manufacturers did not use safer designs, a court might still find that a less dangerous design was economically feasible. The court may believe that the whole industry should have used a safer design.

Dangerous beyond expectations/design defect

This fourth situation is the only one in which a court *may* find a manufacturer liable although it was not at fault. Such an outcome is possible because, regarding complex products, this standard is too vague. Consumers do not have expectations regarding the design of complex products. Thus in this situation the law does not provide courts with adequate guidance. In this situation, therefore, courts have great discretion, and a court may find a manufacturer liable although it was not at fault.

Cars offer a good example. Consumers expect their car to be reasonably safe, but they also know that a car accident may injure them. No one can say precisely how dangerous consumers expect cars to be. Thus, in one case, a court found the Chrysler Corporation liable because it made the side of its car too weak. This weakness, the court said, caused the driver's injuries. Yet, in other types of accidents, weak sides help reduce injuries to drivers. Thus Chrysler may have used a reasonable design. It may not have been at fault.

Strict products liability law does not open manufacturers to limitless liability

Thus, with one possible exception, strict products liability law imposes on firms the liability standard of negligence law. Strict products liability law only holds liable manufacturers who were at fault. Even when suing under strict products liability, injured consumers must still prove that the manufacturer acted unreasonably, that it was at fault. Strict products liability law, therefore, does not make manufacturers liable for all injuries involving their products. Under strict products liability law courts do not impose on manufacturers limitless, irrational, liability.

(c)   Warnings

Manufacturers must warn

In addition to requiring manufacturers to make products which are as safe
as practicable, the law also requires manufacturers to warn customers of
any remaining risks. The warnings must describe both the nature and the
extent of the danger. A manufacturer, however, can never give a warning
instead of making its product as safe as practicable.

Manufacturers need not warn of obvious dangers. But the definition of
obvious is, of course, anything but obvious. In one case, in which a
toddler choked on peanut butter, the court said that the manufacturer
should have issued a warning. The risk of choking on peanut butter, said
the court, was not obvious. Given this an other cases, if in doubt, a
manufacturer should warn.

Strictly enforced

Courts apply this warning requirement strictly. In one case a manufacturer's warning said: "Do not heat or thin. When either is done the
waterproofing qualities are damaged." A court later found this warning
inadequate because it related to waterproofing rather than safety.

Limited to current knowledge

Courts limit the duty to warn to the state of scientific knowledge at time
the manufacturer sold the product. If, at the time of sale, scientists did not
know of a particular danger, or thought it to be extremely unlikely, then
the law will not require the manufacturer to have warned of that danger.

Continuing duty

The law imposes on manufacturers a continuing duty to warn. A manufacturer must certainly warn of any defects or serious health risks relating
to its product which it discovers after it has sold the product. In some
cases the law may also require the manufacturer to repair a defective
product which it has already sold.

Manufacturer should have known

The law requires manufacturers to warn not only about dangers they know, but also about dangers of which they should have known. The law is not always clear, however, about what a manufacturer should have known. A court will certainly expect a manufacturer to know of dangers which other manufacturers know. But even if other manufacturers do not know of a particular danger, a court may still believe that a reasonable manufacturer would know of that danger.

Packaging and advertising claims which nullify warnings

Manufacturers should be careful not to include on a package a claim which nullifies a warning. For example, the claim "Kind to your hands" may nullify the manufacturer's warning about skin damage.

Advertising claims may also nullify warnings. If an advertisement assures consumers that a product is safe, then a court may hold a manufacturer liable despite warnings to the contrary it may have put on its package. A court may find that, overall, the manufacturer did not adequately warn consumers.

Further, a court may hold a manufacturer liable if a consumer relies on the manufacturer's false advertisement. In one case a court found a manufacturer liable when its winch failed to pull the weight its advertising claimed it could pull.

(d) Product misuse and alteration

Product misuse

The law does not expect a manufacturer to sell a product which can do any-thing any consumer may do with the product. However, the law does expect manufacturers to build products which can do what they should reasonably foresee consumers doing with their products. Thus the law expects manufacturers to build chairs on which consumers can stand.

As with many terms, the law cannot precisely define "reasonably fore-see." Examples best illustrate how courts define the term.

Courts have found reasonably foreseeable uses to include the following.

● Screwdrivers used to pop open lids.

- Liquid furniture polish used near children. The manufacturer should have made the bottle child-proof.

- Flammable nightgown worn inside out, with the pockets protruding out. Pockets caught fire as consumer reached over lighted stove.

- Telephone booth stuck, trapping the injured person, who was struck by a car. The telephone company had placed the booth near a dangerous intersection. Others had told the telephone company of a previous incident in which a car almost injured another person because he could not get out of the booth.

Courts have found the following not to be reasonably forseeable uses.

- Tread came off tyres and the driver, instead of stopping, swerved his car left, right, and left again.

- Sewing needle stuck in the injured person's knee and shattered after she brushed against a coffee table.

Product alteration

If a consumer alters a product, then the law will only hold the manufacturer liable if the consumer altered the product in a way the manufacturer should reasonably have foreseen. In this context as well, the law cannot adequately define "reasonably foresee." In one case a court ruled that, because removing a particular guard made a forklift truck more versatile, the manufacturer should have foreseen that consumers would remove the guard.

(e) Disclaiming liability

Manufacturers and others cannot disclaim the obligations strict products liability and negligence law impose on them towards consumers. Thus even if a consumer agrees not to sue a manufacturer in strict products liability or negligence, the consumer may nevertheless sue the manufacturer. If the law did not give consumers this protection, then manufacturers and distributors would only sell to consumers who agreed not to sue.

The law does not offer sophisticated commercial buyers this same protection. Courts will uphold agreements in which sophisticated commercial buyers agree not to sue manufacturers under negligence or strict products liability law. However, courts are reluctant to allow buyers to waive their rights under these laws. A manufacturer trying to enforce an agreement not to sue must therefore prove to the court that the purchaser was sophisticated, had the same bargaining leverage as the manufacturer and made an informed decision to waive its rights.

Thus firms selling non-consumer goods to sophisticated commercial buyers may want to ask these buyers if they will waive their negligence and strict product liability rights. See also, Disclaimer, Warranties and Fraud, Chapter 8.

(f)   Licensors' liability

Licensors, in particular trademark licensors, at times retain some control over their licensees' manufacturing processes. They do this to ensure that their licensees produce goods of sufficient quality but these licensors must be careful. If they retain more than a minimum degree of control over their licensees' manufacturing processes, then a court may hold them liable. A court may see the licensor as a manufacturer of the product.

Patent and other technology licensors must also be sure to give their licensees accurate information. If technology licensors provide their licensees with inaccurate or incomplete information, a court may find this caused the licensee to manufacture defective products. The court may then hold the licensor liable for the consumer's injuries.

(g)   A final note on risk

No one can predict the outcome of lawsuits. The fact that courts apply a negligence standard in strict products liability cases does not change this fact. Further, even if juries are more rational than many people presume, juries nevertheless tend to view injured consumers with sympathy, and they tend to view manufacturers as rich and insured. Thus there remains a casino-like aspect to products liability lawsuits.

Again, managers must see this problem in perspective. All firms doing business face the risk of being sued. There is a casino-like aspect to all lawsuits, not just product liability lawsuits. There is also a casino-like aspect to lawsuits prosecuted outside the United States. Many who fault the American jury system do not appreciate the fallibility of judges. Perceptions and stereotypes influence all persons, judges and juries alike. Judges as well as juries make mistakes.

In short, no system is perfect. The American products liability system is not perfect. But it is less imperfect than many managers, particularly non-American managers, presume.

(iv)   Money compensation for injuries

(a)   Calculating amount owed

This is the area of strict products liability law which strikes fear in some managers. These managers fear that juries deciding strict product liability cases will order their firms to pay millions of dollars. At times juries do indeed award injured consumers a lot of money but these cases are rare. In fact, it is because these cases are rare that they make headlines.

Direct expenses of injury

The two main categories of direct expenses which a court will award an injured consumer are medical expenses and lost wages.

Medical expenses

Medical costs are very high in the United States. Americans therefore buy health insurance. As mentioned above, manufacturers doing business in the United States should also buy appropriate insurance. In this way they will be able to pay any medical expenses for which a court finds them liable.

The injured consumer may need medical and related assistance, such as physical therapy, for a period of time, perhaps even for the rest of his life. If an injured consumer needs such assistance, then a court will order a liable manufacturer to pay for this assistance.

Lost wages

An injured consumer will almost certainly not be able to work for at least some period of time. A court will order a liable manufacturer to compensate the injured consumer for the wages he or she will lose because of this.

Indirect expenses

Pain and suffering

This is the category of compensation which makes headlines. Some jurys award very high amounts of money as compensation for pain and suffering. To compensate the injured consumer for pain and suffering the jury can award whatever amount it feels is appropriate. Because the jury has so much discretion over the amount of money it may award for pain and suffering, lawyers have great difficulty predicting the size of pain and suffering awards.

Emotional distress

In rare cases a court will award compensation to a person who has suffered emotional, but not physical, injury. While courts have historically been very reluctant to award compensation in such cases, over time they have become somewhat less reluctant to award compensation in cases of serious emotional distress. Courts have awarded compensation, for example, to:

- asbestos workers worried that they will contract cancer in the future

- a parent witnessing a very serious injury to his child.

Punitive damages

Reprehensible conduct leads to punitive damages. In the context of selling goods, a court will award punitive damages against a manufacturer which sells a product it knows is very dangerous. Courts will award punitive damages not against a firm which sold a defective product by mistake but against a firm which knowingly sold a very dangerous product.

For example, Ford sold the Pinto even though it knew the car had a design defect. Ford had designed the gas tank in such a way that some rear-end collisions caused the gas tank to explode, burning the car's occupants to death. Ford knew of this problem, could have fixed it at minimal cost, but chose not to fix the problem. In another famous incident, numerous asbestos manufactures discovered that asbestos causes cancer. The companies hid their research, thereby causing many people to contract asbestosis, a deadly form of cancer. In these cases courts rightly awarded punitive damages.

Courts tend to apply the informal rule that punitive damages should be twice the injured consumer's losses. A court applying this rule would therefore award the injured person, in total, three times his actual loss. Lawyers call this the treble damages rule, but it is merely a non-binding rule of thumb. A court can award as punitive damages whatever sum it feels is appropriate.

Attorney's fees

A court also has the discretion to order a party it finds liable to pay the other party's attorney's fees. As with punitive damages, a court will order a party to pay attorney's fees only if its conduct was so reprehensible that the award is appropriate. Courts rarely award attorney's fees.

Sharing compensation

If manufacturer and injured are both responsible, they share costs

If a court finds the injured consumer and the manufacturer both partially responsible for the consumer's injuries, then, in most states, the court will apportion liability appropriately. For example, if a court found the injured consumer 40% at fault for his injuries, then it would order the manufacturer to pay only 60% of the injured consumer's losses. In some states, if a court finds that the injured consumer is more than 50% at fault, then a court will not award the consumer any compensation at all.

One defendant cannot pay, then the others must pay more

A court may find more than one defendant liable. It may, for example, find both a manufacturer and its component supplier liable. One of these defendants, however, may not be able to pay the court award, perhaps because it is bankrupt. In this case the court will usually order the solvent defendant to pay the entire award.

(v)   Product liability reform

Several states have reformed their product liability laws. These reforms change relatively tangential aspects of product liability law, not the main principles of the law. These reforms typically limit one defendant's liability when another defendant cannot pay a court award. These reforms also typically impose limits on the amount of money the jury may award the plaintiff, particularly for pain and suffering or as punitive damages.

7. CONTRACTNG
Creating binding obligations

7. CONTRACTING
Creating binding obligations

(i) Introduction

(a) Courts will not enforce all promises

To create a contract two people must each promise to give the other something of value. This contracting principle distinguishes American law and British law from the civil law of continental Europe. If only one person promises to give the other something of value, then the parties have not created a binding contract. One person has merely made a promise. American courts do not enforce mere promises.

Therefore, to create a binding contract, there must be, first, an offer (I'll sell you my car for $1,000.00), secondly, an acceptance (Yes, I accept your offer), and, thirdly, each party must promise to give the other something of value (here, a car and money).

On the other hand, if an uncle were to promise to buy his nephew a car, and then fail to do as he promises, a court will not require the uncle to buy the car. The nephew promised nothing to the uncle. The uncle therefore made a mere promise, he did not enter into a contract. Perhaps we should all do what we say, but the law will not always require us to do so.

(b) Courts will enforce most oral agreements

Managers, and others, often fail to put their agreements in writing. These oral agreements are, however, usually contracts which courts will enforce. The common belief that courts will only enforce written agreements is not true.

However, a wronged party will often have great difficulty proving the existence and terms of an oral contract, particularly if the other party denies that the contract exists. Given the high cost of lawsuits, therefore, an aggrieved party will probably not, as a practical matter, be able to enforce an oral contract.

(c)   Easy to form contract

Managers should therefore be careful. They can easily, and perhaps accidentally, enter into a formal, binding, oral contract.

To form a contract the law only requires that:

- one party make an offer,
- the other party accept the offer, and
- the parties agree to exchange something of value.

The contract does not necessarily have to be in writing – many oral contracts are binding.

(d)   Uniform commercial code

To encourage trade within the United States, 49 of the 50 states have enacted many identical, uniform laws, including the Uniform Commercial Code (UCC). The UCC regulates:

- only the sale of goods, and
- only among managers.

The UCC's influence in the area of contracts, however, goes beyond these limitations. Courts often apply UCC principles in situations to which the UCC does not technically apply. Thus the UCC regulates the sale of goods among firms, which itself is very important, but also influences the law of contracts generally. The UCC is therefore a critically important part of American contract law.

(ii)   Creating a contract

(a)   Introduction

Three basic requirements

To create a contract:

- one party must **offer** to form a contract,

- the other party must **accept** this offer, and

- each party must give up **something of value**.

This chapter will examine each of these three requirements.

(b) Offer

Contents of offer

Certain and definite

The person making the offer must make a certain and definite offer. The offer must contain all the main terms of the contract, including price.

Sale of goods offers need only identify the goods

The UCC enforces less definite offers. Thus, regarding the sale of goods, the UCC changes general contract law. The UCC requires only that the offer contain the essence, or "heart," of the contract. These can be rather few terms because courts can infer reasonable terms regarding issues the offer does not address. The UCC does not even require that the offer state a price.

In practice, therefore, the UCC requires only that the offer clearly describe the goods. The UCC requires that the offer clearly state:

- the type of goods, and

- the quantity to be sold.

Courts will infer reasonable additional terms

Courts applying the UCC will infer any additional terms beyond the description of the goods which must be necessary to complete the transaction. Courts will infer what they believe are reasonable and fair terms. To determine fairness courts will look at factors such as industry custom and norms, and the parties' previous behavior.

Thus by saying, "I will sell you 1,000 standard windowless business envelopes," for example, one manager, if talking to another, would be making a valid offer. If the other manager said: "I accept," then the parties would have created a binding contract. A court would infer all necessary additional terms: it would infer the market price, for example, and require payment and delivery within a reasonable period, say one month.

On the other hand, if the manager making the offer had merely said that he would sell 1,000 envelopes, then he would not have made a valid offer. Even if the other manager had accepted the offer, the parties would still not have created a binding contract. In this second case the offer does not clearly state the type of good: there are many types of envelopes.

Price is the free market price

Since the UCC requires only an adequate description of the goods, parties could form a valid contract without even discussing price. In this case a court would simply assume that the parties agreed to the fair market price.

Previous behavior creates future contract terms

Managers should keep in mind that the terms of their previous contracts with another firm and their previous actions may "write" the terms of later contracts with that firm. For example, if a seller has always delivered goods within 10 days, a court will infer this requirement in later contracts which do not specify a delivery time.

By not taking an action a manager can also create implied terms of future contracts. For example, if a manager always accepts 10% defective goods, a court will infer that standard in future contracts which do not state otherwise.

To avoid creating implied terms in future contracts, a manager should simply make clear to the other party that he does not intend to do so. For example, a manager may accept 10% defective goods in one shipment but will probably also want to avoid creating a standard for future contracts. To do this the manager should write a letter to the seller stating that while he is accepting the defective goods this one time, he will not do so in the future.

By simply telling the other party – explicitly and in writing – that he did not intend to establish a future standard the manager avoided establishing that standard – but the manager had to act. If a manager had remained silent, then he would have inadvertently created implied terms in future contracts.

Termination of offer

Offer generally cancelable at any time

The person making the offer can cancel it at any time. To cancel an offer, the person making it must simply tell the other person that he is canceling the offer. He must do this before the other person accepts the offer. If the other person had accepted the offer, then the parties would have created a contract and it would then be too late for the person making the offer to withdraw it.

Special situations – cannot withdraw offer

There are three situations, however, in which the person making the offer cannot withdraw it.

Option contracts

In an option contract one sells his right to cancel the offer at any time. An option contract is a contract separate and distinct from the underlying contract. The sale of the right to cancel the underlying contract creates a second contract, the option contract. For example, a seller may offer to sell a parcel of land for $10,000.00, and the person to whom the seller made the offer may then pay the seller $500.00 in return for the seller's promise not to withdraw the offer for, say, one month. During this month the seller, who received the $500 cannot withdraw his offer to sell the land and thereby enter into the underlying $10,000.00 contract. A court will enforce the option contract because each party will have given the other something of value – $500.00 and the right to revoke the offer.

The UCC firm offer

UCC requires that offers not be withdrawn for up to three months if they are:

- from a manager,
- in writing, and
- signed.

Thus under the UCC if a manager – in a signed writing – assures another manager that he will keep the offer open until a specified time, then he must keep the offer open until that specified time. This is true even if the other manager has not paid for the promise to keep the offer open.

Further, if the manager making the offer has not specified a time, a court will require that he keep the offer open for a reasonable time. A court will consider a reasonable time to be, at most, three months. Even if a manager says he will keep his offer open for more than three months, the UCC will still allow him to withdraw the offer after three months.

Reliance

If one party begins to accept the offer by doing what the offer asks, and the person making the offer expected the other person to do this, then the person making the offer cannot withdraw it until the other party has had an opportunity to do what the offer asked of it. Thus if, as the buyer expected, the seller is trying to satisfy the offer by manufacturing the relevant goods, then the buyer cannot withdraw its offer without first giving the seller a reasonable opportunity to manufacture the goods.

Managers should not expect to use this principle to win a lawsuit. Manufacturers, for example, will have great difficulty proving that the buyer expected them to accept the offer by beginning to manufacture rather than by simply saying: "I accept your offer."

(c) Acceptance

Acceptance creates contract

To create a contract one party must accept another's offer. One can accept another's offer in three different ways:

- acknowledging acceptance, such as writing a letter,

- doing what the offer asks, such as shipping the goods, or

- taking some other action which the offer requires for acceptance.

When looking to see if there was a valid offer, and then a valid acceptance of this offer, a court is really trying to discover the parties' intent. If a court believes that the parties intended to enter into a contract, then a court will find that the parties did in fact do so. A court will look for, as the cliché goes, the parties' "meeting of the minds."

The contract's terms are what the parties intended

Since the contract exists only if the parties intended it to exist, it follows that the contract terms are those the parties intended. The contract contains the terms which existed in the parties' minds when they had their "meeting of the minds." If the terms of the written agreement differ from those to which the parties actually agreed, then a court will enforce the terms to which the parties actually agreed and not the terms of the written agreement.

A party will have difficulty proving that the written contract does not state the terms to which the parties agreed. He will have to convince a court that the parties signed contract containing terms different to those which the parties actually agreed.

Mutual mistake

On the other hand, if the two parties had a "meeting of the minds," but based on a mutual mistake of an important fact, then in reality the parties never actually entered into a contract. For this situation to arise both parties must have made the same honest mistake. For example, if the parties based their transaction on the good faith, honest belief that a stone was a diamond, when in fact it was a valueless cubic zirconia, then the parties in reality never entered into a contract. The parties made a mutual mistake of an important fact, they never had a "meeting of the minds" and a court will not enforce a contract based on such a mutual mistake.

In this type of situation, however, the seller must be careful not to inadvertently create a warranty. If the seller described the stone as a diamond, then he may have made an express warranty that it was in fact a diamond. (See Warranties and fraud, Chapter 8.)

The offer and acceptance must be identical

The person accepting the offer can only accept that particular offer. He cannot accept an offer very similar to that offer. He cannot change the offer, however slightly, and then accept the offer he changed. If a party makes one change to the offer, then he has in fact rejected the offer. If he sends the changed offer back to the person who made the original offer, then he will have made a counter-offer, which the person who made the original offer may then accept or reject. The law, appropriately enough, calls this the "mirror image rule." The law requires the acceptance to be the mirror image of the offer.

Thus, if the one party drafts and signs a contract, then forwards it to the other party, who makes just one slight change – such as making delivery one day later – and then signs the contract, there is no contract. The changed contract would then itself be a new offer, which the drafter of the original contract could then accept or reject.

The UCC has special rules regarding the common situation of managers conducting business after exchanging inconsistent invoices and similar documents. This problem is discussed below. See Differing invoices, Section (iii)(b).

(d)   Exchange must be for something of value

General points

To create an enforceable contract, each party must agree to give the other something of value. The law calls this thing of value "consideration." Thus an agreement to exchange a car for $10,000.00 creates an enforceable contract because both parties have agreed to give up something of value – $10,000.00 and a car. By contrast, if one person promises to give away a car he has merely made an unenforceable promise. Unless the person receiving the car agrees to give something of value in exchange, the promise remains just a promise, not part of a contract, and no court will require the person who promised to give away the car to actually do so.

There are many things of value. Money is only the most obvious. Objects can of course be of value. In the discussion to the option contract, above, the thing of value the seller gave up was his right to cancel the offer, which is certainly valuable. One who forgives a debt has also given up a thing of value, and doing so can therefore create a contract. One who surrenders the right to bring a lawsuit has, similarly, given up something of value. In fact, it is because this right has value that surrendering it allows courts to enforce lawsuit settlement agreements.

Unequal exchanges create contracts

A manager should be careful not to agree to exchange items of unequal value. If he agrees to do so, then he will form a contract. In particular, managers should be wary of those who offer to exchange something of nominal value, such as $1.00, for something of real value. Even if the parties agree to exchange things of greatly differing value, they will still create a contract. Courts do not ensure that contracts are fair.

Thus, an attorney may ask a manager to enter into a contract in which the attorney's client agrees to exchange something of nominal value for the manager's promise of something of real value. The attorney is using his offer of nominal value to turn the manager's promise of real value into an obligation courts will enforce.

A "thing of value" must really have value

While courts will enforce agreements to exchange things of unequal value, both things which the parties agreed to exchange must actually have value. Courts will not enforce contracts in which one party agrees, for example, to buy all he may "choose to order." The party might buy nothing. His promise has no value because he has not promised to actually buy something. The parties have not agreed to each give each other "something of value," and the parties have therefore not created a contract.

Requirement contracts enforceable

The UCC, however, will enforce a buyer's promise to buy all he may need of a certain good from a particular seller. The UCC reasons that since all contracts require the parties to act in good faith (see below), the contract actually requires the buyer to operate his business in good faith so that he actually needs and buys some of the good. Then he must buy all he needs of that good from this seller. Therefore the buyer has actually promised to do something and the UCC will enforce the contract.

(iii)   Doing business under American contract law

(a)   Many oral agreements are enforceable

Courts will enforce many oral agreements. Although not written, many oral agreements are nevertheless contracts which courts will enforce as rigorously as they would any written contract. Having a written agreement is certainly the better practice – a written contract will greatly help a wronged party prove the existence and terms of the agreement. However, in many cases the parties create a binding contract without writing anything.

General rule and exceptions

In general, courts will enforce oral agreements. The law makes three major commercial exceptions to this general rule. Courts will not enforce contracts:

- for the sale of *goods* worth $500.00 or more,

- relating to real property, or

- with which it is *impossible* for one party to comply within one year after its signing.

Thus, the party *against whom the court will enforce the contract* (not both parties) must sign one of these types of contracts or a court will not enforce it.

$500.00 contracts

The UCC requires contracts to be in writing if they are for:

- the sale of goods,

- between managers, and

- worth at least $500.00.

Real property

"Real property" includes more than just land. It also includes buildings, easements (the right to use land another person owns) and other interests in real property. Courts interpret this term broadly. The parties should therefore put in writing any contract relating to real property in any way.

Comply within one year

Compliance "within one year" is tricky. If, within one year, a person *could possibly* do all the contract requires of him, then the parties do not need to put their contract in writing. The law does not ask how probable it is that the party will actually comply within one year, the law simply looks at whether compliance is at all *possible*. If the party *could possibly* comply then the contract will not satisfy the exception, and the parties need not put the contract in writing.

For example, someone may hire a nurse to care for him until he is well. Since he may become well within one year, the law does not require that the contract be in writing.

Many "writings" satisfy the writing requirement

Any piece of paper is a writing

Any piece of paper which reflects the deal is a writing. Invoices, memoranda, notes, faxes, etc. could reflect the deal. Notes scribbled on the back of an envelope could reflect the deal. So could several pieces of what might seem to be scrap paper. If a court could read together these pieces of supposed scrap paper, and thereby determine the terms of an agreement, then the papers are not scrap at all. They are a contract.

Confirmation letters

Under the UCC, if one manager sends another a letter confirming the sale of goods, that letter is the written contract unless the other manager objects within 10 days. If the second manager fails to object, then the letter is the contract.

Managers must therefore be alert for confirmation letters. If a manager receives a confirmation letter, and does not respond within ten days, then he has "signed" the contract the confirmation letter describes.

- If a manager enters into an oral contract, then he should send a confirmation letter. He will then be sure that the agreement is in writing and contains the correct terms.

- If a manager receives a confirmation letter and he objects to its terms, he must respond quickly. He has only ten days.

The writing must contain only the essential terms

Recall that general contract law only requires the contract to contain the *essential* terms of the transaction. Further, the law only requires the contract to state these essential terms with *reasonable* certainty. Together, these two qualifications imply that a writing containing much less than a clear statement of all the contract terms will nevertheless be a sufficient "writing" to create a contract.

Regarding the sale of goods, the UCC makes very clear how little the parties must write to create a binding contract. The UCC requires only that the writing state the quantity of goods sold. This requirement is related to the UCC rule that a valid offer need contain no more than an adequate description of the goods. Thus, just as the UCC does not require that an offer contain a price, so too it does not require that a written contract contain a price. A court will simply infer the fair market price and other reasonable terms.

Signature

A contract which the parties must put in writing they must also sign but the law does not require both parties to sign the contract. A court will enforce a contract so long as the party being sued has signed the contract.

Furthermore, the law does not require a full, formal signature. It requires only a mark showing that the person acknowledged and accepted the terms. A party who initials a contract has certainly signed it. Under the UCC, a firm printing a contract on its own letterhead stationery has signed the contract.

Enforcing contracts which should have been written

If a party performs an oral contract, he has in effect "signed" it. By complying with the terms of a contract, one acknowledges and accepts that contract. Thus, delivering goods has the same effect as signing a contract. The act acknowledges that a contract exists.

This is true, however, only to the extent that the party's actions acknowledge the contract. Thus, a buyer accepting one delivery of goods has clearly shown his intent to buy those particular goods. By accepting these goods he has not, however, shown his intent to buy additional goods.

One must still pay for benefits received

The law still requires one to pay for any benefits one may receive. Thus, if a party accepts goods or services based on an oral agreement which the law required the parties to put in writing, the party must still pay for the goods or services he accepted.

Practicalities of contracting

Assume oral contract enforceable

Managers should assume courts will enforce all their oral agreements. They should do so for the following reasons.

- Courts will enforce many oral agreements. The rules regarding when the law requires contract to be in writing are complicated and tricky. This is particularly true regarding the rule that contracts which the parties could perform within one year must be in writing.

- Even if the law requires an agreement to be in writing, existing invoices, letters, notes, etc. may together create a satisfactory writing.

- Even if the parties did not enter into the written agreement the law requires, the party receiving benefits must still pay for them. Since courts will infer a fair market price either as a contract term or simply in the interests of fairness, in many cases in the end it really does not matter whether the parties created a formal, binding contract.

Put agreements in writing

Managers should put all their agreements in writing. They should either draft formal written contracts, or, as a second best option, send confirmation letters. They should do this even though they should also assume that courts will enforce all their oral contracts. They should put their agreements in writing because in this area, as in many others, practical reality is more important than legal theory.

Without a writing, a wronged party will have great difficulty simply proving that a contract exists. He will have even more difficulty proving the terms of the contract. The slow and expensive American court system makes many theoretically enforceable oral agreements unenforceable as a practical matter.

Oral agreements cause misunderstandings. Since each party has not examined the same written agreement, the parties could easily develop honest misunderstandings about the terms of the agreement. Furthermore, there is always the chance that one party will act in bad faith and lie about his recollection of the terms of the agreement. A written agreement will help to eliminate these potential problems.

(b) Differing invoices

A common problem

Managers often base their transactions on purchase orders, invoices and similar documents which contain inconsistent terms. Managers typically ignore these inconsistencies, at least until they have a dispute. At this point each manager of course claims that his document contains the true contract terms.

In such situations the parties will have based their transaction on the mistaken assumption that they formed a contract. Recall the mirror image rule, that for the parties to form a contract the offer and acceptance must be identical. If the parties' invoices differ, then the offer and acceptance are, by definition, not identical. Therefore, technically, the parties never created a contract.

UCC creates contract

For the common situation of managers buying and selling goods based on invoices and similar documents with inconsistent terms, the UCC changes the law. Under the UCC the parties have formed a binding contract. The terms of this contract are:

● the terms of the first invoice, and

● those terms of the second invoice which do not "materially alter" the first invoice.

Materially alter

The UCC cannot precisely define "materially alter." Business situations vary too greatly. The best the UCC can do is to say that terms which "materially alter" an offer are those which, if a court incorporated them into the contract, would cause "unreasonable surprise or hardship."

As a general rule, terms which cause "unreasonable surprise or hardship" are those which are inconsistent with the general practice of the trade or industry. Accordingly, courts will generally not include in contracts additional terms which are inconsistent with industry practice.

Offers may require identical acceptance

The UCC allows a first invoice to state that the terms of any contract it forms must contain only the terms of this first invoice. Technically, the first invoice will offer a contract, and will also say that the other party must either accept or reject this contract but cannot change its terms. If the first invoice will allow no changes, it must say so clearly and explicitly.

Not only the first invoice, but the second as well may state that any contract which it forms must contain only its terms. A manager sending such an invoice would, in reality, be rejecting the contract the first invoice offered, and then offering a new, second, contract. This new offer would require the other party to either accept it or reject it in its entirety.

Practical considerations

Details crucial

The devil is indeed in the details. Lawyers hide terms unfavorable to other parties in the fine print of clients' invoices and other documents. If at all possible, and certainly if the transaction is of great value, a manager should take the time to read the fine print or incur the expense of having his lawyer read it. What the fine print lacks in interest it more than makes up in importance.

Include favorable terms

Every manager should include in his invoices and similar documents as many clauses favorable to his firm as is appropriate. If he is the first to send an invoice, then these favorable terms will form the contract. If he is sending a responding document, then this will at least arguably be part of the contract.

Similarly, a manager should include in his invoice a term stating that any contract the invoice forms will only contain the terms of the invoice. Whether a court will actually enforce this requirement is uncertain. But managers who include the term add to their arsenal during future lawsuit settlement negotiations.

How to respond

A manager receiving another's invoice can respond in several ways. The following lists possible responses, starting with the response which a court is least likely to accept, but which is also least likely to disrupt the underlying sale. The third response is the opposite, it is the one a court is most likely to accept it, but it is also the one most likely to disrupt the sale.

A manager's possible responses are as follows.

- Accept the offer, but, along with the acceptance, send a list of terms which the manager rejects, and which he therefore claims are not part of the contract. The other manager may not respond. If he does not, then the manager will certainly be in a better position than if he had simply ignored the objectionable terms. If the other manager does respond, then the two parties may reach an agreement. Any concessions the manager receives because he objected to the terms will put him in a better position than he would have been in had he not objected. And, as a fall-back position, the manager could accept all the objectionable terms.

- Include additional terms in the responding invoice, and also include in the responding invoice a term stating that the responding invoice forms the contract unless the other party objects. Whether a court will actually enforce this provision and find that the contract contains only the terms of the responding invoice, is uncertain. But it may. The manager who does this will certainly be in a better position than the manager who simply accepts objectionable terms.

- Reject the offer outright, and make a counter-offer. Doing this increases the chances that the entire transaction will collapse but it also puts the manager rejecting the offer on very firm legal ground should there be a later lawsuit.

At times managers have difficulty striking the right balance between enhancing their legal position and ensuring the success of the underlying transaction. Managers must consider their relative bargaining strength, the nature of the business relationship and a myriad of other factors. Many managers do not stop to consider the terms of the contracts they form, with their invoices. Thus managers who consider their options when using invoices to form a contract will have an advantage over the many who do not.

(c)   Changing the contract

Parties must again exchange something of value

If the parties want to change their contract, then they must enter into a second contract. In the second contract the parties will agree to change the first contract. To form this second contract each party must once again give the other something of value. Recall that parties form a contract only if they each give the other something of value. Thus if only one party agrees to change the contract, then that party has merely made a promise, and a court will not enforce a mere promise.

For example, if a construction firm has agreed to put up a building for $100,000.00 and if, perhaps due to rising costs, the building's owner simply agrees to pay an additional $20,000.00, a court will not enforce this change to the original contract. The construction firm already had the obligation to put up the building for $100,000.00. It has not given the owner something of value in exchange for the additional $20,000.00. *Both* parties have not agreed to give up something of value, and therefore a court will not enforce the owner's promise to pay the additional $20,000.00.

The construction firm could give the building owner many things which would be "something of value," and which would therefore allow the parties to create a contract. The firm could, for example, agree to complete construction early. Early completion is certainly something of value, and if the construction firm agreed to provide it in exchange for the $20,000.00, then the parties would have formed a contract.

Promises of managers enforceable

The UCC changes the general rule that a court will only enforce contract changes if each party gives the other something of value. The UCC allows managers to change their contracts even if only one party receives something of value. Thus, regarding contracts only between managers, and only relating to the sale of goods, courts will enforce one party's mere promise to do or provide something. For example, if a supplier's costs suddenly rise, and the buyer therefore agrees to pay more than the contract price, a court will require the buyer to pay the higher price, even if the supplier has not given the buyer anything in return for the extra money.

Managers buying or selling goods must therefore be careful. If they promise to change the contract to benefit the other party, a court will hold them to their promise. This is true even if they do not receive anything of value in exchange for their promise.

Oral changes

Contract requires written changes

Courts often enforce oral agreements to change contracts which state that parties must put all their changes to the contract in writing. Courts often say that when the parties orally agreed to change their contract, they also agreed to change the term requiring them to put changes in writing. Thus courts often enforce oral changes to contracts which state that all changes must be in writing.

Law required written contract

Even if the law required the original contract to be in writing, the law will not necessarily require changes to it also to be in writing. The law of most states does not require changes to contracts to be in writing simply because it required the original contract to be in writing.

Rather, the law sees the change as itself a separate contract. The law will therefore only require the change to be in writing if the change satisfies the exceptions to the general rule that courts will enforce oral contracts. For example, if it is impossible for both parties to comply with the change within one year, then the parties must put the change in writing. See, Courts will enforce most oral agreements, Section (i)(b).

UCC has stricter standard

The UCC is perhaps a little less willing than the general law to enforce oral changes. The UCC will not enforce an oral change to a contract if:

- the original contract had to be in writing, or

- the original contract said that changes must be in writing.

However, if the parties orally agree to change their contract, and acted on the assumption that they changed their contract, then even under the UCC the parties will have in fact changed their contract.

Changes in writing is the better practice

Managers should put their contract changes in writing. This will help both parties to see exactly how they agreed to change their contract. At the very least, a manager who has orally agreed to change a contract should send a letter confirming the contract change. This confirmation letter should say: "This is to confirm that we agree to ... – and we agreed to nothing else."

Further, if a manager orally rejects another's request to change a contract, then he should send a letter confirming that he declined to change the contract.

(d) Contract compliance

Perfect compliance not required

The law does not require parties to comply with every term of their contracts, particularly their complex contracts. Firms must comply only with the essential terms, the "heart" of the contract. The legal term for such compliance, "substantial performance," goes a long way towards describing what courts look for: not complete, but substantial performance. Courts probably apply this principle most commonly to construction contracts, typically finding substantial performance despite delays and minor construction defects.

A party who has substantially performed his contract will, by definition, not be in breach of the contract. Therefore, despite failing to comply with every term of the contract, a court will not order him to pay the awards discussed later in this chapter.

On the other hand, if a firm has not done everything the contract requires of it, then the law will not give it full compensation. For example, if a seller provides services of lower quality than the contract requires, then a court may find that while the seller has not breached the contract, the buyer should still pay less than the contract price. Thus, if a firm failed to construct the exact building the contract required, a court will probably find that the construction firm nevertheless substantially complied with the construction contract, and is therefore not in breach of the contract. But it will still award the firm less money than the contract required, and this lesser amount would reflect the lower value of the building the construction firm actually built.

The UCC requires perfect compliance

The UCC requires that the seller deliver the exact goods it agreed to deliver. Thus, the UCC does not accept the principle of substantial compliance. On the contrary, the UCC does not allow the seller to deviate even slightly from the contract terms. The UCC believes that buyers must be sure that they will in fact receive the exact goods for which they contracted.

Thus, if the seller delivers goods which do not exactly match the contract's specifications the buyer may:

- accept the goods,

- reject the goods, or

- reject some of the goods.

The buyer may accept goods which do not conform to the contract's specifications. If the buyer does so, a court would only expect him to pay the actual value of the defective goods. Thus, if a buyer accepts defective goods, it need only pay the seller the goods' actual fair market price, not the contract price.

Before accepting, buyer may inspect goods

The UCC gives the buyer the right to inspect goods before he accepts them. This allows the buyer to know whether he should accept the goods. The buyer may inspect the goods at any time and place, and in any manner, so long as these are reasonable.

Buyer must actively reject defective goods

If the buyer rejects the goods, he must take the positive, affirmative step of telling the seller. The law places the burden of rejecting the defective goods on the buyer. If the buyer fails to act, then, even if the goods are defective, the law will not consider them defective. If the buyer complains later, it will then be too late.

The buyer must reject defective goods within a reasonable time. This reasonable time is usually the time it should take the buyer to inspect the goods. In the case of a hidden defect the buyer may reject the goods later, when it learns of the defect. But it must reject the goods as soon as it learns of the defect.

Similarly, if the buyer chooses to accept defective goods, and therefore pay less, it must tell the seller as soon as possible that the goods he is accepting are defective.

The buyer's notice telling the seller that the goods are defective must be in writing. While managers should always put their legally significant communications in writing, doing so is particularly important in this context. As discussed below, the seller has the right to correct any defects the buyer may find in the goods. The seller therefore also has the right to demand that the buyer identify those defects – in writing. To speed the process, as well as to create a record of the defects, as soon as the buyer rejects the goods he should tell the seller – in writing – why he believes the goods are defective.

Buyer receiving goods

A buyer receiving goods should:

- inspect the goods as soon as possible – he should not risk losing his right to reject the goods simply because he waited too long before inspecting them;

- if rejecting the goods, do so as soon as possible – again, the buyer should not let time slip, and thereby lose the right to reject defective goods. He should quickly explain – in writing – why he is rejecting the goods.

Seller's right to correct defects

To balance the harshness of its requirement that the seller must deliver the exact goods the contract describes, the UCC gives the seller the right to correct defects in the goods it delivers. Further, the UCC gives the seller the right to demand that the buyer explain, in writing, why it believes the goods are defective. The UCC then limits the buyer to these complaints: only if there are hidden defects can the buyer rightfully later complain about additional defects.

If the time to complete the contract has not expired, then the seller has until that time to correct any defects. If the time has expired, then the seller has an additional, reasonable, time to correct defects – so long as it first notifies the buyer that it will correct the defects. Again, the law requires the seller to put this notification in writing.

Managers' common errors

Firms often make mistakes in this area.

Buyers' errors

Buyers' common mistakes include the following.

- Not realizing they have the right to inspect goods.

- Waiting too long to reject the goods. While managers may have plenty of problems, few must be solved within a legally mandated time period.

- Accepting the seller's promise – made over the telephone – to correct defects.

- To courts, telephone promises never happened. If the seller later fails to do what he promised, the buyer will be stuck with the defective goods.
- Thus, a buyer should write a polite letter to the seller confirming any telephone promises to correct defects: "I enjoyed speaking to you yesterday. Thank you for agreeing to ..." In this way the buyer will have created an obligation which a court will enforce.

● Giving the seller time to correct defects, but failing to state – again, in writing – that the buyer has not waived the right to sue for breach of contract. The UCC makes binding written promises not to sue for breach of contract. It makes these promises binding even if the other party has not paid for this release from liability. Managers must therefore be careful how they phrase letters. They should not inadvertently waive their right to sue later for breach of contract.

Sellers' errors

Sellers must be aware that:

● they have the right to demand that the buyer state – in writing – why it is rejecting the goods.

● they have the right to correct defects, and

● if the time to complete the contract has expired, then they must first notify the buyer – again, in writing – of their intention to correct any defects in their goods.

(e)   Can ask for assurance of performance

If one party takes steps which are clearly inconsistent with an intention to complete the contract, then courts will allow that the other party may take steps as if the first party had already breached the contract. This is so even if the first party has not yet breached the contract. For example, a seller who sells particular goods to a third party has clearly shown its intent not to sell those goods to the buyer.

The UCC allows a party which reasonably suspects that another will not complete a contract to ask the other party for written assurance that it will do as it should. If the party asking for assurance does not receive it within 30 days, then the party failing to give the assurance has breached the contract.

Managers should therefore not hesitate to make sure that other firms are ready to do as their contracts require. If the manager has any doubt, then he should ask for written assurance.

(f)   Seller need not deliver to buyer without money

Relatedly, the UCC does not expect a seller to deliver goods to a buyer who has no money. If, before he is due to deliver the goods, the seller learns that the buyer is insolvent then, despite what the contract may say, the seller may demand cash payment from the buyer before he delivers the goods.

The seller even has the power to require an insolvent buyer to return already delivered goods. If the seller did not learn that the buyer was insolvent until after he had delivered the goods, then the seller may require the buyer to return the goods. But the UCC requires that the seller make his request within ten days of delivering the goods.

The seller can also demand return of goods if the buyer pays with a bad check. To do so, however, the seller must act as soon as the bank returns the check.

(g)   Unforeseen event

If an event, which both parties assumed would not happen, in fact happens, then a court will adjust the parties' contract rights accordingly. A court will only adjust the parties' contract rights if the parties based their transaction on the assumption that the event would not occur. Examples of such unforeseen events include an embargo, a drought, an unforeseen shutdown of supply, or the contract becoming illegal after the parties signed the contract.

The law will excuse performance only for so long as the event hinders performance. The seller must therefore deliver the goods, for example, when the embargo is lifted. Of course, if by then the buyer no longer wants the goods, then the law will not require the seller to deliver the goods.

(iv) Compensation for breach of contract

(a) Money favored

General points

In America, courts are overwhelmingly likely to require liable parties to pay money. Courts are very reluctant to order the alternative, that the liable party perform some act. Thus if a seller fails to deliver the goods the contract requires, then a court will not order the seller to deliver the goods. Instead the court will order the seller to pay the buyer enough money so the buyer can buy the goods from another seller.

Rarely must the liable party actually do something

Only in unusual circumstances will a court order the liable party to do something other than pay money. A wronged party asking the court to order the liable party to perform some act must prove that it, the wronged party, is in an unusual situation and that money will therefore not adequately compensate it.

An unusual situation would exist, for example, if the seller were the only firm able to manufacture the goods the contract required. In this very unusual case a court may order the seller to manufacturer the goods. If a contract required delivery of unique goods, then a court would order the seller to sell to the buyer those unique goods. But a court would only do this if the goods were truly unique. Works of art are unique. While components may also be unique, buyers usually have great difficulty proving that they are so unusual that a court should order the seller to sell the components to the buyer.

On the other hand, the law considers all land to be unique. Therefore, the law requires all those who contract to sell a parcel of land to in fact sell that parcel of land. The law will not allow a seller of land to breach his contract and later give the buyer money instead of the land.

(b)   Amount of money

Reimburse for costs of breach

The breaching party must pay what the breach cost the wronged party. A court will require the liable party to pay the wronged party a sum sufficient to put the wronged party in exactly the same position as it would have been in had the liable party not breached the contract.

For example, if the seller failed to deliver goods and the buyer had to purchase replacement goods, then a court would order the seller to pay the buyer the difference between the price of those replacement goods and the original contract price. The court would also order the seller to reimburse the buyer for any additional transportation costs the buyer incurred. Thus, if the buyer had to pay $15,000 for goods for which the original contract charged only $10,000, then a court would order the seller to pay the buyer $5,000. If the buyer paid $100 to have the goods delivered, then a court would order the seller to pay this cost as well. On the other hand, if the buyer could purchase replacement goods for the same price as the contract price, then, despite his breach, a court would not order the seller to pay any money.

Sale of goods - UCC

Buyer does not actually have to buy

The UCC requires the seller to pay the buyer whether or not the buyer actually purchases replacement goods. If the seller fails to deliver goods, then the law will require it to pay the buyer the difference between the contract price and the market price of the goods. This is true even if the buyer does not actually buy replacement goods.

Seller must keep losses to minimum

However, if the buyer breaches, then the seller must sell the goods the buyer refused to accept. This is an application of the rule, discussed below, that each party must try to keep the costs of a breach to a minimum. A court will therefore order the buyer to pay the seller the difference between the contract price and the price for which the seller actually sold the goods. A court will only require the buyer to pay the full contract price if the seller could not sell the goods to any other buyer, at any price, despite making a good faith effort.

For a discussion of the amount of money recoverable when delivered goods do not match the specifications of the contract, see Compensation for failing to satisfy warranty, Chapter 8(1)(d).

(c)   Liable party must only pay foreseeable costs

Liable party must anticipate cost

A party is only responsible for the consequences of its breach which it could reasonably foresee. For example, a shipping company may deliver a part, vital for the operation of a factory, after the date the contract required. The shipping company has therefore presumably breached the contract. Assume that owing to this breach the factory had to shut down. Despite this breach, under normal conditions a court would not order the shipping company to pay the factory owner the profits the factory owner lost because it closed its factory. Under normal conditions a shipping company could not foresee that if it were late delivering one part, this delay would cause an entire factory to close. Such a loss would not, under normal conditions, be reasonably foreseeable for a shipping company, and it would therefore not be liable for such a loss.

Accordingly if, due to special circumstances, a breach of contract leads to an unusually high loss, the breaching party will only be responsible for this unusually high loss if:

● it knew of the special circumstances (in the above example, that the factory could not operate without the part), or

● such a loss were obvious under the circumstances.

The parties can agree that in case of a breach neither party will have to pay these difficult to foresee costs, which the law calls consequential damages. A court will enforce such an agreement so long as it considers the agreement fair to both parties. Courts usually consider such agreements between firms to be fair.

Managers should notify of special circumstances

Managers should notify other firms of any special costs their firm will incur if the other firm breaches a contract. Managers should, if at all possible, put this notification in writing.

(d) Duty to keep damages to a minimum

All parties must do all they reasonably can to keep the costs of a breach to a minimum. For example, if a buyer improperly refuses to accept delivery of a perishable commodity such as fruit, then the seller must sell the fruit as soon as possible, and for as much money as possible. The seller must also tell the buyer that it is reselling the goods. This will give the buyer the opportunity to accept the goods, or to take other steps to further lower the cost of the breach. If the seller has done all it can to lower the costs of the breach, then a court will order the buyer to reimburse the seller for its remaining costs. To use the above example, a court would order the buyer to pay the seller the difference between the price for which it sold the fruit and the contract price.

(e) Parties may agree in advance to amount payable

Agreement must not impose penalty

The parties may agree that if there is a breach, one party will pay the other a fixed sum or a sum based on a predetermined formula. A court will enforce such a provision so long as, when the parties signed the contract, the provision reflected the parties' reasonable judgment of what would be fair compensation.

By contrast, if a court believed the parties intended to impose a penalty on the breaching party, then it would not enforce the provision. In other words, a court will not enforce a provision which, when the parties signed the contract, seemed to award one party more than enough money to compensate it for the other's breach.

Agreements regarding awards speed lawsuits

Managers should include in their contracts a provision stating how much money each party will pay the other if one were to breach the contract. These provisions should be fair, so courts will enforce them. These provisions help both parties because they make lawsuits simpler, faster, and cheaper.

(f)   Each party responsible for his own attorney's fees

Under the American rule the losing party in a lawsuit does not pay the winning party's attorney's fees. Each party pays its own legal fees. Fraud cases are the major exception to this rule. See Warranties and fraud, Chapter 8.

However, the parties can agree to change this rule. They can agree, for example, that the loser of a lawsuit will pay the winner's attorneys fees.

(v)   Interpreting contracts

(a)   Courts will infer reasonable missing terms

If a contract does not discuss the issues before the court, then the court will do what it thinks is fair and appropriate. In the most common application of this rule, a court will require the buyer to pay the fair market price for the goods it received.

(b)   Implied promise of good faith

The law includes in all contracts an "implied covenant of good faith and fair dealing." In other words, the law implicitly includes in all contracts a provision in which each party agrees to deal fairly with the other. For example, when the UCC requires that, if there is a breach, the non-breaching party must take affirmative steps to keep the costs of the breach to a minimum, it is actually applying this general principle.

(c)   Courts do what they think is fair

A manager trying to imagine what a court would do in a particular situation should ask himself: "What is fair?" He should put legalities aside, try to be objective, and ask himself: "What is the "right" thing to do?" This is what a court would probably do. In fact, some lawyers believe courts decide what to do, then find the legal rationale for that

(vi) Convention on the international sale of goods (CISG)

Most American managers prefer, and some insist, that the UCC, rather than the Convention on the International Sales of Goods (CISG), governs contracts relating to their business within the United States. The CISG is the international equivalent to the UCC. Just as the UCC creates uniform rules to foster interstate trade, the CISG creates uniform rules to foster international trade.

Non-American managers should generally allow the UCC to control contracts relating to business within the United States. This is so for the following reasons.

- Generally speaking, the UCC is as fair to both parties as is the CISG.

- Americans usually request that the UCC applies.

- If any lawsuit or arbitration will take place in the United States, as is usually the case, then the parties should agree to apply the UCC, with which American courts and arbitrators are quite familiar.

- The interplay of the CISG and the UCC can create complex legal issues. The CISG, for example, does not cover all aspects of the sale of goods. To keep lawsuits as quick and inexpensive as possible, the parties should keep the legal issues as simple as possible.

A final note about confirmation letters

This chapter, and others, have consistently stressed the need to put everything in writing. To simplify only a little, if a manager did not put it in writing, then it did not happen. Telephone conversations are therefore not enough – a manager must send a confirming letter. A confirmation letter will greatly help a manager who must later prove his version of events. It will help the manager both in court and during lawsuit settlement negotiations. In fact, if the other party knows that the manager sent a confirmation letter, and can therefore prove his version of events, then it may choose not to bring a lawsuit at all.

Confirmation letters therefore help managers win in court, reach favorable lawsuit settlements, and avoid lawsuits. They save managers many thousands of dollars. And they are so easy to write. Confirmation letters are always good investments.

) Practical Appendix

(a) Some practical aspects of contract negotiation

- For the non-price terms of the agreement, reasoning and custom, rather than sheer bargaining leverage, usually determine of the outcome of negotiations.

- If the negotiations are going well do not break, either for a meal or for any other reason. On the other hand, if negotiations are going poorly, find an excuse to stop, and try again later.

- Never take anything personally.
  This applies, in particular, to lawsuits. Managers should do what makes business sense, not what they find emotionally satisfying. Thus managers should usually settle.

- Always show the utmost respect for persons involved in the negotiations, especially those from the other firm.

- Let lawyers deal with lawyers.

- Managers should make a list of their minimum requirements. Before negotiations begin, they should prepare themselves to walk away from the deal if they cannot achieve these minimum requirements.

(b) Sales checklist
Main terms of typical sale of goods contract

Description of goods

The seller should describe the goods in enough detail that the buyer, and a court, will know what he is selling.

Quantity

- The quantity sold, and

- any deviation from this quantity the buyer may allow.

Price

While the price is not an essential contract term, it is of course the better practice for the contract to state the price of the goods.

Timing of payment

- The buyer must usually pay either:
  - when the seller delivers the goods to the shipper, or
  - when the buyer receives the goods.

- Payment may be due a period of time, such as 30 days, after the goods are delivered.

- Many contracts provide for a lower price if the buyer pays early or promptly. The implicit rate of return in such provisions is usually very favorable for the buyer.

Place of delivery

- If the contract does not say where the buyer should deliver the goods, then the seller need only make the goods available for pick up at his place of business. In other words, unless stated otherwise, transportation is the responsibility of the buyer.

- The seller could make more than one instalment delivery.

Risk of loss

- One party must assume the risk of loss. This really means one party must buy insurance. Some parties split the responsibilities of buying the insurance and paying for the insurance. This is a poor practice. It is awkward, can lead to mistakes, and the party buying the insurance may not have the appropriate incentive to find the lowest-priced policy.

- One party, particularly the buyer, may have a floating insurance policy covering all goods shipped to or by it.

Time of delivery

- The parties should agree when the seller will deliver the goods.

- The parties should also agree on the consequences of late delivery. For example:
  - there may be no breach, so long as the seller delivers within a reasonable time, or
  - if late delivery does cause a breach, then the seller may be responsible for the buyer's lost profits.

Warranties

- The seller could make explicit promises to the buyer about the quality of his products.

- The contract will contain the implied warranties unless the seller disclaims these. If the seller disclaims these warranties, he must do so conspicuously. See Warranties and Fraud, Chapter 8.

Compensation for breach

- The parties could agree to the amount of money the seller will pay the buyer if he does not deliver:
  - the goods on time, or
  - goods of appropriate quality.

- The parties could agree to the amount of money the buyer will pay the seller if the buyer breaches the contract.

- The parties could agree to other financial terms such as:
  - whether the buyer must pay interest if he pays the seller late, and
  - if so, what the interest rate will be.

Changing and canceling the contract

- The parties must agree on whether they may:
  - change the contract, or
  - cancel the contract.

- If the parties may change or cancel the contract, then they must agree on how they may do so. They may, for example, require that all changes and notices of cancellation be in writing.

Length of agreement

The parties may agree not only how much is sold, but also if the buyer may purchase more goods at the same price. In effect, this would give the buyer the right to renew the contract.

Corporate approval

Often a subsidiary or low ranking official must obtain approval of higher ranking corporate officials. If this is the case, then before shipping the goods the seller must be sure that the buyer has obtained the appropriate approval from the appropriate officials. The seller should be sure that the appropriate official has given his approvals in writing.

Sample to be approved

Parties sometimes agree that the buyer will first forward a sample of his goods, and the buyer has not accepted the offer until it acknowledges that the sample is acceptable.

State of lawsuit

- The parties must choose a state in which they will conduct any lawsuit. The buyer and seller will each prefer the state it knows best.

- The parties may also agree to:
  - arbitration, and
  - meditation.

8. WARRANTIES AND FRAUD
The promises you make

8. WARRANTIES AND FRAUD
The promises you make

(i) Warranties

(a) Introduction

The law calls the guarantee a seller makes to a buyer a warranty. Some warranties are explicit, affirmative statements which sellers make to buyers. Other warranties are implicit, implied by law. The seller can disclaim these implied warranties, but, if he does so, his disclaimer must be very clear. If the parties do not discuss warranties, then the law will assume that the seller gave the implied warranties to the buyer.

(b) Unstated promises (implied warranties)

The implied warranties

Title

When one sells something he implicitly promises that he owns what he is selling.

Not used as collateral

When selling a product a seller also implicitly promises that he has not used the product as collateral for a loan, or for a similar purpose. The seller promises that no other person has an ownership interest in the product, and that no one can repossess the product.

Patents and trademarks

Those who sell products as part of their regular business implicitly promise that what they sell does not infringe any third party's patent or trademark rights.

Seller must be in business

The law does not impose this warranty on all sellers. It imposes the warranty only on sellers who are in the business of selling the relevant product.

Packaging

Sellers implicitly promise that they have adequately packaged and labelled their products.

Seller must be in business

The law also does not impose this warranty on all sellers. It again imposes the warranty only on sellers who are in the business of selling the relevant product.

Adequate quality

Sellers promise that their products are of adequate quality. A seller does not have to sell the best possible product but a firm which is in the business of selling a particular product cannot sell a product which does not work at all. In other words, while the law does not require the seller to sell the best product, it cannot sell junk.

The law uses two different terms to describe the level of quality it requires:

- "fair adequate quality," and

- "fit for ordinary purposes for which such goods are used."

These two terms mean what they say. "Adequate quality" means just that, and not top quality. For example, one court found that fish soup containing some bones was nevertheless of adequate quality.

"Ordinary purposes" means the uses to which most consumers would ordinarily put a product. The seller must make products which consumers can use for these ordinary purposes.

Seller must be in business

The law also does not impose this warranty on all sellers. It only imposes the warranty on sellers who are in the business of selling the product.

Fit for a particular purpose

Through this warranty the law holds sellers to the specific promises they make to specific buyers. If a seller made a specific promise to a specific buyer, the law will probably hold the seller to its promise. One could call this a warranty for a special purpose, in contrast to an ordinary purpose.

Courts will find that the seller gave a warranty for a particular purpose if:

- given the context of the transaction, the specific purpose to which the buyer would put the product was clear to the seller,
- the buyer believed that the seller was an expert, and
- the buyer relied on the seller's expertise.

Avoid being seen as an expert

A seller may be able to take steps to limit the chances that a court will see it as an expert. For example, if a seller's advertising or stationery highlights the seller's expertise, then the seller should disclaim the warranty for a particular purpose in its invoice, standard contract, or similar document.

History of dealings

To determine whether the buyer relied on the seller's advice, courts look at the entire context of the transaction. Courts, in particular, look at the parties' business relationship and the history of their dealings together. Thus a seller should be careful when developing a relationship and pattern of doing business with a buyer. If a customer once relied on a seller's recommendation regarding one product, then this may establish that the buyer believes the seller is an expert.

Applies to all sellers

In contrast to the warranty of adequate quality, the law imposes the warranty for a particular purpose on all sellers, not just those in business. In other words, the law holds all sellers to their word.

Put warranties in writing

If a seller is aware of the particular needs of a particular buyer, and recommends a product, then it may have given the buyer a warranty of fitness for a particular purpose without intending to do so. To be safe, a seller should state, in writing, that it is either providing no such warranty, or if it is, precisely what it is promising. Because courts tend to favor unsophisticated buyers, a seller dealing with an unsophisticated buyer should be particularly careful to put in writing either the appropriate disclaimer or whatever warranty it may be giving the buyer.

Disclaiming implied warranties

Disclaim explicitly

Sellers can sell products "as is." Sellers can disclaim implied warranties and thereby sell products without making any promise whatsoever about the ability of the product. While sellers can disclaim warranties, the law requires that they do so explicitly and conspicuously.

Courts require a very conspicuous disclaimer. Courts want to ensure that the buyer knows that the seller is disclaiming the implied warranties the buyer usually receives. Since in this context courts tend to favor the buyer, a seller disclaiming an implied warranty must be sure that a sceptical court will enforce the disclaimer. He must therefore make the disclaimer truly conspicuous. For example, sellers often print disclaimers in capital letters and bold print.

To disclaim the warranty of general product quality ("fair adequate quality," "ordinary purpose") the seller must use the word "merchantability" in his disclaimer. The law imposes this obligation on sellers because the law's technical term for this warranty is the "warranty of merchantability." The law wants to ensure that buyers realize that sellers are not offering them the warranty of merchantability.

Disclaim through inspection

If a seller gives the buyer the opportunity to examine its goods, or a sample of the goods, then the seller has in effect disclaimed any warranty that the goods are in any way different from what the buyer would learn if it inspected the goods. In other words, if the buyer can examine the goods before buying, then it must. It will then know what it is getting, and cannot expect more.

Business practice as disclaimer

Patterns of business activity can also disclaim implied warranties. Just as a court will look at the parties' relationship to see if the buyer believed that the seller was an expert, so too will it look at the parties' relationship to see if the seller has disclaimed the implied warranties. If the seller has disclaimed warranties during the parties' past business transactions, then, unless the parties agreed otherwise while conducting a later transaction, a court will apply the terms of the previous transactions to the later transaction. It will therefore find that the seller disclaimed the implied warranties. See Contracting, Chapter 7.

Limits on right to disclaim

The law imposes the following restrictions on the seller's right to disclaim warranties.

- If the parties signed a contract, then if the seller is to disclaim the warranty it must include the disclaimer in the contract.

- Courts may choose not to enforce a disclaimer. Courts tend to favour unsophisticated buyers. A court may therefore decide that:
  – the disclaimer was not sufficiently conspicuous, or
  – it would be unfair to enforce the disclaimer against the buyer. (The court would find the disclaimer "unconscionable.")

- The federal Magnuson-Moss Warranty Act further limits sellers' rights to disclaim warranties made to consumers. For example, if a seller provides any warranty to the consumer, then it may not disclaim the implied warranties. This Act applies only to retail firms selling to consumers.

Disclaimers and bargaining leverage

A seller should disclaim all implied warranties which it appropriately can. Should the seller have a dispute with the buyer after selling the product, the disclaimer will give the seller bargaining leverage during the inevitable lawsuit settlement negotiations.

Warranties and consumers

Historically, the law did not allow consumers to sue manufacturers for breach of warranty. Manufacturers usually sell to intermediaries such as distributors or wholesalers who in turn sell to retail stores, who sell to consumers. Consumers do not buy directly from manufacturers and manufacturers therefore make no promises directly to consumers.

Nevertheless, over the last several years courts have expanded manufacturers' liability. In many states consumers can now bring breach of warranty actions against manufacturers. States also developed strict products liability law to allow injured consumers to sue manufacturers directly. See Strict products liability, Chapter 6 (iii).

(c)   Explicit promises (express warranties)

Not required

The law does not require a seller to promise explicitly that its product
has particular features. But if a seller does make such an explicit promise,
then the law will hold the seller to his promise. An express warranty
is very similar to a warranty for a particular purpose. In both cases a
seller makes a promise to a buyer, and in both cases a court will hold the
seller liable if the product cannot do what the seller promised.

One important difference between express and implied warranties,
however, is that a court will, without doubt, allow a consumer to sue a
manufacturer for breach of an express warranty.

Samples and descriptions

A seller showing a sample of his product, or giving a description of his
goods, can create an express warranty. If a seller shows a sample, for
example, then courts will expect all the seller's goods to be the same as
the sample. Thus sellers must be careful – either they should make sure
that all their goods match their samples, or they should tell buyers the
extent to which their goods do not match their samples.

Writings

If the seller puts his promise in writing, then a court will hold the seller
to the exact wording of his promise. The court will look at the wording of
the promise, not the seller's intent when signing the document containing
the promise. Thus, if a seller does offer its buyers an express warranty, it
should put the warranty in writing. In this way it will be sure of the terms
to which a court will hold it.

The Magnuson-Moss Act regulates express warranties sellers make
to consumers. Its most important feature is that it defines "full" and
"limited" warranties and requires sellers to offer consumers one of these
two defined warranties.

Advertising and sales claims

A seller's advertising and sales claims can create express warranties. The law calls common sales techniques, such as expressing a positive opinion of a product, "puffing." This "puffing" does not create a warranty.

In theory a sales representative expressing an opinion is merely "puffing" while one stating a fact is creating an express warranty. In practice the courts cannot always distinguish between opinion and fact. Since a court may find that the seller made an express warranty even if it did not use words such as "warranty" or "guarantee," sellers should always be very careful not to inadvertently create an express warranty.

Write down sales talk

For example, unless they do in fact intend to create a warranty, sellers should include in their standard sales talk a statement that they are not creating a warranty. Sellers should write down their standard sales talk. Thus, if they have to, they will be able to prove that their sales representatives do not make statements which create express warranties.

Further, if the seller does intend to create a warranty, then the seller should be just as sure that it writes down its standard sales talk. In this way it will be able to prove to a court what it did promise, and what it did not promise.

(d) Compensation for failing to satisfy warranty

Pay costs to repair or replace

If the seller's goods do not satisfy the seller's warranty, then the seller has not provided the goods the contract requires. The seller has sold inadequate goods and has breached its contract. A court will hold it liable according to the general rules for paying compensation for breach of contract.

A court will order the seller to reimburse the buyer for the costs of the breach. The buyer may, for example, have bought replacement goods, or may have paid someone to repair the inadequate goods. A court will hold the seller liable for these costs. A court may also order the seller to pay other costs, so long as the seller could foresee that its failure to satisfy its warranty would force the buyer to incur these costs. Thus, in one case, a driver parked a car in a garage. Inadequate wiring in the car caused the house to catch fire. A court held the seller liable for burning the house down. See Contracting, Chapter 7.

Seller limits its liability to replacing defective goods

Sellers often limit their liability, for example, simply to replacing defective goods. In some circumstances courts enforce such limitations. In other cases, particularly those involving unsophisticated buyers, courts will find such limitations unfair, and refuse to enforce them.

Limitations, like disclaimers, give sellers bargaining leverage during lawsuit settlement negotiations. Thus, sellers should try to include in their warranties a term limiting their liability should they breach the warranty.

(ii)   Fraud and misrepresentation

(a)   Fraud

Those who commit fraud pay punitive damages

Television and newspapers, at times, pay a great deal of attention to cases in which one party, alleges or proves fraud. Courts order those who commit fraud to pay punitive damages. Courts usually set punitive damages at twice the other costs which the court has ordered the liable party to pay. Thus courts usually order parties who commit fraud to pay, in total, three times the wronged party's losses. Thus, at times, courts order those who commit fraud to pay quite a considerable sum. These considerable sums, at times, attract great media interest.

Because proving fraud can be lucrative, it is hard to do

Because proving fraud can be lucrative the law makes it difficult to do so. To prove fraud the wronged party must prove that the accused's acts satisfy each of the seven requirements of fraud. While parties can often prove three or four of these requirements, they usually have great difficulty proving all seven.

The seven requirements of fraud are as follows.

1. Making a false statement. The defendant must have stated something to the wronged party, and this statement must have been false.

2. Knowing the statement was false. The defendant must have made this misrepresentation knowingly. In other words, the defendant either:
    - knew the statement was false, or
    - knew it may be false, and did not bother to learn the truth. The law calls this "utter disregard for the facts".

3. Regarding a fact. The defendant's misrepresentation had to be of a fact. The law considers statements of opinion or statements about future events to be too unsure to be facts.
    - The law has one exception to this rule, however. The law considers the opinion of an expert to be as sure as a fact. Thus, if an expert expresses his opinion, then the law will treat this as a fact.

4. When the fact is material, or important. The misrepresentation must have been about an important fact.

5. Said with the intent to cause reliance. The accused had to make his misrepresentation with the intent that the wronged party would rely on the false statement. A mere idle comment will not satisfy this requirement.
    - Parties find it particularly difficult to prove the accused's intent. Divining intent is always subjective and difficult. Given the severe penalties for committing fraud, courts usually only find fraudulent intent when the evidence is clear.

6. The wronged party had to rely on the false statement. The wronged party must have actually relied on the false statement.

7. The wronged party's reliance on the false statement had to be justified. The wronged party's decision to rely on the accused's false statement must have been reasonable. Courts, for example, expect managers to act with common sense and appropriate scepticism, and not to naively believe every claim they hear.
    - On the other hand, if the accused has taken active steps to conceal evidence, then a court is more likely to find fraud.

Lawsuit tactics

For tactical reasons, lawyers representing someone with another type of claim not infrequently include a fraud claim in their lawsuit. These lawyers believe that the fraud claim will increase their bargaining leverage during future lawsuit settlement negotiations.

These lawyers run two risks. First, a lawyer who includes a weak claim in his lawsuit may make all his claims look weak, including his strong claims. A court may therefore discount all his clients claims, and the other party, knowing this, may actually offer less money to settle, not more. Secondly, if the attorney makes a claim against another in bad faith, then a court may impose sanctions and penalties on the attorney. See Court system: lawsuits and arbitration, Chapter 9.

(b) Negligent and faultless (strict liability) misrepresentation

Accused made a mistake

Wronged parties alleging negligent misrepresentation claim that the accused made a false statement, but did so without intending to cause harm to the plaintiff. The accused was simply negligent, says the wronged party, and a court should hold the accused liable for the mistake the accused made. The wronged party is therefore basing his claim on the general law of negligence, which holds everyone liable for the costs of their mistakes. Regarding negligence law generally, see Strict products liability, Chapter 6 (iii).

To prove negligent misrepresentation the wronged party must prove all the requirements of fraud, but one. Instead of proving that the accused knew his statement was false, the wronged party must prove that the accused made his false statement because he acted unreasonably. In other words, the accused made his statement with negligent disregard for the facts.

Negligence v. utter disregard for the facts

In many cases courts have difficulty deciding if an accused has acted with utter disregard for the facts, or merely with unreasonable, or negligent, disregard for the facts. For example, if a corporation's president announced that his firm had earned $500,000.00 in profits last year, when in fact he did not know the true figure, and did not bother to look at his firm's records, then he would have acted with utter disregard for the facts. If he had looked at the accounts, however, but they were inaccurate because he had acted unreasonably when hiring a clearly incompetent accounting firm, then a court would probably find that he had acted with negligent disregard for the facts.

Compensation

Those who violate an express warranty and those who make a negli-gent misrepresentation of fact have committed very similar acts. Courts will accordingly order both to pay the costs the wronged party incurred because these parties acted improperly. A court will not, however, order a party who negligently misrepresented a fact to pay punitive damages.

9. Court system: lawsuits and arbitration

9. Court system: lawsuits and arbitration

(i) Introduction

(a) The parties do battle, which is expensive

The American legal system is adversarial. Like other common law systems, it is based on the belief that if the two parties do battle, then the truth will emerge from the fight. The American judge regulates this battle. He supervises not only the trial, but also the pre-trial process in which both parties gather information and prepare themselves for the coming battle at trial.

Doing battle is expensive. Arming oneself with information is expensive. Therefore, after each party's attorney has obtained enough information to evaluate his and his opponent's case, and after a few legal bills have calmed the parties' emotions and focused their attention on costs, the parties usually settle.

Business lawsuits in the United States are exploding. The common impression that personal injury, and particularly product liability, claims are driving the American lawsuit explosion is not accurate. Business lawsuits are driving the explosion. Businesses are more likely than ever to sue each other. Those firms choosing to do business in the United States should expect to sue or be sued at one time or another. Lawsuit expenses are a cost of doing business in the US.

To keep these costs down, more and more managers are turning to arbitration. Filings in the main arbitration service, the American Arbitration Association, are increasing steadily. As discussed below, with the court systems becoming increasingly clogged, arbitration is indeed an attractive alternative.

(ii) The structure of the court system

(a) Introduction

Federal and state systems have equal authority

The United States has many parallel court systems: the system of the federal government and the system of each state government. In general, the federal system does not have more authority than the state systems. Federal courts simply hear cases involving federal law, such as federal securities law. State courts hear cases involving state law, such as the UCC. Federal courts will, however, at times hear cases involving state law. As described below, a federal court will at times hear a state law case.

Trial courts

Both the federal and state systems have essentially the same structure. The lowest level general authority court is the trial level court. Naturally enough, this court hears trials. The federal system calls its trial level court the District Court, and states typically call it the District or Superior Court. Each trial court has authority over only a limited geographical area. The trial level court supervises the pre-trial process of exchanging information which this chapter discusses in greater detail below.

Appeal

The party losing at trial always has the right to appeal the court's decision. His first appeal is to a court which the federal system, and most state systems, call the Court of Appeals. This is an intermediate level court, above the trial court but below the highest court in the system.

The federal system, and most state systems, call their highest level court the Supreme Court. Parties do not have a right to have a Supreme Court hear their appeal. Each Supreme Court decides for itself which cases it will hear. These high courts hear cases which will allow them to rule on the great social and legal issues of the day. They will not hear a case merely because a lower court decided it incorrectly. Since few cases involve great social issues, few cases reach a Supreme Court.

Inferior and specialized courts

Most state systems, but not the federal system, have courts below the general authority trial level court. These are city courts, small claims courts, traffic courts, landlord and tenant courts, etc. They hear minor cases, sometimes of only a specific type. A party losing in one of these courts must usually first take his appeal to the general authority trial level court.

Most state systems, and the federal system, have courts which have the same authority as the general authority trial level court but which only hear cases relating to one type of claim. For example, most state systems have a court specializing in wills or family matters. The federal system has the Court of International Trade. An appeal from one of these courts is usually first to the intermediate level Court of Appeals.

Terminology: plaintiff and defendant

A final note about terminology. In a lawsuit, the party making the claim, the one complaining, is the plaintiff. The party defending his actions is the defendant.

(b)   Choosing between state and federal court

At times, a federal court can hear a state law claim

Most lawsuits involve state, not federal, law. For example, most of the areas of law discussed in this book, such as contracts and product liability, are areas of state law. Since state courts usually decided matters of state law, state courts decide most lawsuits.

In some cases, however, a federal court may hear a state law claim. It may do so if:

- the amount in dispute is at least $50,000.00, and

- the parties are from different states.

The law considers a non-American to be from a different state than that of any American. Thus, federal courts may hear a dispute between a non-American and an American citizen. The law considers corporations to be residents of both the state in which they are incorporated and the state in which they have their major production or service facility. Thus a federal court cannot hear a case between a corporation and a person residing in either the corporation's state of incorporation or the state in which it has its major facility.

Practical differences between state and federal court

In theory, it should not matter whether a federal or state court hears a particular case. A federal court must still apply the relevant state law and so in theory would reach the same decision as would a state court.

In the real world whether a federal or state court hears a case can make a great deal of difference. Most observers believe the federal and state systems differ in the following ways.

- Federal courts are faster.
  - This is to be expected, since state courts decide most lawsuits.
  - As is discussed in greater detail below, in general plaintiffs prefer speed and defendants prefer delay.
- Some attorneys feel that federal court judges have a better appreciation of the law.
- Federal courts may be more neutral.
  - Out-of-state parties often fear that a state court will favor a party from its state. Sometimes this fear is justified.

(iii)   The reach of courts outside their state (long-arm jurisdiction)

(a)   Defendant must take a purposeful act

In some cases a federal or state court will have the authority to order an out of state defendant to come to the court to stand trial. For the court to have this authority, the defendant must have taken, as the law calls it, a "purposeful" act. This is an act which should lead him to anticipate that he may be sued in that state.

For example, in one case a court said that a car dealer should not anticipate that selling a car in New York would lead it to being sued in Oklahoma. By contrast, if a party enters into a contract which will require regular contacts with a particular state, he should anticipate being sued in that state. In this area, as in many others, courts do what they think is fair and fairness varies from case to case.

(b)   For the sake of convenience, a court may decline to hear a case

Even if a court could order a defendant to come to the court to stand trial, it may choose not to do so. A court may decide that a trial before it would be too inconvenient, to either the defendant or to possible witnesses.

Typically, a court will decline to hear a case if another court could more easily hold the trial. To decide whether it should hold the trial, a court will consider all the practical aspects of the lawsuit, such as the defendant's convenience, the witnesses' convenience, the location of evidence, and so on. These considerations of ease and convenience are usually particularly relevant to cases involving non-Americans.

A court would only decline to hear a case, for the sake of convenience, if another court would hear the case. A court will not decline to hear a case which it could hear if doing so would leave the plaintiff with no place to press his claim. Thus, to persuade a court to decline to hear a case, a defendant may have to agree not to challenge the authority of another court to hear that case. This other court could be outside the United States.

(c) A defendant can usually be sued in a state in which he owns property

If a party owns land in a state, then he should probably anticipate being sued in that state. A court clearly has the authority to determine ownership of land located within its state. However, even if the dispute does not involve the land directly, the simple fact that the defendant owns land in the state will usually give the defendant enough contacts with the state for him to be sued in that state.

Regarding property other than land, a court cannot order a defendant to stand trial simply because he owns personal property within the state. However, as with land, if a defendant owns personal property within a state, then he usually also has sufficient contacts with the state that he should anticipate being sued there. This is particularly true if the personal property is related to the dispute.

Enter state only to deny court's authority

A defendant may object to a plaintiff's argument that the courts of a particular state have the power to order him to come to that state to stand trial. A defendant making such an objection must be very careful. If he rushes into the state to defend himself he may inadvertently admit that the court has the very authority he wants to claim it does not have.

Instead of rushing into the state, the defendant should first apply to make a "special appearance." This special appearance gives him the right to come to the state simply to argue that the court cannot order him to come to the court to stand trial. If the defendant does not make a special appearance, then the court will consider his act of coming to the state to defend himself as acknowledging that the court has the authority to order him to come to the state–he would be admitting the very point he intends to challenge.

To avoid inadvertently admitting that the court has authority over him, a defendant should never respond–in any way–to a complaint (the document which begins a lawsuit, see below). He should always contact his attorney.

(iv)   The lawsuit process

(a)   Starting the lawsuit

Serving the complaint begins the lawsuit

A lawsuit begins when the plaintiff delivers the "complaint" to the defendant. The complaint is the fundamental document of the lawsuit. In it the plaintiff lays out his entire claim. He lists each separate act of the defendant which, he believes, leads to the defendant's liability. In the complaint the plaintiff lists each legal theory under which he believes the defendant is liable. These legal theories may be inconsistent among themselves and the complaint may contain many different claims. The complaint can therefore be quite long and complex.

To begin the lawsuit the plaintiff must give the complaint to the defendant. He must "serve" the complaint, as the law puts it. In the movies defendants dramatically, or comically, try to avoid receiving the complaint, as if running away will protect them. But few defendants can avoid lawsuits by simply running away.

Plaintiffs can easily serve complaints on corporate defendants. When granting a corporation permission to do business in the state, all states require the corporation to either identify an office where a plaintiff may serve a complaint on it or authorize the state to receive the complaint on its behalf. In either case, a plaintiff will thereafter be able to easily serve a complaint on a corporate defendant.

Regarding individuals, the law prefers that the plaintiff hands the complaint to the defendant. If this were not possible, perhaps because the defendant ran away, then the plaintiff may use one of several alternative means of service. While the rules of each state differ, in general, the plaintiff can hand the complaint to someone else living in the defendant's home, can leave it in the defendant's home or mailbox, or can leave it at the defendant's place of work. Firms specializing in serving complaints know the rules of their state. In the end few defendants successfully avoid service.

Parties can change rules of service

The parties can agree to change the rules of service. In their contract they can agree to alternative methods by which one party may serve a complaint on the other. Under these alternative methods of service the defendant is usually less likely to actually receive the complaint. Therefore, when entering into a contract, one should be very careful not to sign away one's right to have the other party serve a complaint in a manner by which one is likely to actually receive it.

The defendant responds in the answer

The defendant responds to the complaint in his "answer". In the answer the defendant admits or denies that he committed each of the specific acts which the complaint alleges. Thus, by comparing the complaint and the answer one can easily see the points on which the parties agree, and the points on which they disagree. Together, therefore, the complaint and the answer make the issues of the lawsuit very clear.

In the answer the defendant may also lay out "affirmative defenses." These are "yes, but..." claims. In essence, the defendant says: "Yes, what you say is true, but I am still not liable because...(for example, the plaintiff waited too long before beginning the lawsuit)." Even though it may seem contradictory, a defendant can both deny a claim, and present an affirmation defense.

The defendant may also make claims against the plaintiff

In his answer the defendant may also make claims against the plaintiff. The law calls these counterclaims. The counterclaim section of an answer looks like what it really is, a complaint. In this section the defendant lays out the specific acts which, he claims, lead to the plaintiff's liability. Counterclaims may relate to the plaintiff's original claim, or they may present entirely new claims.

The plaintiff must respond to any counterclaims the defendant may make. He does so in a "response." A response has the same function as an answer, and, perhaps unsurprisingly, looks like an answer.

DOING BUSINESS IN THE US

(b) Freezing the defendant's assets

Almost all plaintiffs wish to freeze the defendant's assets – film-makers love to show the plaintiff trying to doing so. In the movies the plaintiff will run to the courthouse and demand an emergency court order forbidding the defendant from taking his money out of the state. The plaintiff will claim that if the defendant can move his money, he will take it and run from the state and thereafter ignore the court's orders, including its future order that the defendant pay the plaintiff.

The plaintiff's true motivation is usually much more practical and immediate. If the plaintiff is successful, then the defendant will lose use of what may be a considerable sum of money. Thus, as soon as the plaintiff wins, the defendant will usually enter into serious settlement negotiations.

When employing this tactic, however, the plaintiff both runs a risk and is sure to incur an additional expense. He runs a risk because if he eventually loses the underlying lawsuit, a court may order him to pay the costs the defendant incurred because the defendant could not use his money. Of course, if the parties settle, then the plaintiff will have avoided this risk.

The plaintiff will incur an additional expense because a court will not freeze the defendant's assets until the plaintiff posts a bond. A bond is an obligation to pay money if a certain event occurs. Before freezing the defendant's assets a court will want to be sure that if the defendant does win the underlying lawsuit and, if the court does order the plaintiff to reimburse the defendant, then the plaintiff will have enough money to make the payment. By requiring the plaintiff to post the appropriate bond, the court will be sure that the plaintiff will make any future payment it may order. A bond firm will post this bond for the plaintiff, naturally for a fee.

If the court does freeze the defendant's assets, it will immediately thereafter hold a hearing to decide if it should keep the assets frozen. At this hearing the defendant will argue that the court should not freeze his assets because to do so would cause him great hardship, that he would pay any court award and that, in any case, he will win the underlying lawsuit. The court will then decide.

(c) How parties exchange information

Broad standard

After the complaint and answer have outlined the issues of the lawsuit, the parties can begin to exchange information relevant to these issues. The law requires this exchange of information so the parties can prepare for trial. Hopefully, this exchange will also highlight areas of agreement and thereby narrow the issues in dispute.

Exchanging information is more than exchanging evidence. Each party must provide the other not only with evidence but also with information which *may lead* to relevant evidence. This is a very broad standard: the information each party must provide need not itself be evidence, nor must the information be certain to lead to relevant evidence, nor must it even be likely to lead to relevant evidence. If the information merely *may possibly lead* to evidence, then a party must provide it. For example, an internal memorandum of a corporate defendant may not by itself be relevant, but it *may* mention another document, or contain a statement, or explain an aspect of the party's business, which *may* help the plaintiff learn of additional evidence. The defendant must give this memorandum to the plaintiff. The parties therefore typically exchange quite a lot of information.

The standard is broad because the law believes that both sides should be fully prepared for trial. They should have all relevant information, so they can track down all relevant evidence. They should be fully armed for the coming clash of ideas, the battle, which is the trial. The law believes that from this battle of ideas the truth will emerge.

Because the process is expensive parties often settle

This extensive information exchange process is time consuming and therefore expensive. Rather than face mounting legal bills, during the information exchange process parties involved in a business dispute almost invariably settle. The parties usually settle after their attorneys have gathered sufficient evidence so they can evaluate the strengths and weaknesses of each party's case. They may settle sooner if, for example, one party does not want to reveal confidential information or trade secrets.

As discussed below, one important advantage of arbitration is that it limits the amount of information the parties must exchange, and therefore cuts the time and cost of resolving a dispute. But these savings come with a cost–the parties may be unprepared for their arbitration trial. See Arbitration and mediation, Section (vi).

Ways of exchanging information

Parties exchange information in the following ways.

Testimony of potential witnesses (depositions)

At a deposition, each party will question the other party's witnesses, including the other party himself. Further, just as at trial, each witness must answer deposition questions "under oath." Under oath means that if the person testifying knowingly lies, then he would be committing perjury. While prosecutors rarely seek jail sentences for witnesses who perjure themselves, they sometimes do. Perjury can be a serious felony. Most deposition witnesses, aware of the risk of criminal prosecution, therefore tell the truth–or at least some shade of it.

Depositions therefore usually provide valuable information and evidence. This is particularly true because attorneys usually take depositions after they have served interrogatories and examined the appropriate documents (see below). Each attorney can therefore ask the deposition witness to explain various facts and circumstances of the case, including any relevant documents. At a deposition an attorney can evaluate the demeanor, confidence, and credibility of each witness. Therefore, after the attorneys have taken the depositions of all potential witnesses, they usually have a good appreciation of the strengths and weaknesses of both sides of a case.

A lawyer will be reluctant to evaluate a case before taking depositions. Quite rightly, a lawyer will hesitate to base his opinion and legal strategy solely on his client's version of events. Sometimes clients do not know important facts. Often clients do not appreciate the legal significance of events or statements. Clients usually can not evaluate the credibility of potential witnesses. Sometimes clients fail to tell their lawyer all they know – and clients are always emotionally involved in their case.

Along with being informative, depositions are also time consuming. A single deposition can easily take one or several days. Attorneys for both the plaintiff and the defendant must be present at all depositions, no matter which party is actually conducting the deposition. Furthermore, before he takes a deposition an attorney must prepare his questions and this alone could take a full day. All this time consuming work increases the parties' legal bills.

Thus, after the parties' attorneys have taken their depositions both parties are usually ready to enter into serious settlement negotiations. The attorneys will have seen enough evidence and the parties will have seen enough legal bills.

Lawyers usually conduct depositions in a law office, not the court-house. A court reporter will record the deposition testimony and will later provide a transcript to the parties.

Written questions

Each party can ask potential witnesses written questions by using either:

- deposition upon written questions

- interrogatories.

Attorneys usually do not find the answers to written questions very helpful. An attorney must send the questions to the opposing witness long before the witness must answer the questions. This large time interval allows the opposing attorney, rather than the witness himself, to actually answer the questions. Attorneys can artfully answer questions so they either fail to reveal relevant information, create a false impression, or do both. Further, written questions lack spontaneity: the attorney asking the question cannot pose follow-up questions or evaluate the witness' demeanor and credibility.

Attorneys tend to use interrogatories at the beginning of a lawsuit, but tend not to use depositions upon written questions. An attorney can easily draft interrogatory questions, and the answers may help him begin to prepare his case. They can help him develop an initial impression of a case, learn of documents he should request, and prepare for depositions. Attorneys therefore tend to use interrogatories to begin the information exchange process.

On the other hand, attorneys rarely take depositions upon written questions. They almost always take depositions upon oral questions instead. In fact, they take this type of deposition so frequently that they call it simply "the deposition".

Requests for documents and objects

Document requests are usually crucial to commercial lawsuits. Recall that each party must give the other not only relevant evidence but also information which may lead to relevant evidence. Documents, particularly company documents, often contain a significant amount of evidence and even more information which may lead to evidence. In the typical com-mercial lawsuit, therefore, the parties exchange quite a large number of documents.

A party may make a document request at any time during the evidence gathering process. Thus as each attorney learns more and more about a case he is likely to make more and more document requests. In fact these repeated document requests are one reason why lawsuits are so time consuming.

In business disputes objects are usually not relevant. Objects relevant to lawsuits are usually cars and similar items relevant to accident cases. However, if in a particular business case an object should be relevant, then the party who has it will have to show it to the other party.

(d) Delays

Typically caused by the defendant

Defendants often try to slow the lawsuit process. The defendant is typically not at all anxious for the court to hold the trial – at the trial it is he who the court may find liable. Thus, for most defendants the next best thing to winning the trial is avoiding the trial. Further, defendants sometimes reason that if they make the lawsuit process as slow and expensive as possible, then the plaintiff will either drop the lawsuit or accept a low settlement offer. This is particularly true if the plaintiff cannot afford to finance his lawsuit.

Object to document request

To delay the lawsuit a defendant will often object to a plaintiff's document request. While the standard for exchanging information is quite broad, it does impose some limits. The requested information must at least arguably lead to relevant evidence. A party requesting a document must have some rationale for requesting that particular document. He cannot simply say "give me all relevant evidence." As the cliché says, a party cannot go on a "fishing expedition."

A defendant will therefore typically claim that the plaintiff has no rationale for requesting a particular document, that he is on the proverbial fishing expedition. At this point a court will intervene in the process for the first time. It will hold a hearing to decide if the defendant must comply with the plaintiff's document request. The plaintiff must of course wait for this hearing, and may also have to wait for the court's decision. Some courts are rather slow to render decisions. The defendant's objection could drag the lawsuit out for quite some time.

To further delay the lawsuit, and increase the plaintiff's costs, defendants also supply the plaintiff with an excess number of documents. The plaintiff's attorney will therefore have to spend an excessive amount of time analyzing all these documents. Furthermore, buried in all this paper, the plaintiff's attorney may miss a vitally important piece of evidence.

Unintentional delays

Not only some defendants' purposeful acts but also honest practical problems delay lawsuits. Parties sometimes have honest difficulty locating documents. Scheduling conflicts among attorneys and witnesses are rampant. For example, even after all the attorneys and witnesses have set a date for, say, a deposition, very often one asks to reschedule, and the next mutually convenient date may be several months away. Thus even a simple lawsuit can drag on for years.

Courts trying to solve problem

Courts are trying to quicken the lawsuit process but often have great difficulty doing so. Courts find it difficult to write clear rules which stop defendants' abuse without also stopping legitimate claims. A defendant may, for example, quite legitimately oppose the plaintiff's document request. Because courts can not write clear rules limiting defendants acting, they tend to write vague rules. And these vague rules tend to lead to more hearings and more court decisions–in other words to more courtroom activity, not less.

Encourage settlement

Courts are generally best able to speed lawsuits not by trying to stop abuse but by helping the parties settle. Courts therefore often encourage the parties to settle. For example, a judge may call a hearing to resolve outstanding issues regarding the exchange of information but at this hearing he may also act as an informal mediator, pushing the parties to settle. In fact, judges are often successful mediators because attorneys are often afraid that if their client does not accept what the judge believes is a reasonable settlement offer, then the judge will remember this when making a crucial ruling at trial.

(e)   Court determination without trial

Not only is the pre-trial exchange of information process slow and expensive but, as is discussed below, so too is the trial itself. Therefore, if a judge could decide a case without holding a trial, he would certainly speed-up the lawsuit and make it less expensive. In fact, the mere possibility that the judge may either find the defendant liable or dismiss the case without holding a trial will have a great impact on the parties' settlement negotiations.

In the following two situations a judge could decide the case himself. He would not need a jury, and would therefore not need to hold a trial.

Parties agree what happened

If the parties agree about the events which lead to their dispute, but disagree only about the legal consequences of these events, then a judge could resolve the dispute. As is discussed in greater detail below, at trial the judge interprets the law and the jury determines what happened. If the parties agree about what happened, then there will be nothing for a jury to do. The judge himself, when interpreting the law, could determine the legal consequences of what happened. Thus the judge could decide the case and there would be no need to form a jury or hold a trial.

Court assumes party's claims are true

A court could dismiss a party's claims even if the parties do not agree about the events which lead to their dispute. A court could instead assume for the sake of argument that a party's version of events is true. The court could then go on to say that even if the party's version of the events is true, that party still loses the lawsuit. A court could say, for example, that even if the defendant did what the plaintiff claims, the law will still not hold the defendant liable. The court would then dismiss the plaintiff's claim without holding a trial.

A party lacks supporting evidence

If, after the parties have had the opportunity to gather all their evidence, one party lacks evidence to support his version of events, then a judge will rule in favor of the other party. The judge will reason that, without sufficient evidence, a jury could not possibly find for that party, and a judge will therefore dismiss his claims without holding a trial.

(e) The trial

The judge and jury

As all Americans are quick to point out, everyone in the United States has the right to a trial by jury. Jurors are ordinary citizens who live in the trial court's district. At one time or another their local court will call almost all Americans to jury duty, at which time they will come to the courthouse and sit among the pool of potential jurors. From this pool either the judge or the attorneys, depending on the court system, select actual jurors.

As mentioned above, the judge and the jury have very different roles. The jury's job is to determine what happened, to "find the facts," as the law puts it. The jury will determine, for example, whether a party entered into a contract with fraudulent intent. The judge, on the other hand, finds, or interprets, the law for the jury. The judge would, for example, tell the jury the legal requirements of fraud.

The parties can agree that a judge rather than a jury will hear a case. Sometimes, perhaps because the case is complex, both parties prefer that a judge hears the case. Usually, however, at least one party insists on its right to a trial by jury.

In commercial cases, unlike criminal cases, the size of juries varies among the states. Some states use 12 jurors, but some use fewer. Also, unlike criminal cases, in civil cases many states do not require that all jurors agree on the verdict. These states usually require that only two-thirds or three-quarters of the jurors agree.

The trial process

Trials begin, just as they do on television, with opening statements. In his opening statement each party's attorney will tell the jury what evidence he will present, and why this evidence proves that his client should win. The plaintiff then begins the main part of the trial by presenting his evidence. He will call witnesses and show the jury relevant documents. The defendant can challenge this evidence by, for example, questioning the admissibility of the evidence (see below) and cross-examining the plaintiff's witnesses.

After the plaintiff has presented his evidence, the defendant will present his evidence. The plaintiff will naturally challenge the defendant's evidence. Finally, each attorney will make his closing arguments to the jury, in which he summarizes his case and again explains why his client should win.

After each party has made his closing arguments, the judge will tell the jury the relevant law. For example, in a case regarding the delivery of goods, the judge may tell the jury the relevant UCC rule. The jury will then determine what happened. It will determine, for example, if the buyer purchased appropriate replacement goods.

The judge retains final control over the jury's verdict. He can overturn the verdict if he believes the jury acted unreasonably. He can usually lower the amount of money the jury awarded. Judges, however, are very reluctant to change a jury's verdict.

Admissible evidence

To introduce evidence at trial, a party must show that it is admissible. Film directors almost always use the rules of evidence for dramatic effect – in movies one attorney will inevitably object to the admission of a piece of evidence with the familiar: "Objection, Your Honor!"

In reality the rules of evidence are mundane, technical, and usually not very interesting. The most important rule of admissibility requires evidence to be not only relevant to the issues of the trial but also to be not overwhelmingly prejudicial to a party. This rule is important in business lawsuits, for example, when one party seeks to show that the other has engaged in unethical business practices in the past. The other party will argue that his past dealings, in other matters, are irrelevant to the issues of the current trial.

The other party will also argue that if the jury learns of the past dealings, then it will be prejudiced against him. The judge will then decide whether the jury will hear the evidence.

The burden of proof

The plaintiff has the burden of proof. In the typical business case, the plaintiff must prove that it is more likely than not that he is right. In other words, he must convince the judge or jury that it is more than 50% likely that his version of events is accurate. This burden of proof is lower than the "beyond a reasonable doubt" standard of criminal law.

Trials can take a long time

Trials can be time consuming and expensive. They can take from a few days to several months. Besides the time spent actually on trial, attorneys can spend many additional hundreds of hours preparing for trial. The attorneys must, for example, review and organize all the documents and other evidence they have gathered during the entire evidence gathering process. They must prepare their challenges to the other party's witnesses. A lawyer may be able to show, for example, that a witness' deposition testimony differs from the witness' previous statements. Lawyers must also be prepared for witnesses who testify at trial differently from how they testified at their deposition. The lawyer must therefore know–and have readily available–all deposition testimony of all witnesses.

(g) The appeal

General points

The party losing at trial will generally appeal against the court's decision. This appeal will typically be to the lowest level appellate court. Most state systems call this the Court of Appeals. A party losing at this court can then appeal to the highest court in the system, which most systems call the Supreme Court. These top courts decide for themselves which appeals they will hear. They hear cases which allow them to rule on important legal and social issues. They will not agree to hear a case merely because a lower court made an incorrect decision.

Appeals courts have several judges. The federal Courts of Appeal vary the number of judges who hear different cases. The number depends on the importance of the case. Some state Courts of Appeal also vary the number of judges who hear different cases. All judges of a system's top court, however, hear all appeals to that court.

Appeal before trial ends

In general, parties cannot appeal until after the trial. Were parties able to appeal against all the trial court's decisions, during both the exchange of information process and the trial itself, then lawsuits would truly never end. Also, since the winning party will typically not appeal, this rule requiring the parties to wait cuts the number of issues appealed by about half.

However, a few pre-trial decisions are so important and so time-sensitive that, despite these practical considerations, the losing party may appeal against these decisions before trial. While the exact exceptions vary from state to state, the principle does not: the issue's importance and the time pressure must both be great. For example, a party can usually immediately appeal against a trial court's decision to freeze his assets. He may lose control of a considerable sum of money–and he may lose control of his money for many years.

Appeals court supervises trial court

Appeals court judges ensure that the trial court judge followed the law. Recall that the trial court judge supervises the pre-trial exchange of information then conducts the trial, including interpreting the law for the jury. Appellate court judges make sure that the trial court judge did all this properly. If the appellate court decides that the trial court judge did make a mistake, and that this mistake may have affected the outcome of the trial, then the appellate court will "overturn" the trial court's decision.

Appeals court cannot reject jury's verdict

The law allows appellate court judges to substitute their judgment for that of the trial court judge. The law allows appellate court judges to do this because it believes that they are in as good a position as a trial court judge to analyze and interpret rules of law. By contrast, the law does not allow appellate court judges to substitute their judgment for that of jurors. The jurors saw all the evidence presented to them, studied the demeanor of the witnesses, and discussed the evidence among themselves. Appeals courts judges, isolated some time later in their offices are, the law believes, in no position to reject the collective wisdom of the jury. The law therefore does not allow appellate court judges to overturn a jury's decision.

Appeals usually unsuccessful

Because appeals courts cannot overturn juries' decisions, appeals courts actually overturn few verdicts. The key to most trials is what happened, not how to interpret the law. For example, the key question at trial is far more likely to be: "Did the defendant act with fraudulent intent?" than it is likely to be: "What is the definition of fraud?"

Further, even if a party wins its appeal, it usually receives not a judgment in its favor but merely the right to a new trial. Thus, since appellate courts cannot overturn jury decisions and can usually only give the appealing party a new trial, appeals change the outcome of few cases.

The appellate process is faster than the trial process. For the appeal the parties need not gather evidence or question witnesses. The appellate judges must only read documents and hear a short oral argument from each lawyer. Appellate courts therefore usually render their decisions without too much delay.

Thus, even if the losing party's chances of winning on appeal are not very great, neither is the expense of appealing. Many losers therefore appeal.

(v) Courts will decide only real disagreements between the parties actually before it

(a) Introduction

Very often parties wish to know the legal consequences of actions they are considering. An attorney can look at past cases and express his opinion about what the court might do, but only the court itself can say for certain what it would do. Many people therefore want to ask the court what it would do in a given hypothetical situation.

Courts refuse to answer such hypothetical questions. To control their workload, courts require an actual "case or controversy" between the parties before they will decide a legal issue. Thus to have a court decide a legal issue the parties must have a real, current dispute.

(b) Declaratory judgment–avoid aggravating a dispute.

This rule, requiring a real, current dispute, could put a firm in a very uncomfortable position. The firm may plan to take an action which may, for example, violate a contract term. Before taking this action the firm will want to know if the action it is planning does in fact violate the contract term. However, a court may choose not to interpret the contract until the firm takes the action. The court may say that until the firm takes the action and the other party then brings a lawsuit the parties will not have a real, current dispute.

If the firm does take the action, and the court later rules that the action breached the contract, then the firm will have to pay money to the other party. If the court had told the firm before it took the action that the action would have violated the contract, then the firm could have avoided breaching the contract and paying the money.

To help firms in such difficult positions, the law allows federal courts, and most state courts, to issue what it calls declaratory judgments. When a court issues a declaratory judgment it declares the rights of the parties. It says what the parties may and may not do.

This rule, allowing courts to declare the rights of the parties, merely allows courts to do so. It does not require them to do so. For example if a court feels that another court, when it decides a pending lawsuit, will resolve the dispute, then it will decline to issue a declaratory judgment. This other lawsuit may be pending outside the United States.

This rule allowing courts to declare the rights of the parties does not violate the principle that courts will only decide real, current disputes. A court will only issue a declaratory judgment if one of the parties to the lawsuit, presumably the plaintiff, proves that unless the court says it cannot, it will in fact take the action it says it will take and a lawsuit will certainly follow.

(c)   Cannot sue on behalf of others

Relatedly, for a court to decide a case, the parties before the court must be the ones whom the court's decision will actually affect. One cannot sue on behalf of someone else. One cannot sue someone who owes one's brother money.

(d)   No nominal claims

For a court to decide a case, the parties must have a significant dispute. For example, unless the law specifically provides otherwise, a plaintiff cannot challenge a governmental action simply because as a taxpayer the action allegedly wastes his money. The harm to him personally must be much more real and substantial.

(vi) Arbitration and mediation

(a) Generally faster, cheaper, and better

Parties are increasingly choosing to arbitrate their disputes. Arbitration has many advantages over the traditional lawsuit process. It is faster. It is less expensive. Also, as non-Americans in particular may appreciate, it is less formal. It is also the logical compromise when parties from different countries cannot decide which national court system should hear their dispute.

Because of these advantages, non-Americans doing business in the US should generally prefer to arbitrate any possible dispute. Arbitration, however, is no panacea. As this section makes clear, it also has its disadvantages. Therefore some parties, rather than arbitrate, mediate their disputes.

Parties usually arbitrate because they agreed to do so before their dispute arose. They included an arbitration clause in their contract. After the dispute arises the defendant will usually not agree to arbitrate. As explained above, the defendant usually wants to delay a hearing at which he may be found liable and the court system usually provides him a better opportunity to do this. Thus if the parties do agree to arbitrate, they usually do so when they sign their contract and before they know which one will be the defendant.

(b) The strengths and weaknesses of arbitration

Exchange less information

Parties in arbitration usually exchange less information than they would if they resolved their dispute using the traditional court system. Parties in arbitration must usually give one another either only their most significant evidence or only summaries of this evidence. Each party must usually also give the other a list of his potential witnesses. The arbitrator usually also has some limited authority to order each party to supply other relevant information.

Exchanging less information has its advantages but also its disadvantages. By exchanging less information the parties will certainly have made the information exchange process faster and less expensive. However, this saving comes with a price. As mentioned above, the information exchange process helps lawyers evaluate, and therefore usually settle, a case. If the parties exchange less information, the lawyers may know less about the case and they may be less willing to settle. In addition, courts require the parties to exchange information so they both are fully prepared for trial. If the parties exchange less information, they may be less prepared for the arbitration trial. This could lead to an unfair outcome.

Preserve confidentiality

By arbitrating the parties are better able to preserve the confidentiality of their records. They may even be able to keep confidential the very fact that they are having a dispute. Preserving confidentiality is usually particularly important to parties involved in trade secret and patent-related disputes.

Arbitrators need not be lawyers

Another advantage of arbitration, many managers believe, is that the arbitrators need not be lawyers. A technical expert, these managers reason, is better able to evaluate a technical dispute. This view is not always accurate.

Lawyers and judges are trained to evaluate evidence and credibility. By forgoing a traditional trial the parties have already lost the safeguards of this time-tested means of resolving disputes. By using engineers and scientists as arbitrators the parties may further increase the chances that the person resolving their dispute will do so incorrectly.

While some engineers and scientists make fine arbitrators, many do not. Technically trained arbitrators sometimes ignore the law. They also have a tendency to "split it down the middle"–award $50,000.00 for a $100,000.00 claim, for example. Many technically trained arbitrators focus on the technical, rather than the human relations, aspects of a dispute. But human relations problems are at the core of most disputes. With the parties having only a very limited right to challenge an arbitration award (see below), the parties will usually not be able to correct any mistakes like these which an arbitrator may make.

The arbitration hearing can be slow

The arbitration hearing itself can be slower than some realize. The hearing, for example, may not be one continuous session. Particularly if there is more than one arbitrator (see below) all the arbitrators, lawyers, and witnesses may not be able to find more than a few days every several weeks or months on which they can all meet. The arbitration hearing can therefore stretch over a considerable period of time.

Stretching out the hearing wastes time and money. Every time the arbitration starts the arbitrators must review their notes and refresh their memories. The parties will find this expensive because the arbitrators are typically professionals whom the parties are paying several hundred dollars an hour. Further, the parties' lawyers will also have to prepare every time the arbitration starts. Witnesses will also have to re-prepare: the parties will have to pay professional expert witnesses for this additional time, and employee-witnesses will miss many hours of work. Finally, repeated sessions require repeated travel, further increasing costs.

In an attempt to quicken the arbitration process, some parties include in their arbitration clauses incentives, deadlines and other terms which encourage or require both the parties and the arbitrators to resolve the arbitration quickly. If the parties can structure such a clause appropriately, then the clause will indeed help the parties resolve their dispute quickly.

Informal

An arbitration hearing will not use the rigid procedural rules of court. It will instead be informal. Typically the arbitrators will sit at the head of a conference table and each party will sit at one end. The attorneys, parties and arbitrators will speak in a manner only slightly more formal than a discussion. The participants can speak in any order they choose. The arbitrators can ask questions. Most significantly, the arbitrator may consider evidence which a court would find inadmissible.

This informality helps in two ways. It speeds the decision making process. It also helps to decrease tension between the parties. On-going relationships, such as joint ventures, are therefore more likely to survive arbitration than they are a traditional lawsuit.

Number and selection of arbitrators

The parties can agree to any number of arbitrators. One arbitrator is usually enough for smaller cases. For complex cases the parties usually prefer a larger number, such as three arbitrators. While three arbitrators may make a better joint decision, using three arbitrators will also increase the costs and scheduling difficulties described above. Usually the arbitration service (see below) provides a list of possible arbitrators, from which the parties select the arbitrator or arbitrators. In some cases the arbitration service will make the selection itself.

Flexible

The parties can structure their arbitration agreement to fit their particular needs. They can decide where they will hold their arbitration. They can decide which arbitration service (see below) will hear their dispute. They can choose the number of arbitrators. They can agree to keep the arbitration confidential. They can agree on the language of the arbitration.

The parties can change almost all the general rules of arbitration. For example, regarding the exchange of information, the parties can agree, at one extreme, not to exchange any information, or, at the other extreme, to exchange all the information a court would require. The parties can limit arbitration to only some types of disputes. And while the parties can certainly include an arbitration clause in their contract, they can also agree to arbitrate after the dispute arises. In short, the parties can decide to resolve their dispute in almost any manner they chose.

Limited right to challenge

The losing party can rarely challenge an arbitration decision. Such a challenge would be to a trial court. This court would only overturn an arbitration decision if the arbitrators acted in an obviously improper manner, such as exceeding their authority or taking a bribe. Courts are overworked and therefore very reluctant to reopen already resolved disputes. Thus a court will almost always order the losing party to pay the arbitration award and a court will enforce this order as strongly as it would any of its orders.

(c) Arbitrators may not decide important public policy issues

Courts will not allow arbitrators to decide important issues of public policy. While overworked courts are generally happy to let arbitrators ease their workload, courts are also reluctant to let arbitrators play too important a role in developing public policy and the law. In a common law legal system such the American system, courts apply general principles of law to specific cases. Many of these general principles reflect important public policy decisions. For example, one such general principle, which reflects an important public policy, is the rule that an employer may not overly restrict its employees' ability to obtain alternative employment.

When deciding a case, an arbitrator may have to apply one of these important principles of public policy. Since the principle is by definition important, a court may not let an arbitrator decide the issue. A court may rule that, even though the parties agreed to resolve their dispute in arbitration, because the public policy involved in the case is so important, the court will nevertheless decide the case itself.

Defendants raise public policy issues to avoid arbitration

Simply to avoid arbitration, a defendant may raise an important issue of public policy. In a licensing dispute, for example, a defendant may raise an issue relating to an employee's right to obtain subsequent employment. The defendant will hope that the court will rule that due to this important public policy issue the court, and not the arbitrator, must decide the case.

However, courts are becoming increasingly suspicious of defendants' motives when they raise such issues. Increasingly, courts resist allowing defendants to use public policy issues to avoid arbitration. Thus, a court may decide that instead of deciding the entire case itself, the court will only decide the important issue of public policy and will let the arbitrator decide the rest of the case. Alternatively, a court may let the case proceed in arbitration but review its public policy implications after the arbitrator has made his decision. In fact, regarding international arbitration proceedings, federal courts must use this second option rather than stop the arbitration proceeding.

(d)   Arbitration services

Many services

There are several arbitration services, both in the United States and throughout the world. Among the prominent international services are the International Chamber of Commerce, the Zurich Chamber of Commerce, and the London Court of International Arbitration.

AAA largest

There are also several services within the United States. The largest is the American Arbitration Association (AAA). Almost all non-Americans doing business in the United States, who have agreed to arbitrate, should agree to so under the AAA's direction. The AAA offers the following advantages.

It is nationwide.

It has offices in all the major cities of the United States. Therefore, no matter which city in the US turns out to be the most convenient for the arbitration, the AAA will have an office nearby.

It is well known

All the parties and attorneys negotiating a contract should, once they have agreed to arbitrate, readily agree to do so under the auspices of the AAA.

It is experienced

It has established relationships with many potential arbitrators. As a group, these arbitrators have wide ranging knowledge and experience.

It has also developed its procedural rules over a long period of time and in response to many different situations. It has therefore established procedures to handle many different types of disputes, including disputes about the arbitration itself.

International rules require written opinions

Finally, the AAA has two sets of rules, domestic and international. The most significant difference between the domestic and international rules is that the AAA's international rules, but not its domestic rules, require the arbitrators to explain their decision in writing.

Written opinions have several advantages. Arbitrators who have to explain themselves in writing usually reach more logical and reasonable conclusions. Written decisions also provide guidance to the parties for future action. Lastly, and not insignificantly, written opinions allow the parties to check that the arbitrators have not made a simple calculation error. But arbitrators must take the time to write these opinions which therefore increase costs and cause delays.

(e) Mediation

To avoid the disadvantages even of arbitration, the parties could choose to mediate their dispute. If the parties mediate then a mediator will work with both parties, talking to each separately or both together, as many times as necessary, to try to resolve the dispute.

A mediator may help the parties to reach a settlement which makes business sense, but which neither an arbitrator nor a judge would have the authority to order. A successful mediation will almost certainly save the parties time and money. The parties will probably pay less than `they would to arbitrate their dispute and almost certainly less than if they resolved their dispute in the traditional court system. Mediation is also quicker than either arbitration or the traditional court system.

Just as parties should usually prefer arbitration to the traditional court system, so too should they prefer mediation to arbitration. In fact many parties include in their arbitration clauses a term requiring the parties to first try to mediate their dispute. The AAA routinely asks parties beginning an arbitration proceeding if they would like to first mediate their dispute. Both these are good practices. Managers should focus on earning profits, not fighting one another.

Index

Compiled by Gillian Delaforce